COFF
HILL

VOLUME 3

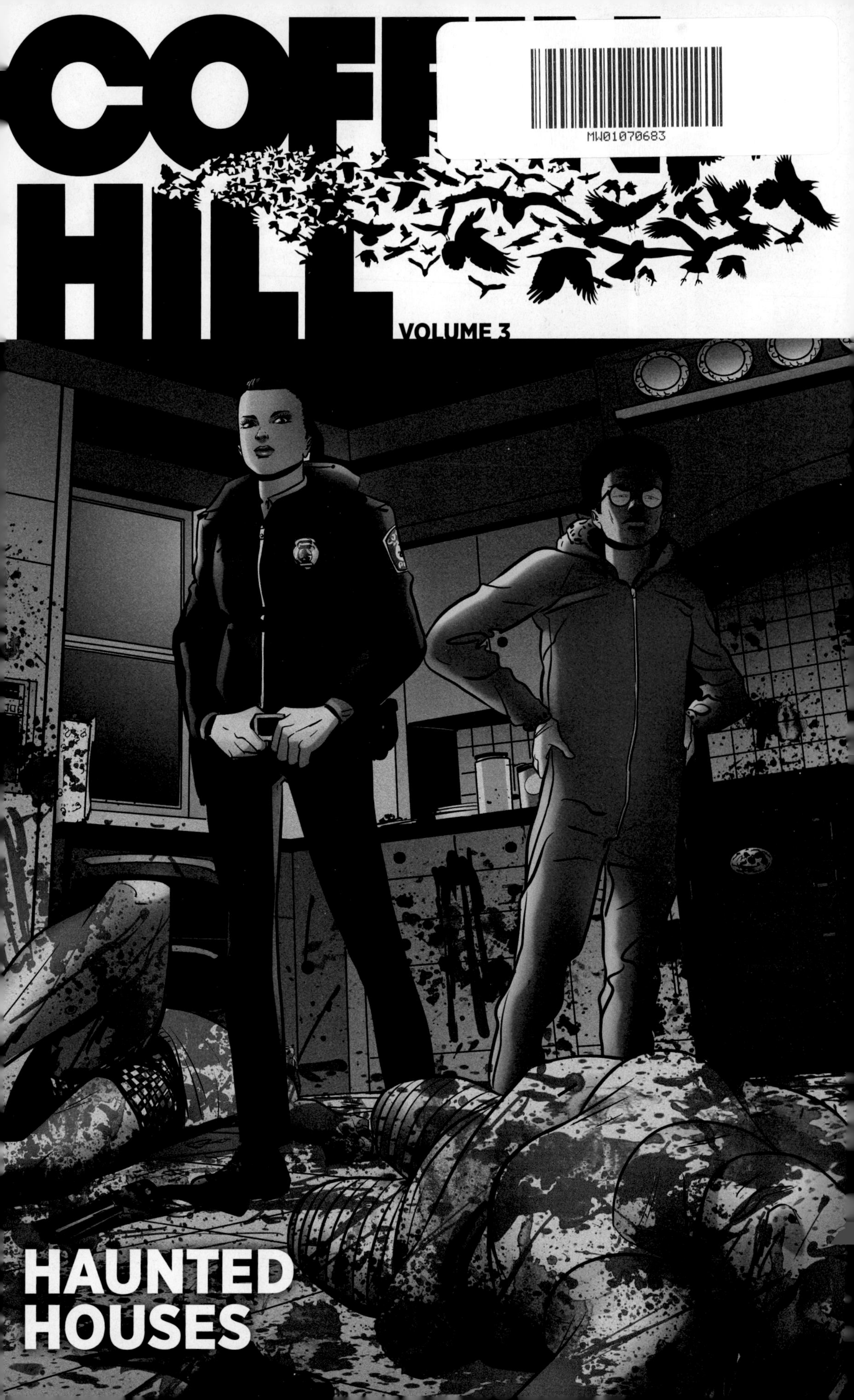

HAUNTED HOUSES

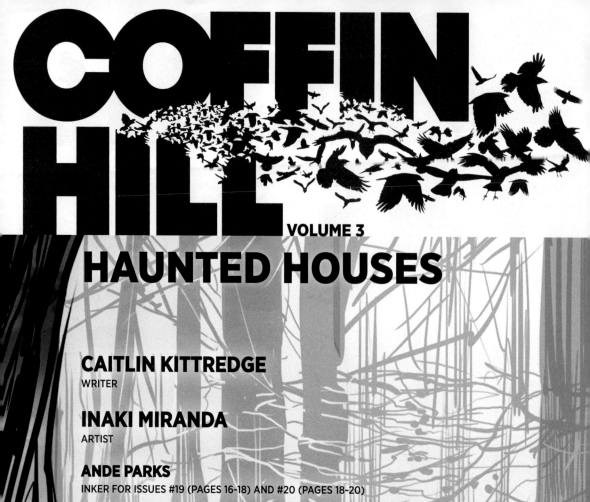

COFFIN HILL

VOLUME 3
HAUNTED HOUSES

CAITLIN KITTREDGE
WRITER

INAKI MIRANDA
ARTIST

ANDE PARKS
INKER FOR ISSUES #19 (PAGES 16-18) AND #20 (PAGES 18-20)

EVA DE LA CRUZ
COLORIST

TRAVIS LANHAM
LETTERER

DAVE JOHNSON
COVER ART AND ORIGINAL SERIES COVERS

COFFIN HILL CREATED BY
CAITLIN KITTREDGE AND INAKI MIRANDA

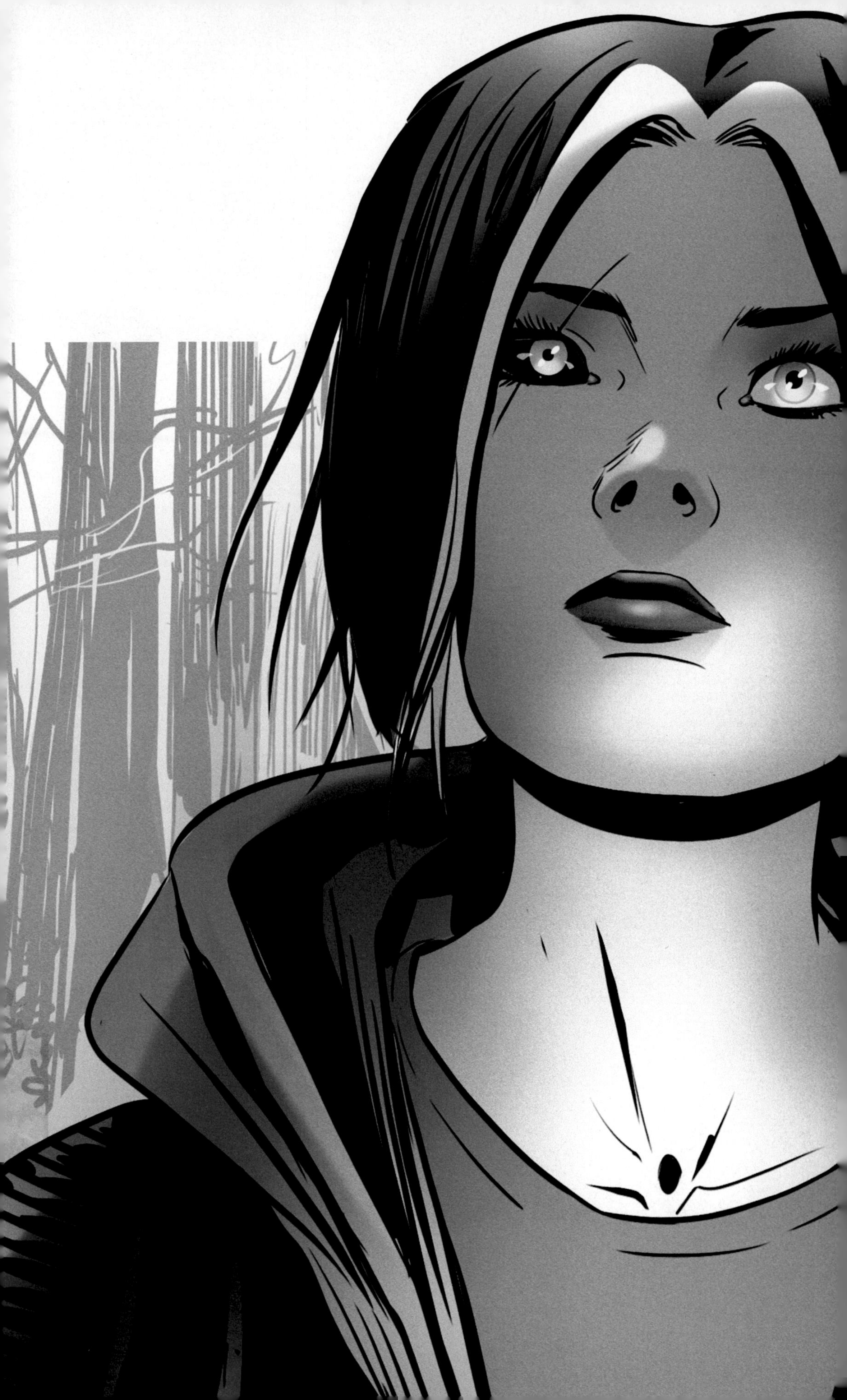

ELLIE PYLE
EDITOR – ORIGINAL SERIES
SARA MILLER
ASSISTANT EDITOR – ORIGINAL SERIES
JEB WOODARD
GROUP EDITOR – COLLECTED EDITIONS
SCOTT NYBAKKEN
EDITOR – COLLECTED EDITION
CURTIS KING JR.
PUBLICATION DESIGN

SHELLY BOND
VP & EXECUTIVE EDITOR – VERTIGO

DIANE NELSON
PRESIDENT
DAN DIDIO AND JIM LEE
CO-PUBLISHERS
GEOFF JOHNS
CHIEF CREATIVE OFFICER
AMIT DESAI
SENIOR VP – MARKETING & GLOBAL FRANCHISE MANAGEMENT
NAIRI GARDINER
SENIOR VP – FINANCE
SAM ADES
VP – DIGITAL MARKETING
BOBBIE CHASE
VP – TALENT DEVELOPMENT
MARK CHIARELLO
SENIOR VP – ART, DESIGN & COLLECTED EDITIONS
JOHN CUNNINGHAM
VP – CONTENT STRATEGY
ANNE DEPIES
VP – STRATEGY PLANNING & REPORTING
DON FALLETTI
VP – MANUFACTURING OPERATIONS
LAWRENCE GANEM
VP – EDITORIAL ADMINISTRATION & TALENT RELATIONS
ALISON GILL
SENIOR VP – MANUFACTURING & OPERATIONS
HANK KANALZ
SENIOR VP – EDITORIAL STRATEGY & ADMINISTRATION
JAY KOGAN
VP – LEGAL AFFAIRS
DEREK MADDALENA
SENIOR VP – SALES & BUSINESS DEVELOPMENT
JACK MAHAN
VP – BUSINESS AFFAIRS
DAN MIRON
VP – SALES PLANNING & TRADE DEVELOPMENT
NICK NAPOLITANO
VP – MANUFACTURING ADMINISTRATION
CAROL ROEDER
VP – MARKETING
EDDIE SCANNELL
VP – MASS ACCOUNT & DIGITAL SALES
COURTNEY SIMMONS
SENIOR VP – PUBLICITY & COMMUNICATIONS
JIM (SKI) SOKOLOWSKI
VP – COMIC BOOK SPECIALTY & NEWSSTAND SALES
SANDY YI
SENIOR VP – GLOBAL FRANCHISE MANAGMENT

LOGO DESIGN BY STEVE COOK

COFFIN HILL VOLUME THREE: HAUNTED HOUSES

PUBLISHED BY DC COMICS. COMPILATION COPYRIGHT © 2015 CAITLIN KITTREDGE AND INAKI MIRANDA PANIAGUA. ALL RIGHTS RESERVED.

ORIGINALLY PUBLISHED IN SINGLE MAGAZINE FORM AS COFFIN HILL 15-20. COPYRIGHT © 2015 CAITLIN KITTREDGE AND INAKI MIRANDA PANIAGUA. ALL RIGHTS RESERVED. ALL CHARACTERS, THEIR DISTINCTIVE LIKENESSES AND RELATED ELEMENTS FEATURED IN THIS PUBLICATION ARE TRADEMARKS OF CAITLIN KITTREDGE AND INAKI MIRANDA PANIAGUA. VERTIGO IS A TRADEMARK OF DC COMICS. THE STORIES, CHARACTERS AND INCIDENTS FEATURED IN THIS PUBLICATION ARE ENTIRELY FICTIONAL. DC COMICS DOES NOT READ OR ACCEPT UNSOLICITED SUBMISSIONS OF IDEAS, STORIES OR ARTWORK.

DC COMICS, 4000 WARNER BLVD., BURBANK, CA 91522
A WARNER BROS. ENTERTAINMENT COMPANY.
PRINTED IN THE USA. FIRST PRINTING.
ISBN: 978-1-4012-5436-0.

Library of Congress Cataloging-in-Publication Data

Kittredge, Caitlin, author.
  Coffin Hill. Volume 3 / Caitlin Kittredge, writer ; Inaki Miranda, artist.
    pages cm
  ISBN 978-1-4012-5436-0 (paperback)
1. Graphic novels. I. Miranda, Inaki, illustrator. II. Title.
  PN6728.C597K6 2015
  741.5'973—dc23
                                2015014146

PEFC Certified

Printed on paper from sustainably managed forests and controlled sources

PEFC/29-31-75   www.pefc.org

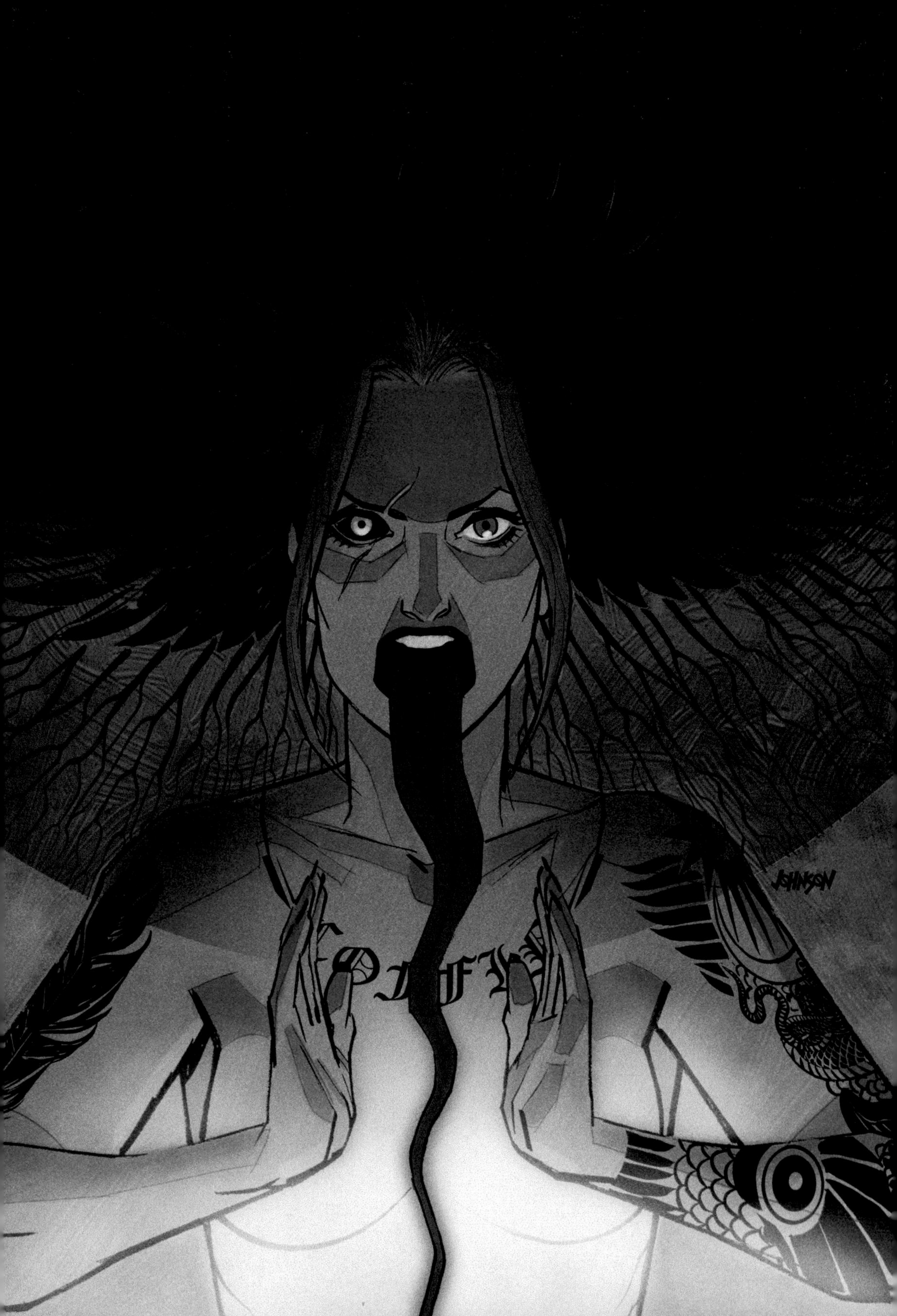
JOHNSON

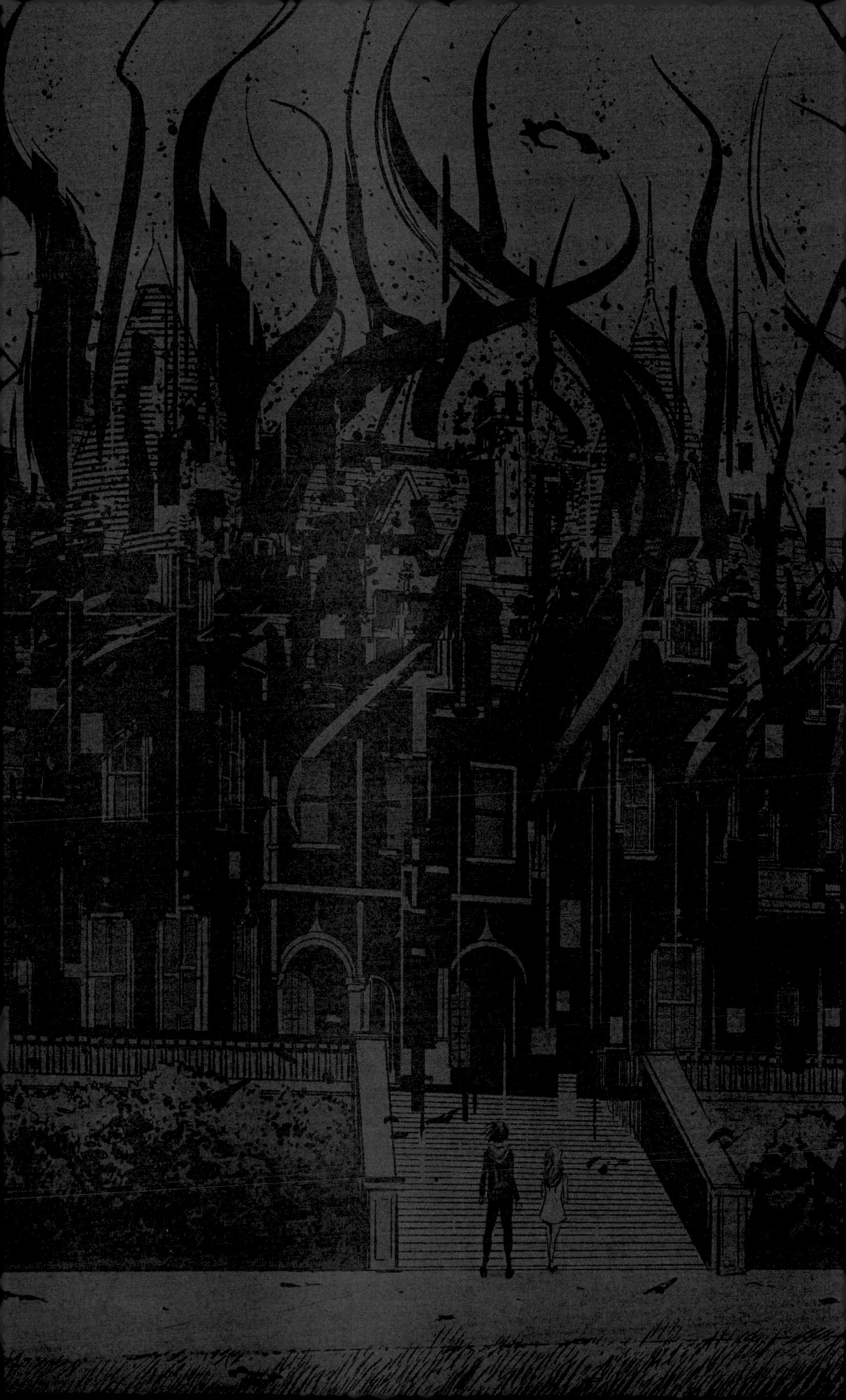

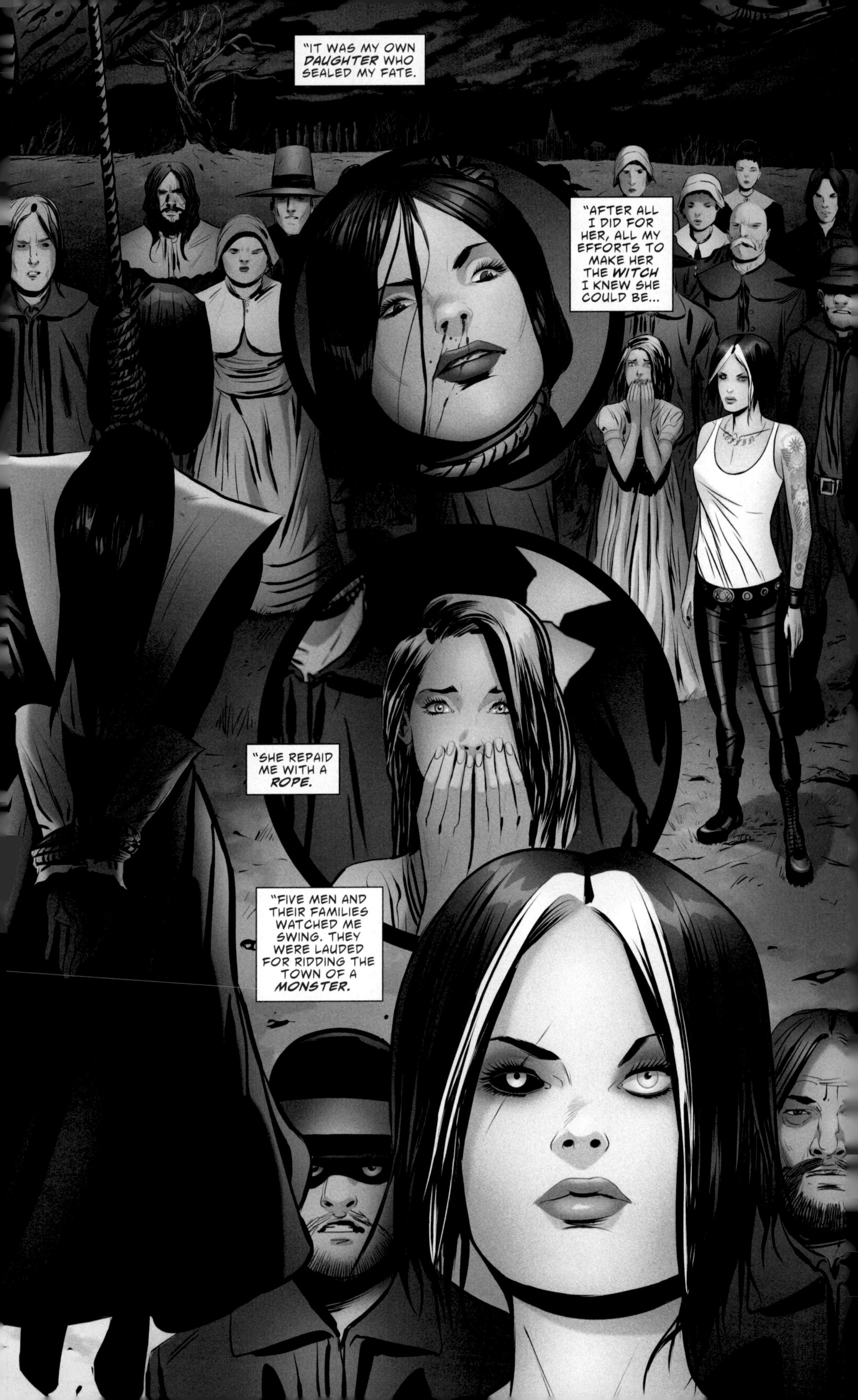
"IT WAS MY OWN DAUGHTER WHO SEALED MY FATE.
"AFTER ALL I DID FOR HER, ALL MY EFFORTS TO MAKE HER THE WITCH I KNEW SHE COULD BE...
"SHE REPAID ME WITH A ROPE.
"FIVE MEN AND THEIR FAMILIES WATCHED ME SWING. THEY WERE LAUDED FOR RIDDING THE TOWN OF A MONSTER.

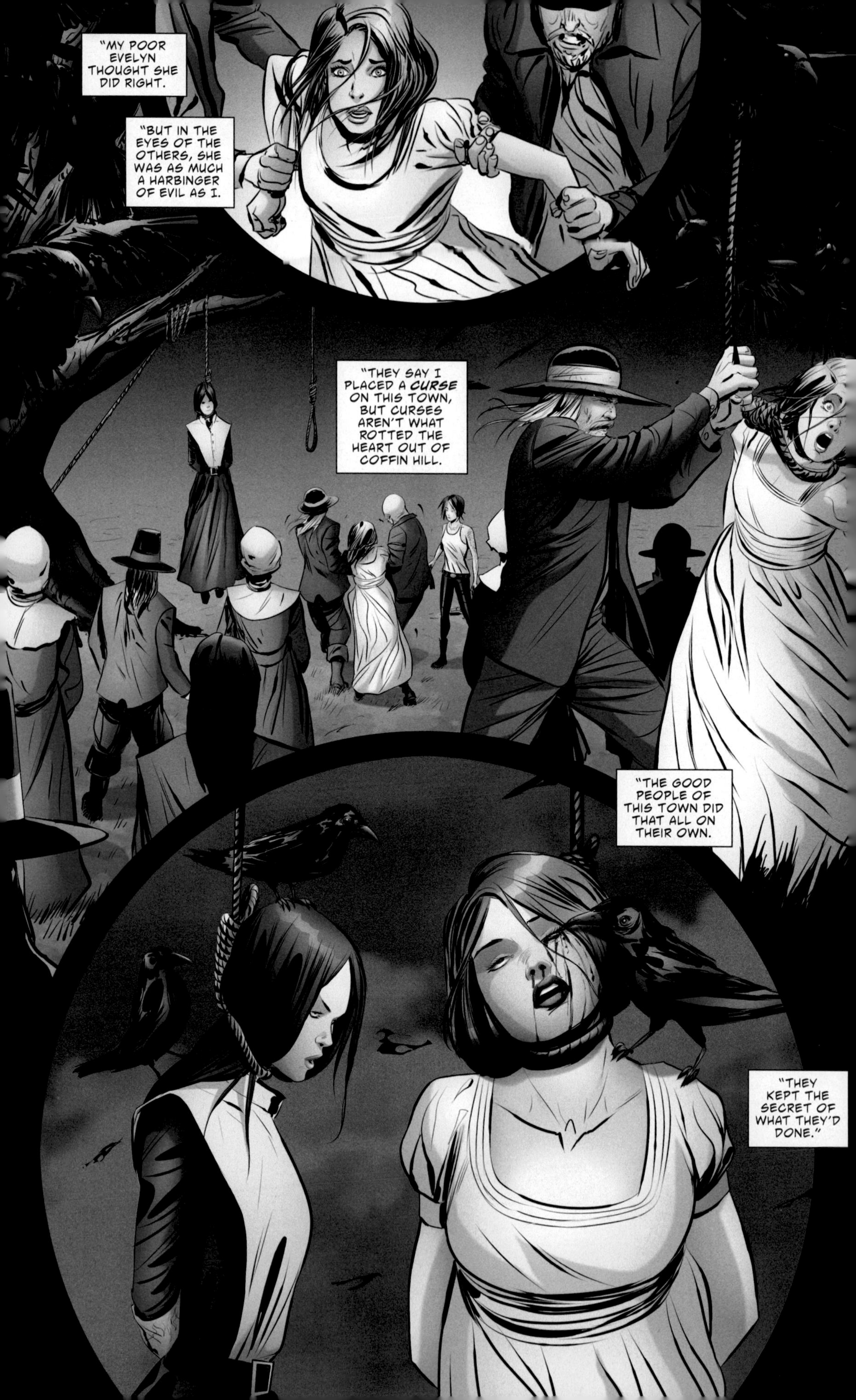
"MY POOR EVELYN THOUGHT SHE DID RIGHT.
"BUT IN THE EYES OF THE OTHERS, SHE WAS AS MUCH A HARBINGER OF EVIL AS I.
"THEY SAY I PLACED A CURSE ON THIS TOWN, BUT CURSES AREN'T WHAT ROTTED THE HEART OUT OF COFFIN HILL.
"THE GOOD PEOPLE OF THIS TOWN DID THAT ALL ON THEIR OWN.
"THEY KEPT THE SECRET OF WHAT THEY'D DONE."

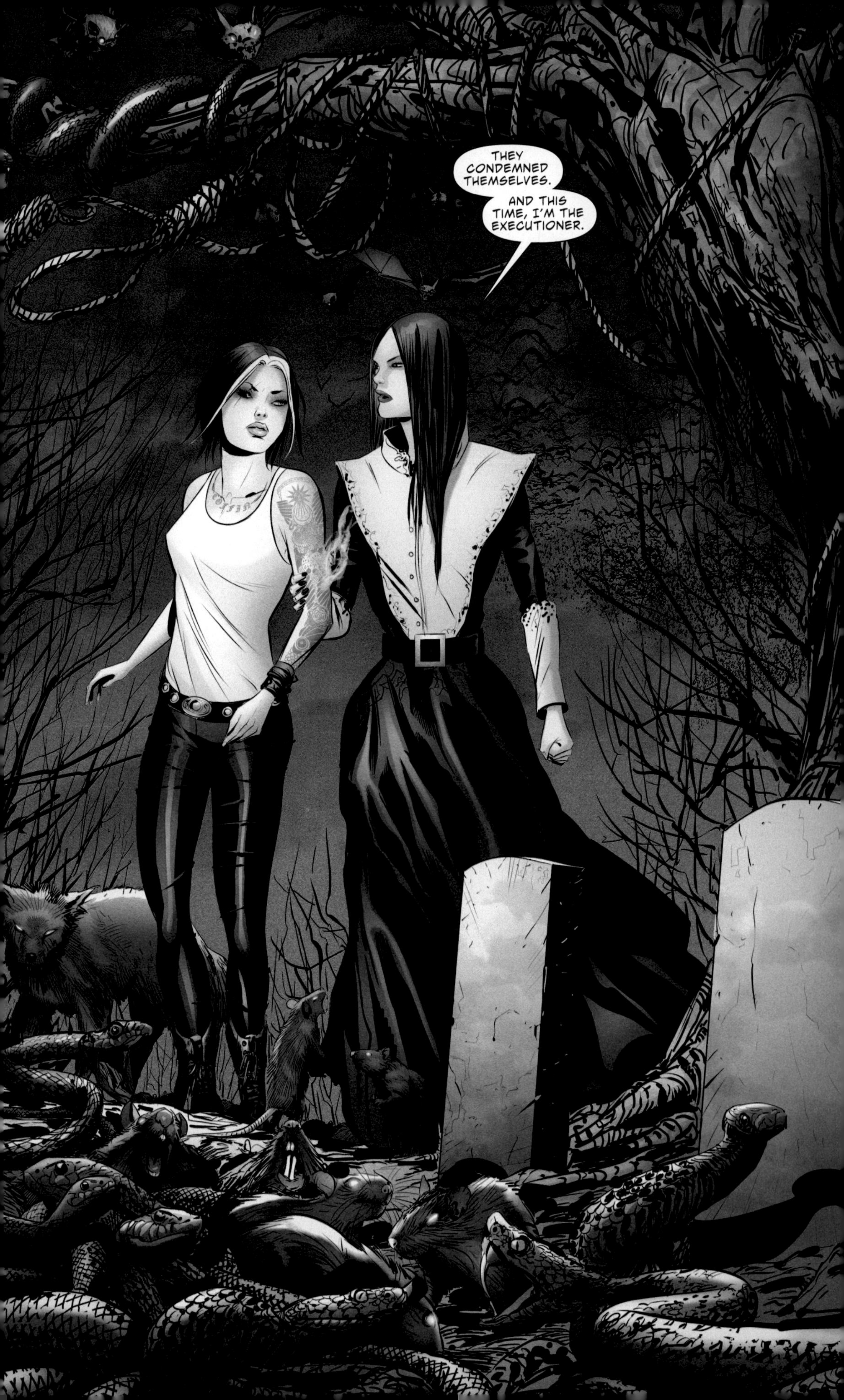
THEY CONDEMNED THEMSELVES.
AND THIS TIME, I'M THE EXECUTIONER.

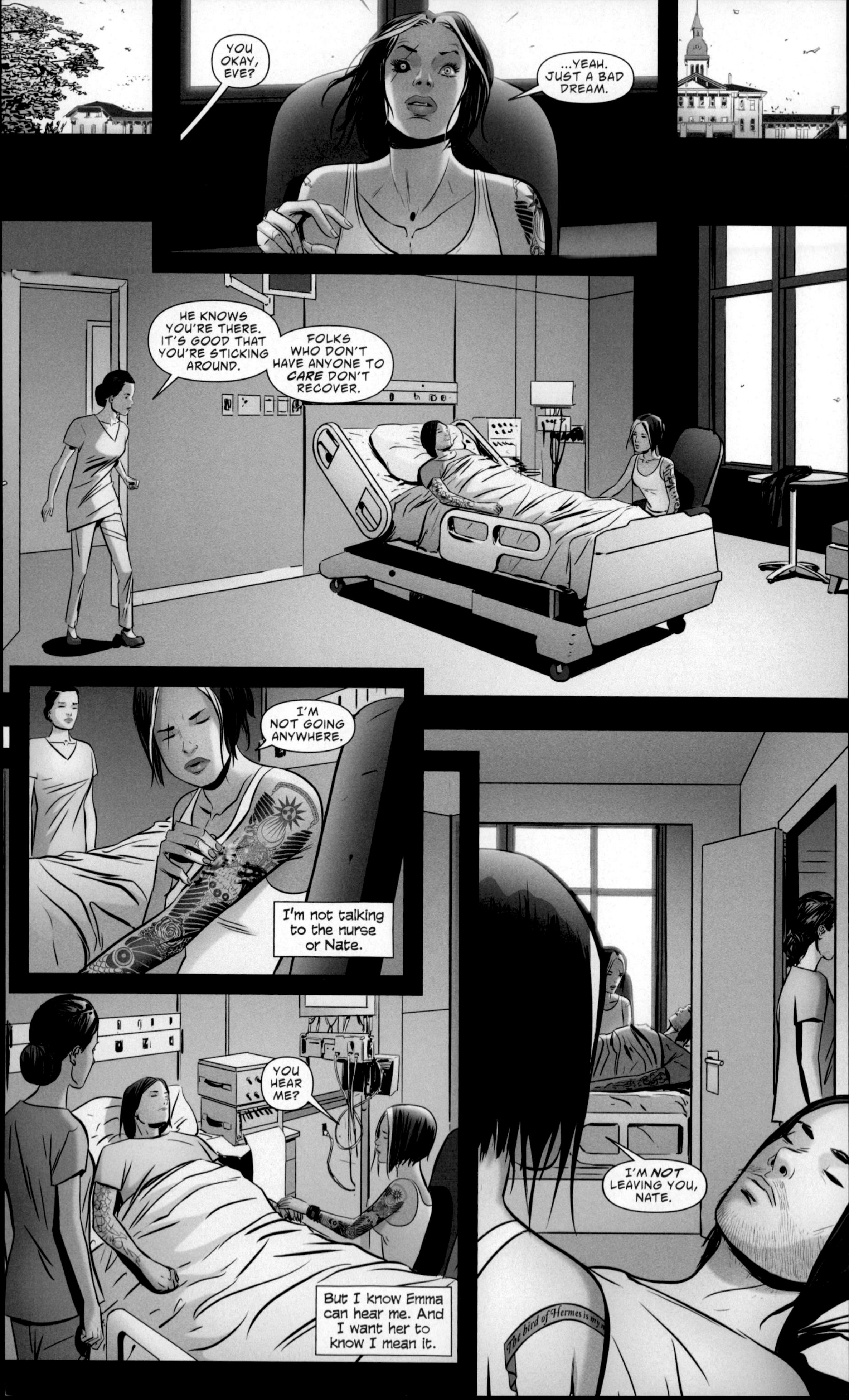
YOU OKAY, EVE?
...YEAH. JUST A BAD DREAM.
HE KNOWS YOU'RE THERE. IT'S GOOD THAT YOU'RE STICKING AROUND.
FOLKS WHO DON'T HAVE ANYONE TO CARE DON'T RECOVER.
I'M NOT GOING ANYWHERE.
I'm not talking to the nurse or Nate.
YOU HEAR ME?
But I know Emma can hear me. And I want her to know I mean it.
I'M NOT LEAVING YOU, NATE.

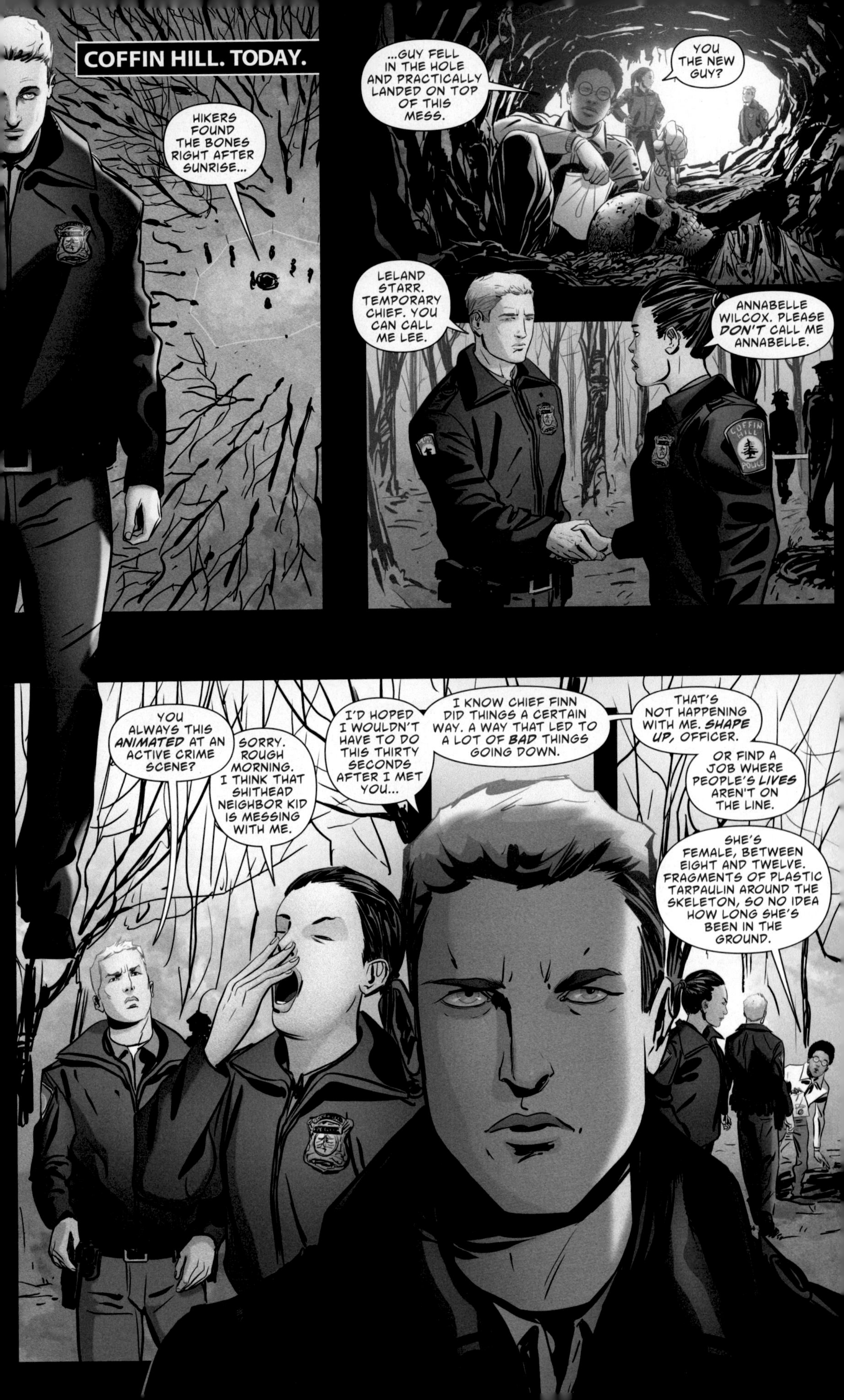
COFFIN HILL. TODAY.
HIKERS FOUND THE BONES RIGHT AFTER SUNRISE...
...GUY FELL IN THE HOLE AND PRACTICALLY LANDED ON TOP OF THIS MESS.
YOU THE NEW GUY?
LELAND STARR. TEMPORARY CHIEF. YOU CAN CALL ME LEE.
ANNABELLE WILCOX. PLEASE DON'T CALL ME ANNABELLE.
COFFIN HILL POLICE
YOU ALWAYS THIS ANIMATED AT AN ACTIVE CRIME SCENE?
SORRY. ROUGH MORNING. I THINK THAT SHITHEAD NEIGHBOR KID IS MESSING WITH ME.
I'D HOPED I WOULDN'T HAVE TO DO THIS THIRTY SECONDS AFTER I MET YOU...
I KNOW CHIEF FINN DID THINGS A CERTAIN WAY. A WAY THAT LED TO A LOT OF BAD THINGS GOING DOWN.
THAT'S NOT HAPPENING WITH ME. SHAPE UP, OFFICER.
OR FIND A JOB WHERE PEOPLE'S LIVES AREN'T ON THE LINE.
SHE'S FEMALE, BETWEEN EIGHT AND TWELVE. FRAGMENTS OF PLASTIC TARPAULIN AROUND THE SKELETON, SO NO IDEA HOW LONG SHE'S BEEN IN THE GROUND.

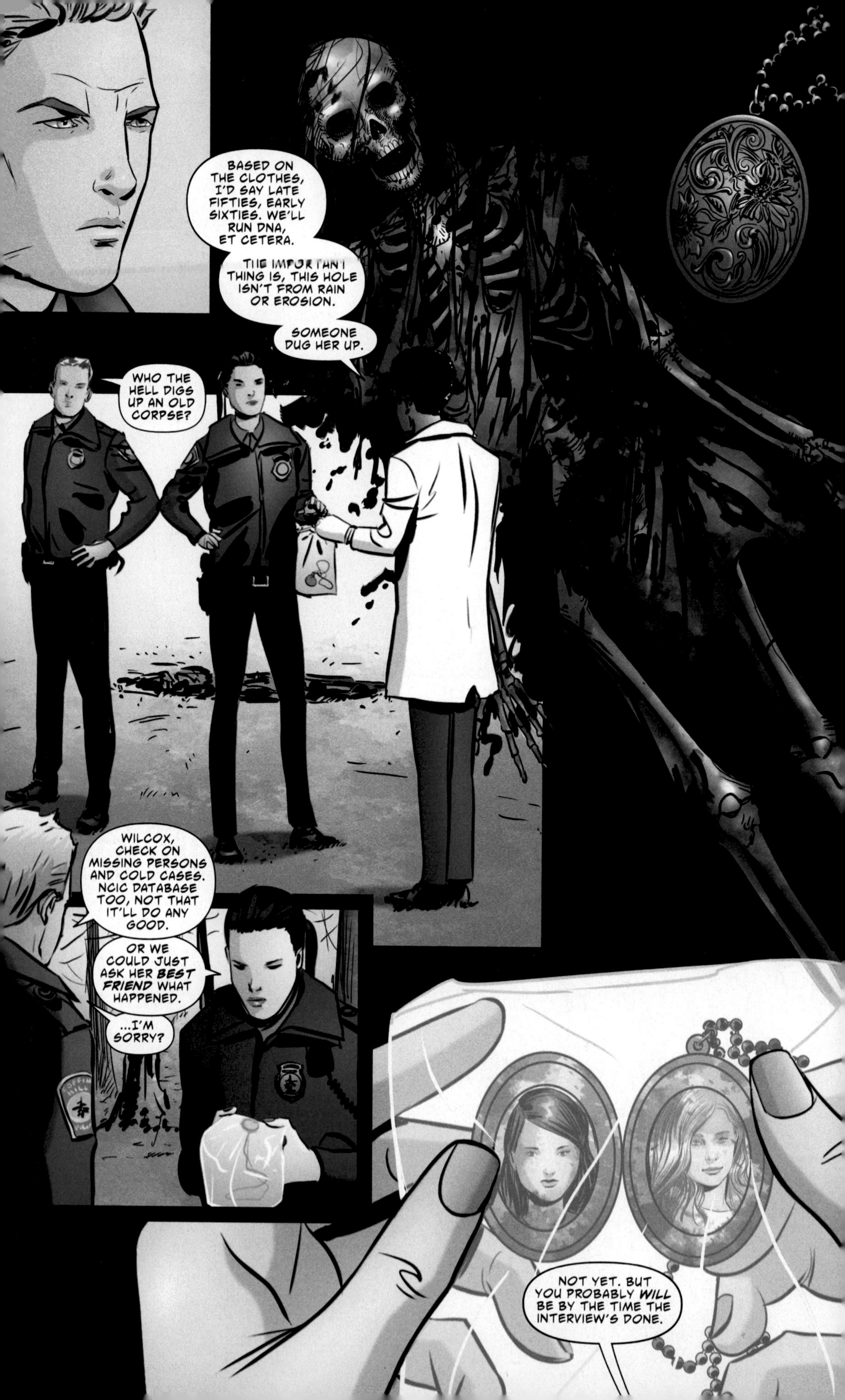
BASED ON THE CLOTHES, I'D SAY LATE FIFTIES, EARLY SIXTIES. WE'LL RUN DNA, ET CETERA.
THE IMPORTANT THING IS, THIS HOLE ISN'T FROM RAIN OR EROSION.
SOMEONE DUG HER UP.
WHO THE HELL DIGS UP AN OLD CORPSE?
WILCOX, CHECK ON MISSING PERSONS AND COLD CASES. NCIC DATABASE TOO, NOT THAT IT'LL DO ANY GOOD.
OR WE COULD JUST ASK HER BEST FRIEND WHAT HAPPENED.
...I'M SORRY?
NOT YET. BUT YOU PROBABLY WILL BE BY THE TIME THE INTERVIEW'S DONE.

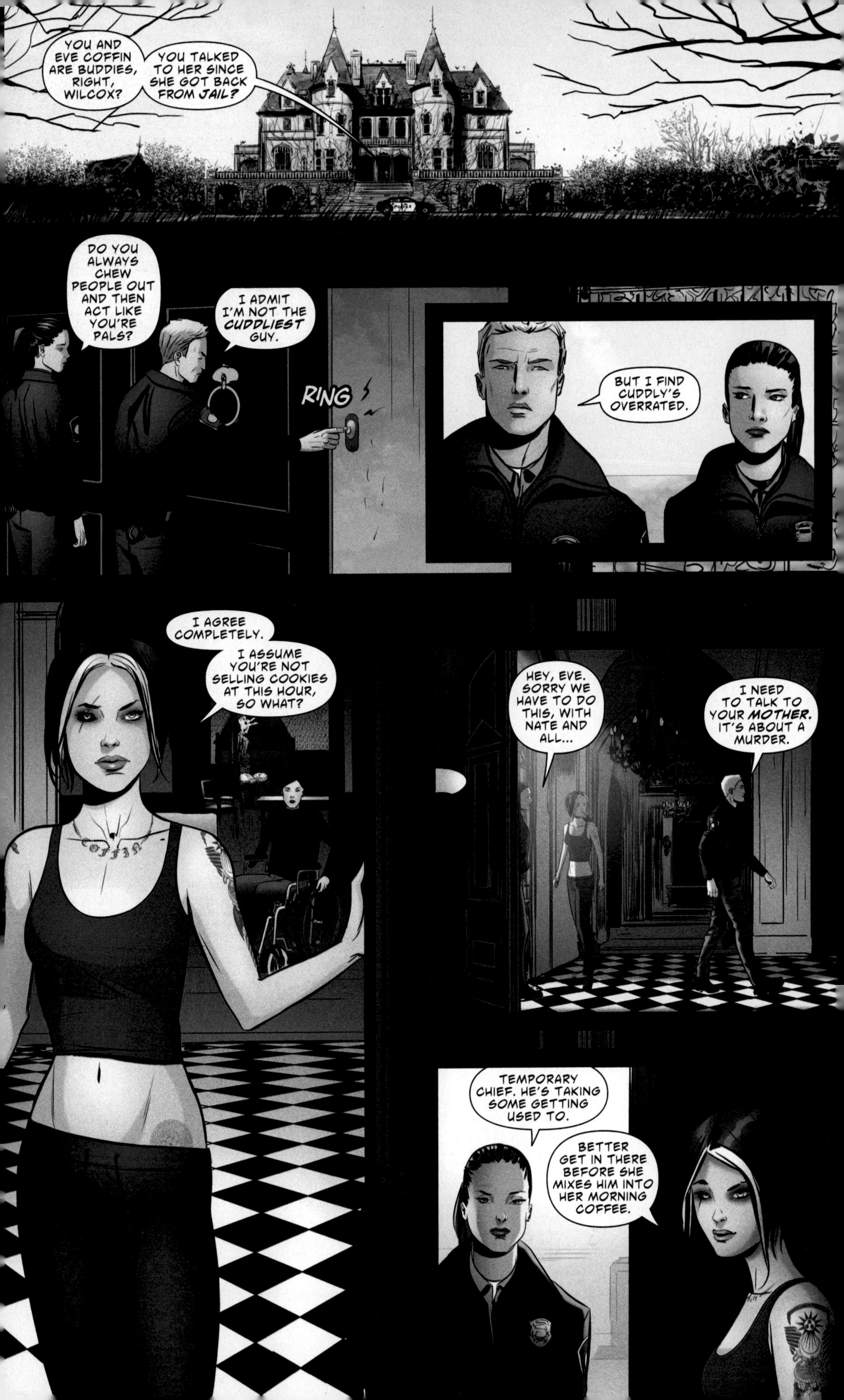
YOU AND EVE COFFIN ARE BUDDIES, RIGHT, WILCOX?
YOU TALKED TO HER SINCE SHE GOT BACK FROM JAIL?
DO YOU ALWAYS CHEW PEOPLE OUT AND THEN ACT LIKE YOU'RE PALS?
I ADMIT I'M NOT THE CUDDLIEST GUY.
RING
BUT I FIND CUDDLY'S OVERRATED.
I AGREE COMPLETELY.
I ASSUME YOU'RE NOT SELLING COOKIES AT THIS HOUR, SO WHAT?
COFFIN
HEY, EVE. SORRY WE HAVE TO DO THIS, WITH NATE AND ALL...
I NEED TO TALK TO YOUR MOTHER. IT'S ABOUT A MURDER.
TEMPORARY CHIEF. HE'S TAKING SOME GETTING USED TO.
BETTER GET IN THERE BEFORE SHE MIXES HIM INTO HER MORNING COFFEE.

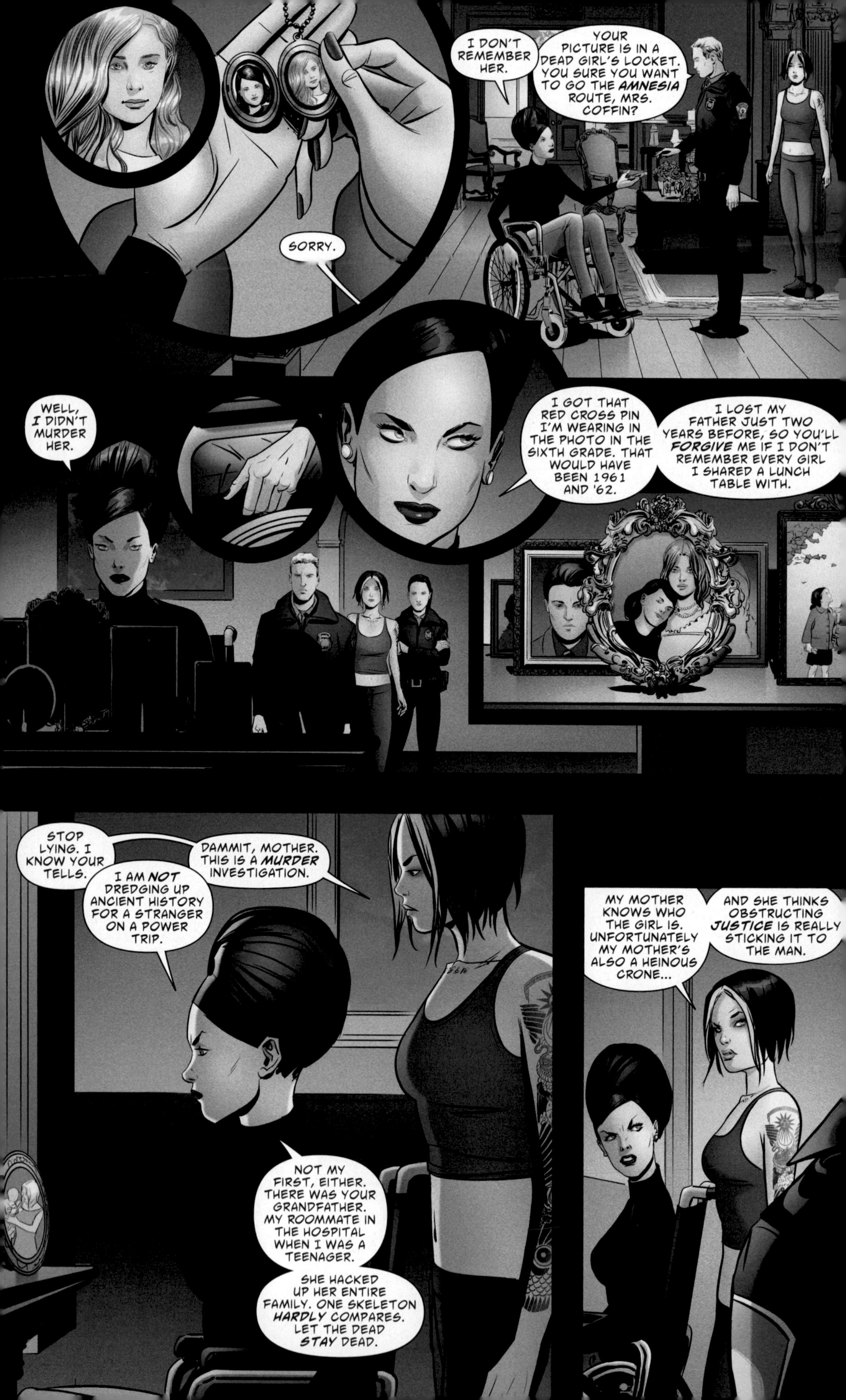
SORRY.
I DON'T REMEMBER HER.
YOUR PICTURE IS IN A DEAD GIRL'S LOCKET. YOU SURE YOU WANT TO GO THE AMNESIA ROUTE, MRS. COFFIN?
WELL, I DIDN'T MURDER HER.
I GOT THAT RED CROSS PIN I'M WEARING IN THE PHOTO IN THE SIXTH GRADE. THAT WOULD HAVE BEEN 1961 AND '62.
I LOST MY FATHER JUST TWO YEARS BEFORE, SO YOU'LL FORGIVE ME IF I DON'T REMEMBER EVERY GIRL I SHARED A LUNCH TABLE WITH.
STOP LYING. I KNOW YOUR TELLS.
DAMMIT, MOTHER. THIS IS A MURDER INVESTIGATION.
I AM NOT DREDGING UP ANCIENT HISTORY FOR A STRANGER ON A POWER TRIP.
NOT MY FIRST, EITHER. THERE WAS YOUR GRANDFATHER. MY ROOMMATE IN THE HOSPITAL WHEN I WAS A TEENAGER.
SHE HACKED UP HER ENTIRE FAMILY. ONE SKELETON HARDLY COMPARES. LET THE DEAD STAY DEAD.
MY MOTHER KNOWS WHO THE GIRL IS. UNFORTUNATELY MY MOTHER'S ALSO A HEINOUS CRONE...
AND SHE THINKS OBSTRUCTING JUSTICE IS REALLY STICKING IT TO THE MAN.

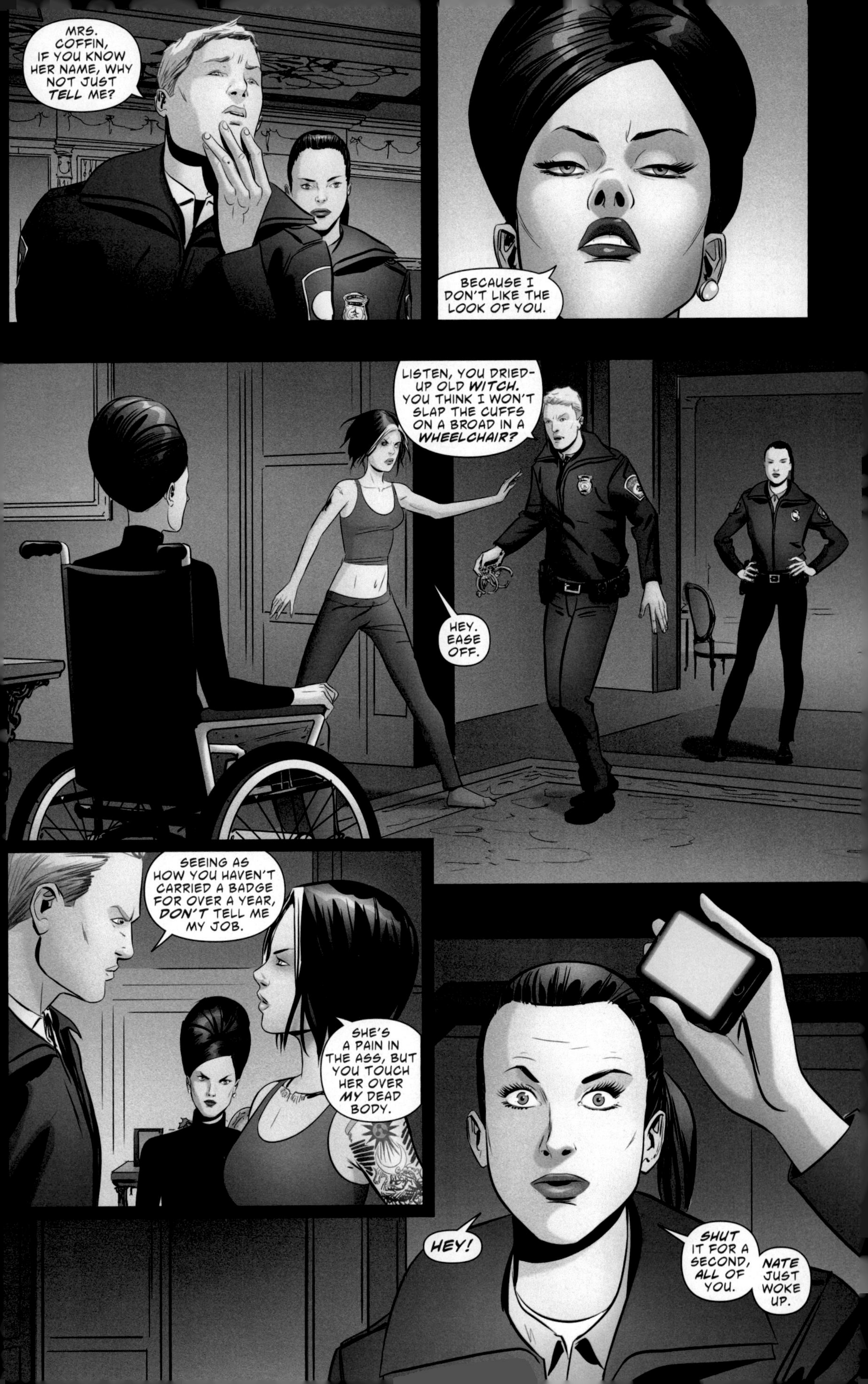
MRS. COFFIN, IF YOU KNOW HER NAME, WHY NOT JUST TELL ME?
BECAUSE I DON'T LIKE THE LOOK OF YOU.
LISTEN, YOU DRIED-UP OLD WITCH. YOU THINK I WON'T SLAP THE CUFFS ON A BROAD IN A WHEELCHAIR?
HEY. EASE OFF.
SEEING AS HOW YOU HAVEN'T CARRIED A BADGE FOR OVER A YEAR, DON'T TELL ME MY JOB.
SHE'S A PAIN IN THE ASS, BUT YOU TOUCH HER OVER MY DEAD BODY.
HEY!
SHUT IT FOR A SECOND, ALL OF YOU.
NATE JUST WOKE UP.

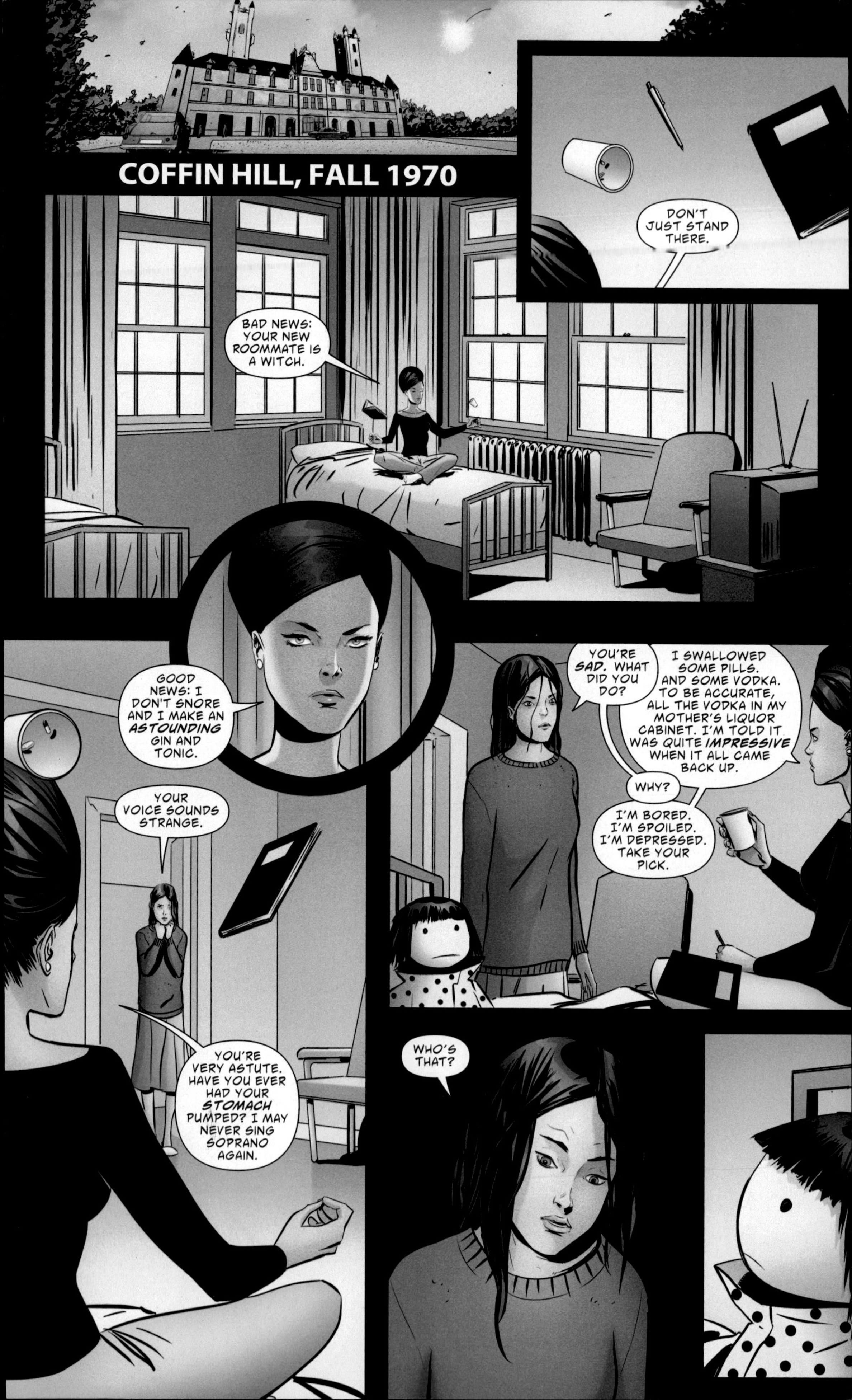

COFFIN HILL, FALL 1970
DON'T JUST STAND THERE.
BAD NEWS: YOUR NEW ROOMMATE IS A WITCH.
GOOD NEWS: I DON'T SNORE AND I MAKE AN ASTOUNDING GIN AND TONIC.
YOUR VOICE SOUNDS STRANGE.
YOU'RE VERY ASTUTE. HAVE YOU EVER HAD YOUR STOMACH PUMPED? I MAY NEVER SING SOPRANO AGAIN.
YOU'RE SAD. WHAT DID YOU DO?
I SWALLOWED SOME PILLS. AND SOME VODKA. TO BE ACCURATE, ALL THE VODKA IN MY MOTHER'S LIQUOR CABINET. I'M TOLD IT WAS QUITE IMPRESSIVE WHEN IT ALL CAME BACK UP.
WHY?
I'M BORED. I'M SPOILED. I'M DEPRESSED. TAKE YOUR PICK.
WHO'S THAT?

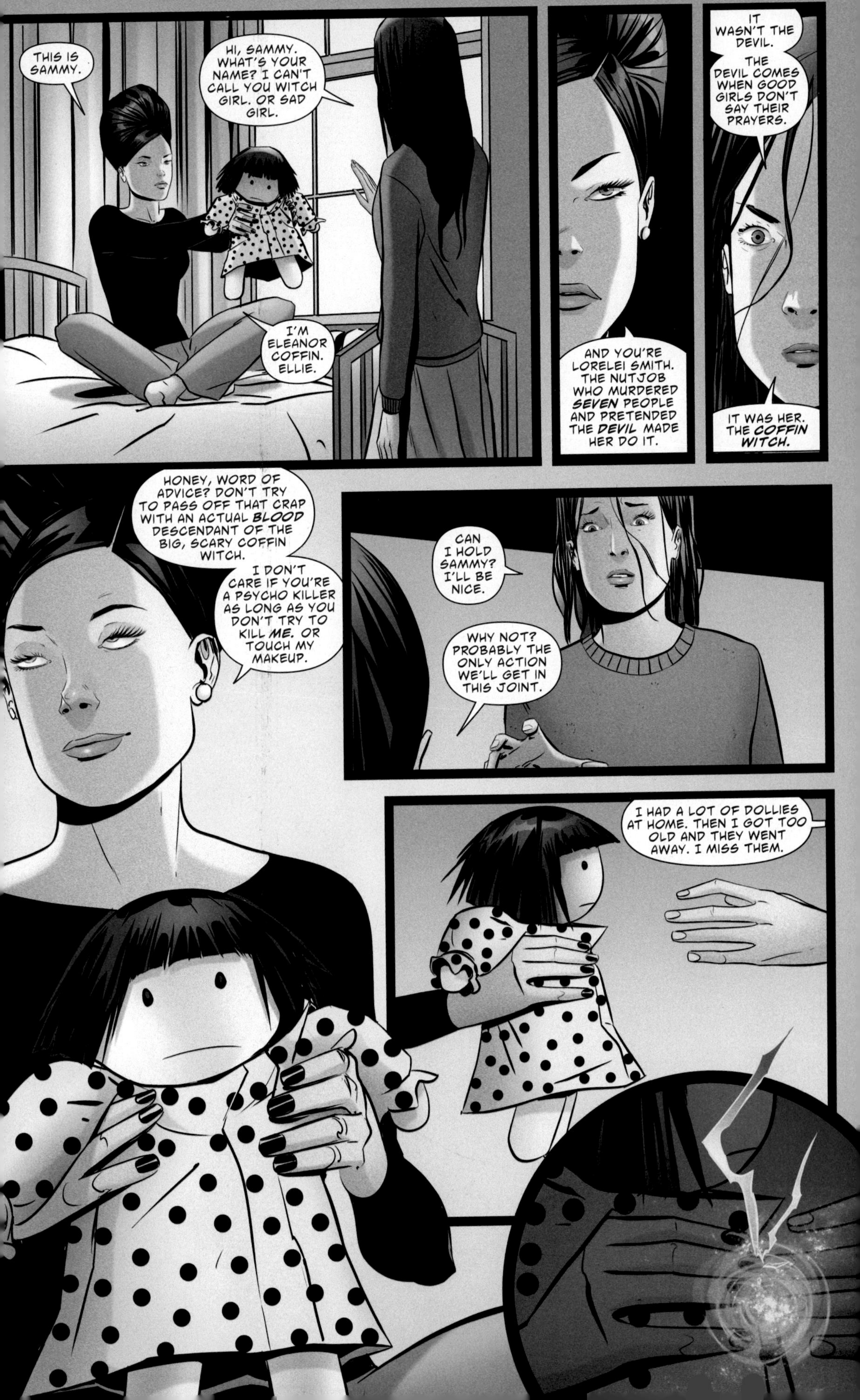
THIS IS SAMMY.
HI, SAMMY. WHAT'S YOUR NAME? I CAN'T CALL YOU WITCH GIRL. OR SAD GIRL.
I'M ELEANOR COFFIN. ELLIE.
AND YOU'RE LORELEI SMITH. THE NUTJOB WHO MURDERED SEVEN PEOPLE AND PRETENDED THE DEVIL MADE HER DO IT.
IT WASN'T THE DEVIL.
THE DEVIL COMES WHEN GOOD GIRLS DON'T SAY THEIR PRAYERS.
IT WAS HER. THE COFFIN WITCH.
HONEY, WORD OF ADVICE? DON'T TRY TO PASS OFF THAT CRAP WITH AN ACTUAL BLOOD DESCENDANT OF THE BIG, SCARY COFFIN WITCH.
I DON'T CARE IF YOU'RE A PSYCHO KILLER AS LONG AS YOU DON'T TRY TO KILL ME. OR TOUCH MY MAKEUP.
CAN I HOLD SAMMY? I'LL BE NICE.
WHY NOT? PROBABLY THE ONLY ACTION WE'LL GET IN THIS JOINT.
I HAD A LOT OF DOLLIES AT HOME. THEN I GOT TOO OLD AND THEY WENT AWAY. I MISS THEM.

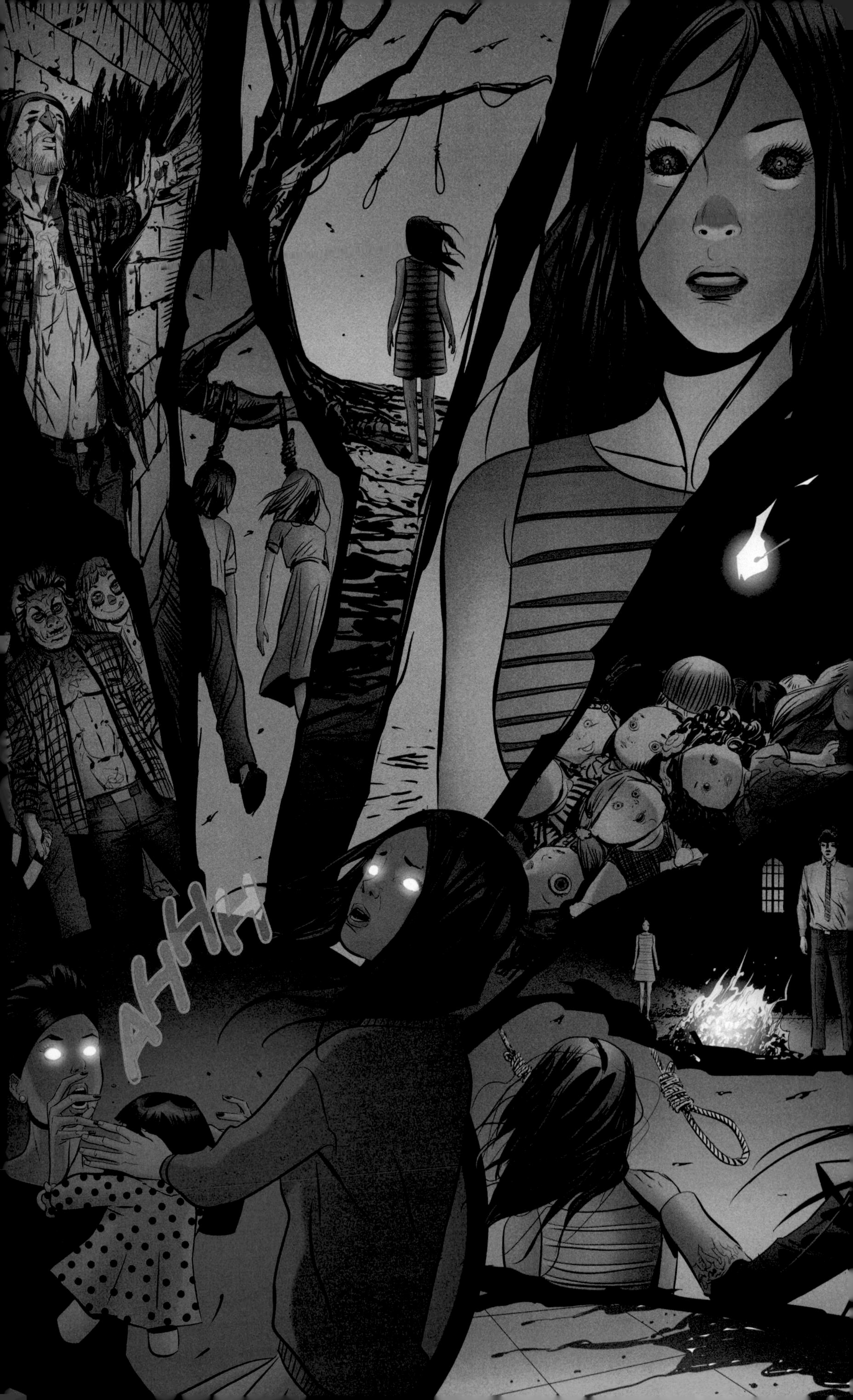
AHHH

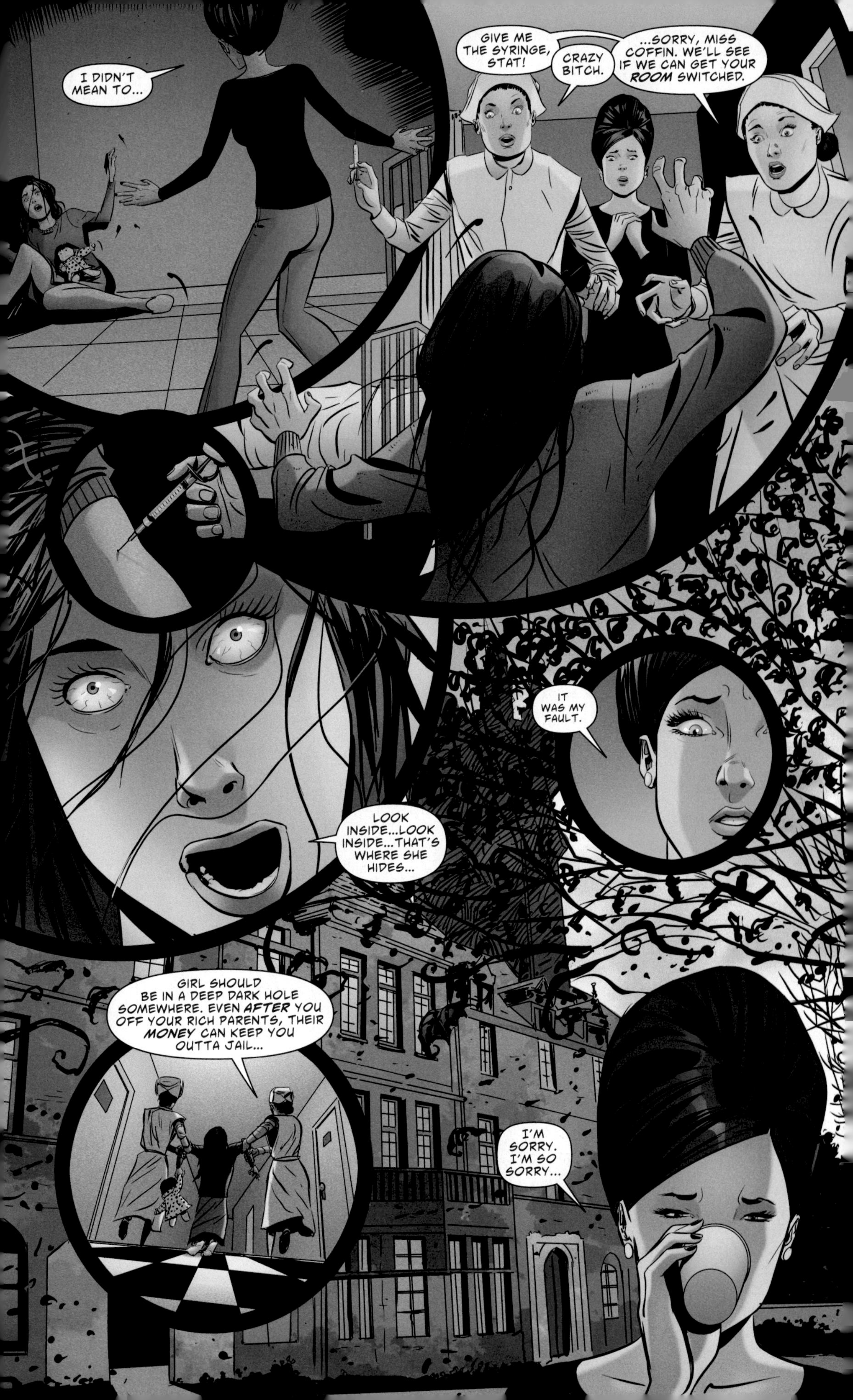
I DIDN'T MEAN TO...
GIVE ME THE SYRINGE, STAT!
CRAZY BITCH.
...SORRY, MISS COFFIN. WE'LL SEE IF WE CAN GET YOUR *ROOM* SWITCHED.
IT WAS MY FAULT.
LOOK INSIDE...LOOK INSIDE...THAT'S WHERE SHE HIDES...
GIRL SHOULD BE IN A DEEP DARK HOLE SOMEWHERE. EVEN *AFTER* YOU OFF YOUR RICH PARENTS, THEIR *MONEY* CAN KEEP YOU OUTTA JAIL...
I'M SORRY. I'M SO SORRY...

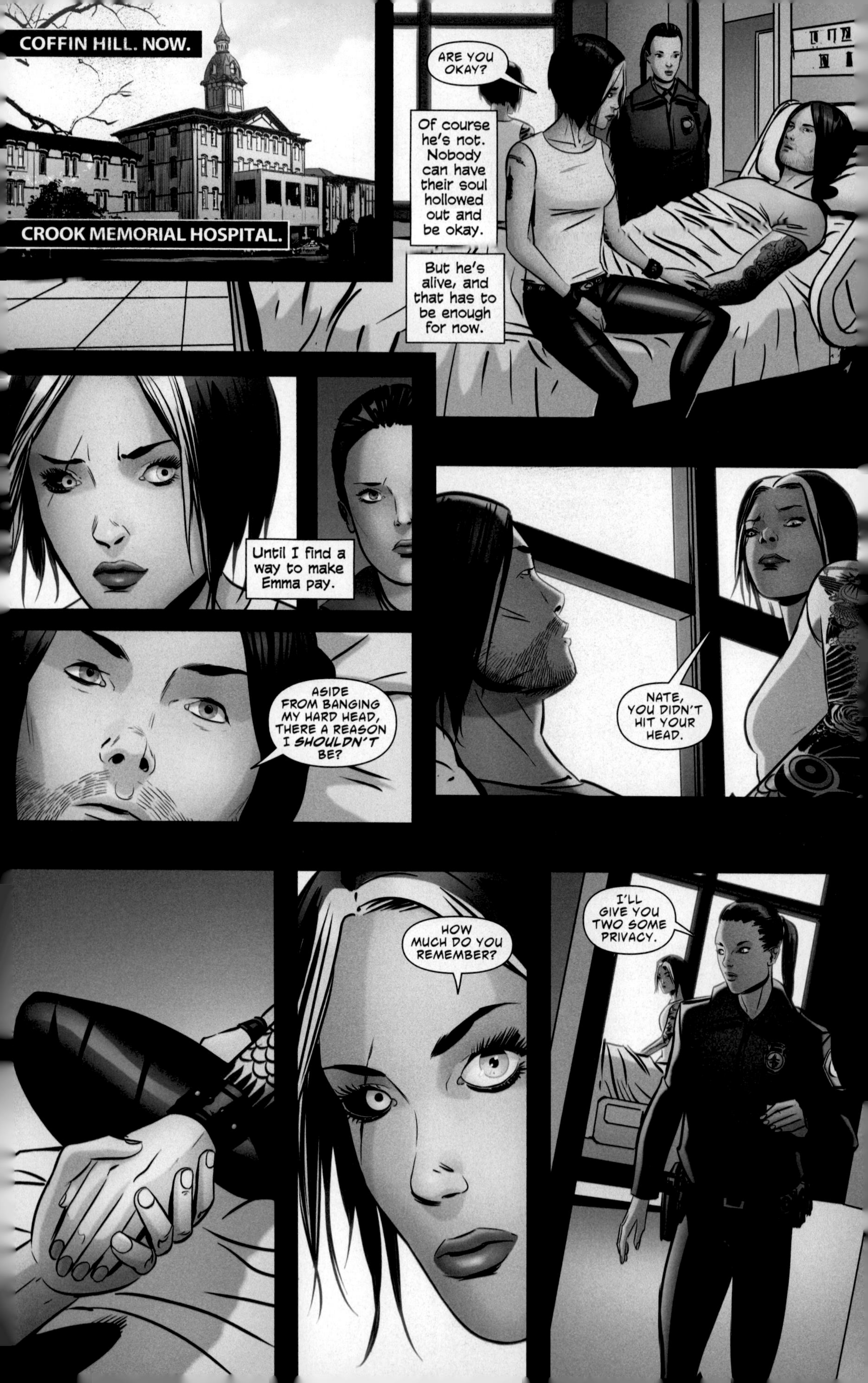
COFFIN HILL. NOW.
CROOK MEMORIAL HOSPITAL.
ARE YOU OKAY?
Of course he's not. Nobody can have their soul hollowed out and be okay.
But he's alive, and that has to be enough for now.
Until I find a way to make Emma pay.
ASIDE FROM BANGING MY HARD HEAD, THERE A REASON I SHOULDN'T BE?
NATE, YOU DIDN'T HIT YOUR HEAD.
HOW MUCH DO YOU REMEMBER?
I'LL GIVE YOU TWO SOME PRIVACY.

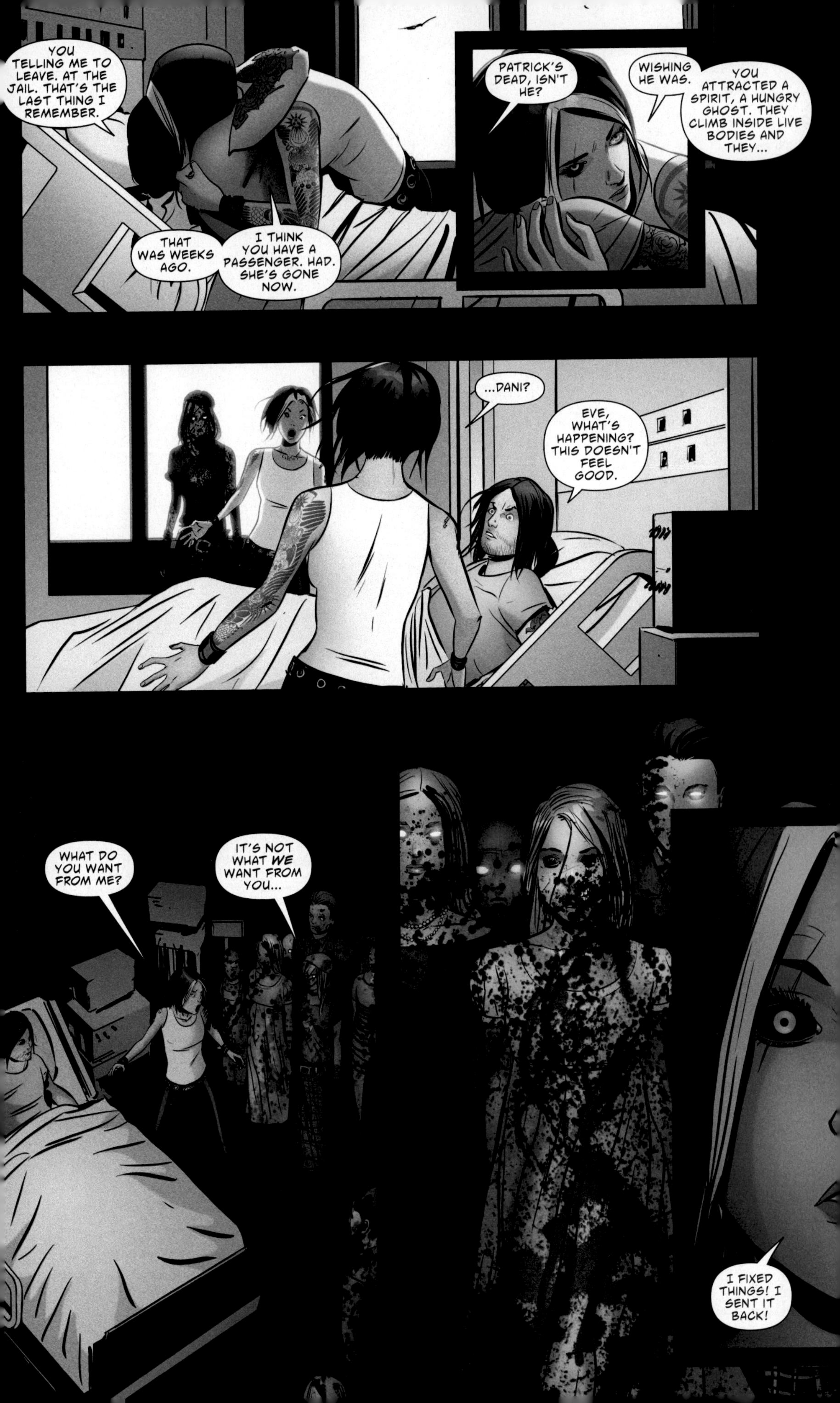

YOU TELLING ME TO LEAVE. AT THE JAIL. THAT'S THE LAST THING I REMEMBER.
THAT WAS WEEKS AGO.
I THINK YOU HAVE A PASSENGER. HAD. SHE'S GONE NOW.
PATRICK'S DEAD, ISN'T HE?
WISHING HE WAS.
YOU ATTRACTED A SPIRIT, A HUNGRY GHOST. THEY CLIMB INSIDE LIVE BODIES AND THEY...
...DANI?
EVE, WHAT'S HAPPENING? THIS DOESN'T FEEL GOOD.
WHAT DO YOU WANT FROM ME?
IT'S NOT WHAT WE WANT FROM YOU...
I FIXED THINGS! I SENT IT BACK!

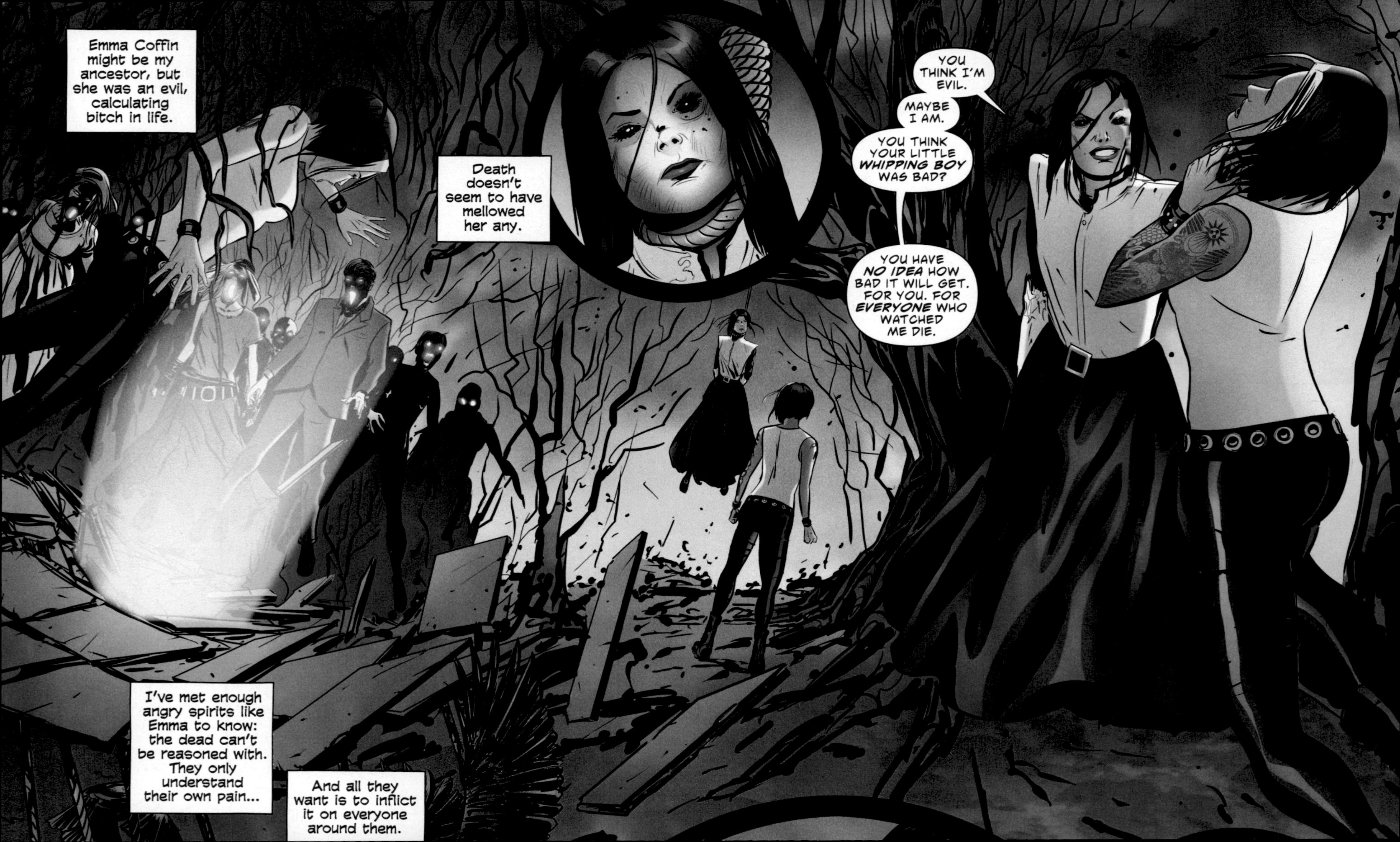
Emma Coffin might be my ancestor, but she was an evil, calculating bitch in life.
Death doesn't seem to have mellowed her any.
YOU THINK I'M EVIL.
MAYBE I AM.
YOU THINK YOUR LITTLE *WHIPPING BOY* WAS BAD?
YOU HAVE *NO IDEA* HOW BAD IT WILL GET. FOR YOU. FOR *EVERYONE* WHO WATCHED ME DIE.
I've met enough angry spirits like Emma to know: the dead can't be reasoned with. They only understand their own pain...
And all they want is to inflict it on everyone around them.

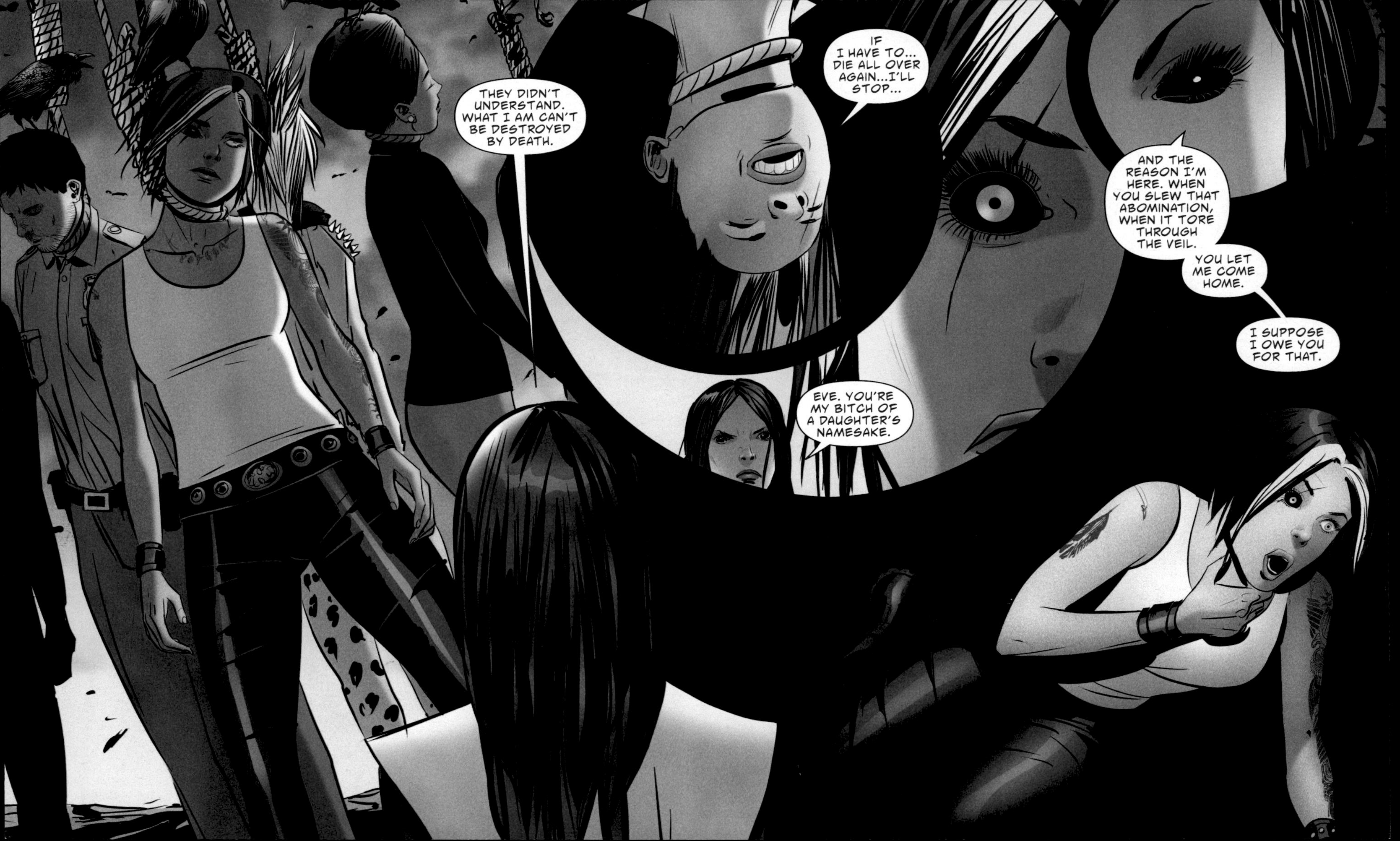
THEY DIDN'T UNDERSTAND. WHAT I AM CAN'T BE DESTROYED BY DEATH.
IF I HAVE TO... DIE ALL OVER AGAIN...I'LL STOP...
EVE. YOU'RE MY BITCH OF A DAUGHTER'S NAMESAKE.
AND THE REASON I'M HERE. WHEN YOU SLEW THAT ABOMINATION, WHEN IT TORE THROUGH THE VEIL.
YOU LET ME COME HOME.
I SUPPOSE I OWE YOU FOR THAT.

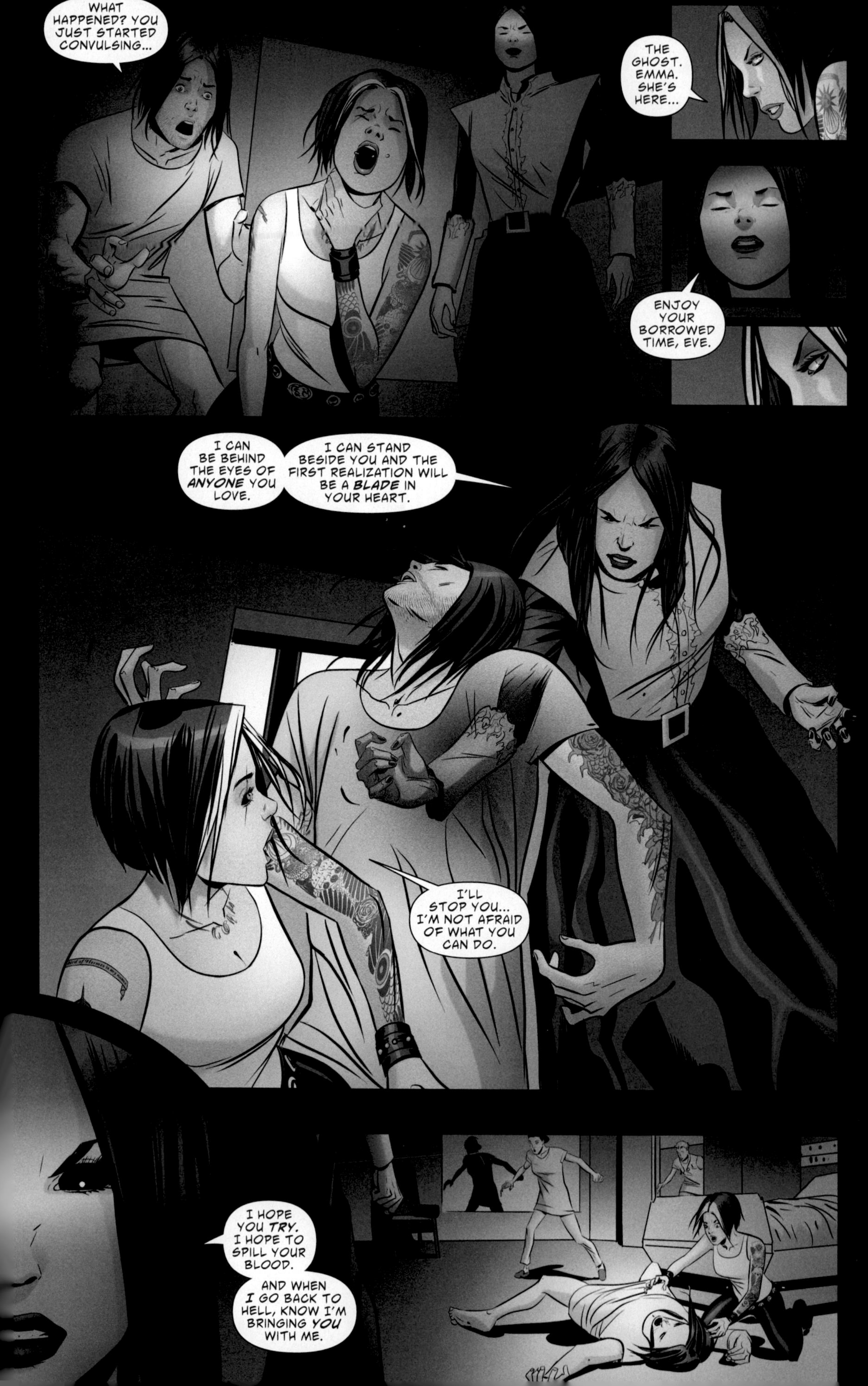
WHAT HAPPENED? YOU JUST STARTED CONVULSING...
THE GHOST. EMMA. SHE'S HERE...
ENJOY YOUR BORROWED TIME, EVE.
I CAN BE BEHIND THE EYES OF *ANYONE* YOU LOVE.
I CAN STAND BESIDE YOU AND THE FIRST REALIZATION WILL BE A *BLADE* IN YOUR HEART.
I'LL STOP YOU... I'M NOT AFRAID OF WHAT YOU CAN DO.
I HOPE YOU *TRY*. I HOPE TO SPILL YOUR BLOOD.
AND WHEN *I* GO BACK TO HELL, KNOW I'M BRINGING *YOU* WITH ME.

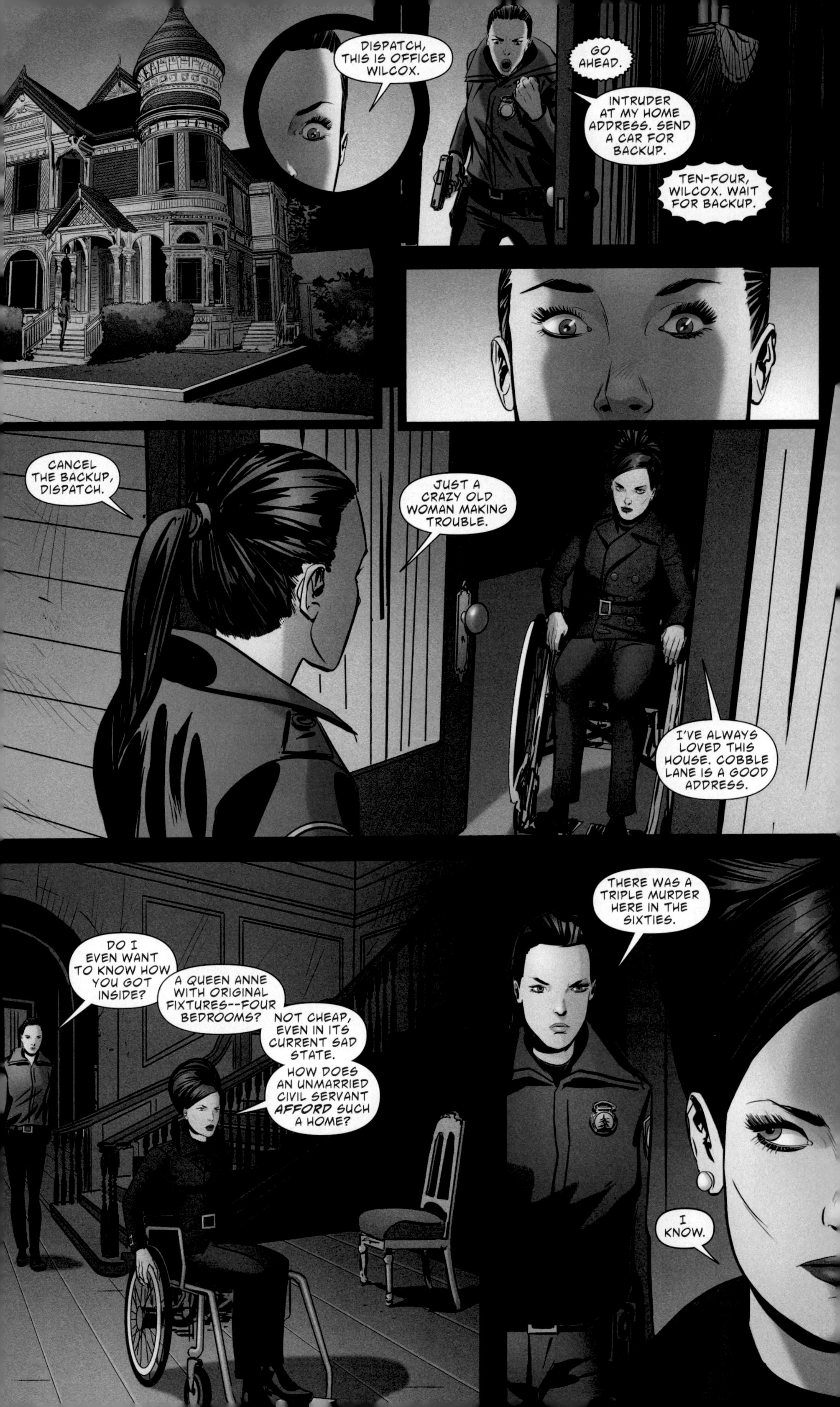
DISPATCH, THIS IS OFFICER WILCOX.
GO AHEAD.
INTRUDER AT MY HOME ADDRESS. SEND A CAR FOR BACKUP.
TEN-FOUR, WILCOX. WAIT FOR BACKUP.
CANCEL THE BACKUP, DISPATCH.
JUST A CRAZY OLD WOMAN MAKING TROUBLE.
I'VE ALWAYS LOVED THIS HOUSE. COBBLE LANE IS A GOOD ADDRESS.
DO I EVEN WANT TO KNOW HOW YOU GOT INSIDE?
A QUEEN ANNE WITH ORIGINAL FIXTURES--FOUR BEDROOMS?
NOT CHEAP, EVEN IN ITS CURRENT SAD STATE.
HOW DOES AN UNMARRIED CIVIL SERVANT *AFFORD* SUCH A HOME?
THERE WAS A TRIPLE MURDER HERE IN THE SIXTIES.
I KNOW.

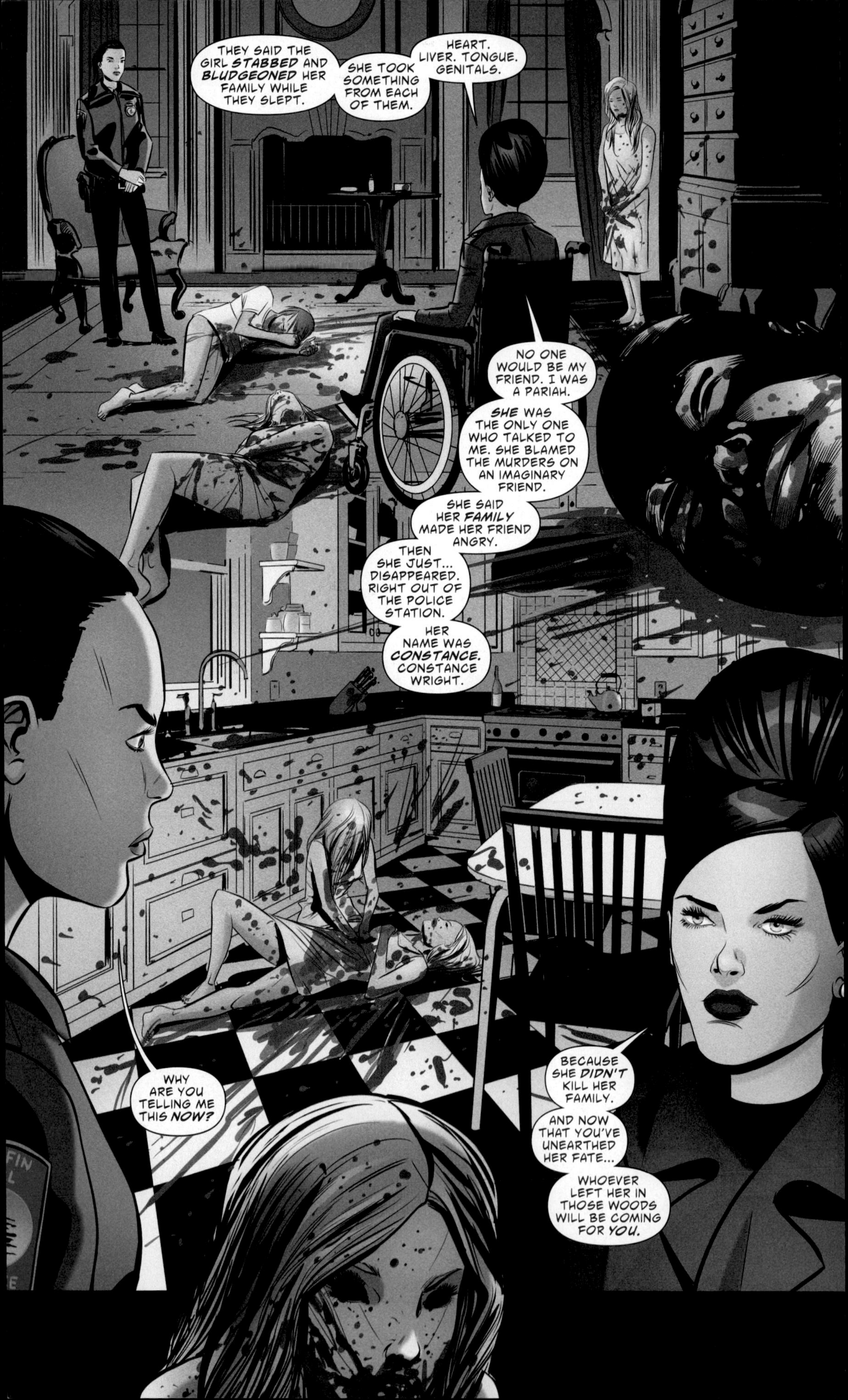
THEY SAID THE GIRL STABBED AND BLUDGEONED HER FAMILY WHILE THEY SLEPT.
SHE TOOK SOMETHING FROM EACH OF THEM.
HEART. LIVER. TONGUE. GENITALS.
NO ONE WOULD BE MY FRIEND. I WAS A PARIAH.
SHE WAS THE ONLY ONE WHO TALKED TO ME. SHE BLAMED THE MURDERS ON AN IMAGINARY FRIEND.
SHE SAID HER FAMILY MADE HER FRIEND ANGRY.
THEN SHE JUST... DISAPPEARED. RIGHT OUT OF THE POLICE STATION.
HER NAME WAS CONSTANCE. CONSTANCE WRIGHT.
WHY ARE YOU TELLING ME THIS NOW?
BECAUSE SHE DIDN'T KILL HER FAMILY.
AND NOW THAT YOU'VE UNEARTHED HER FATE...
WHOEVER LEFT HER IN THOSE WOODS WILL BE COMING FOR YOU.

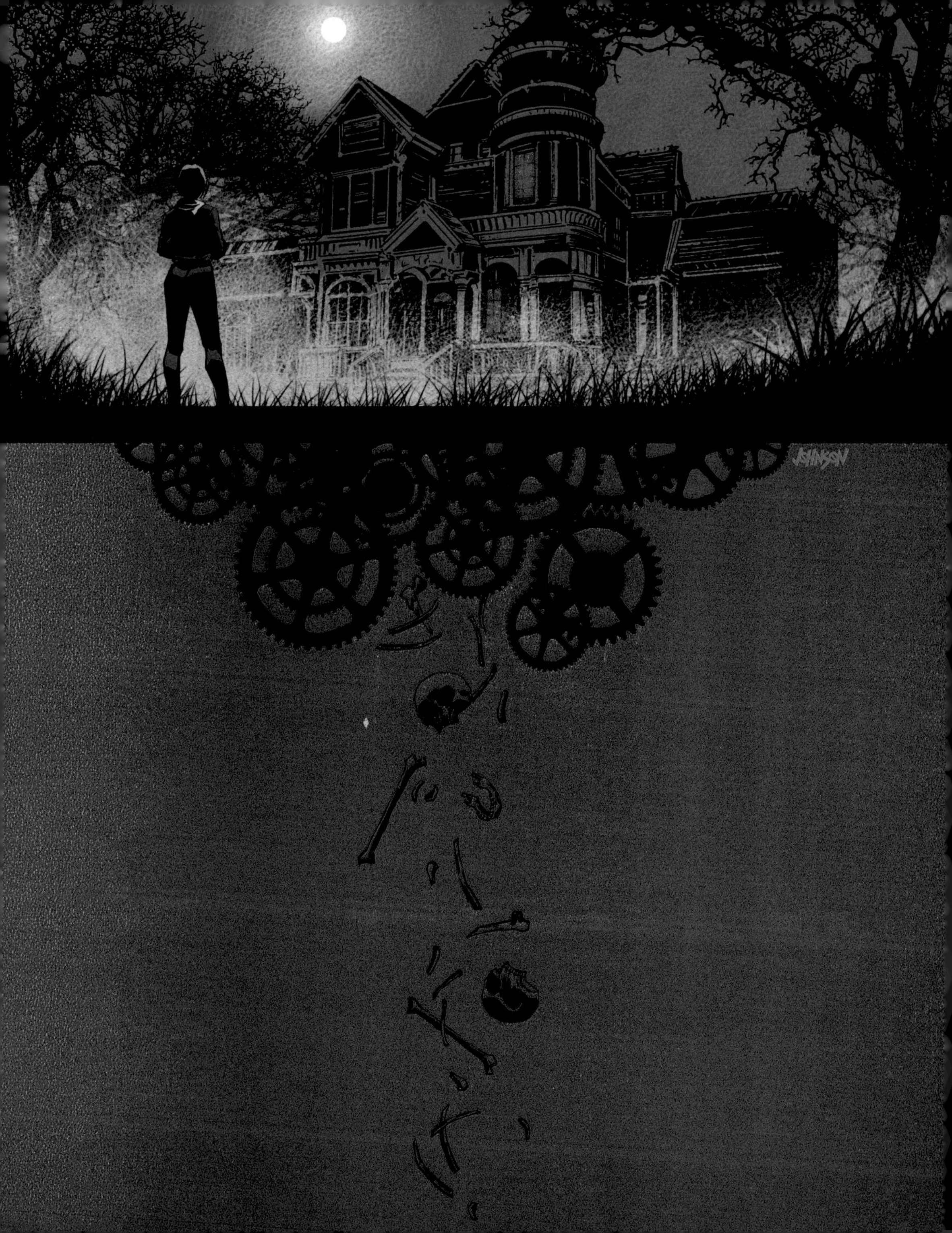
JOHNSON

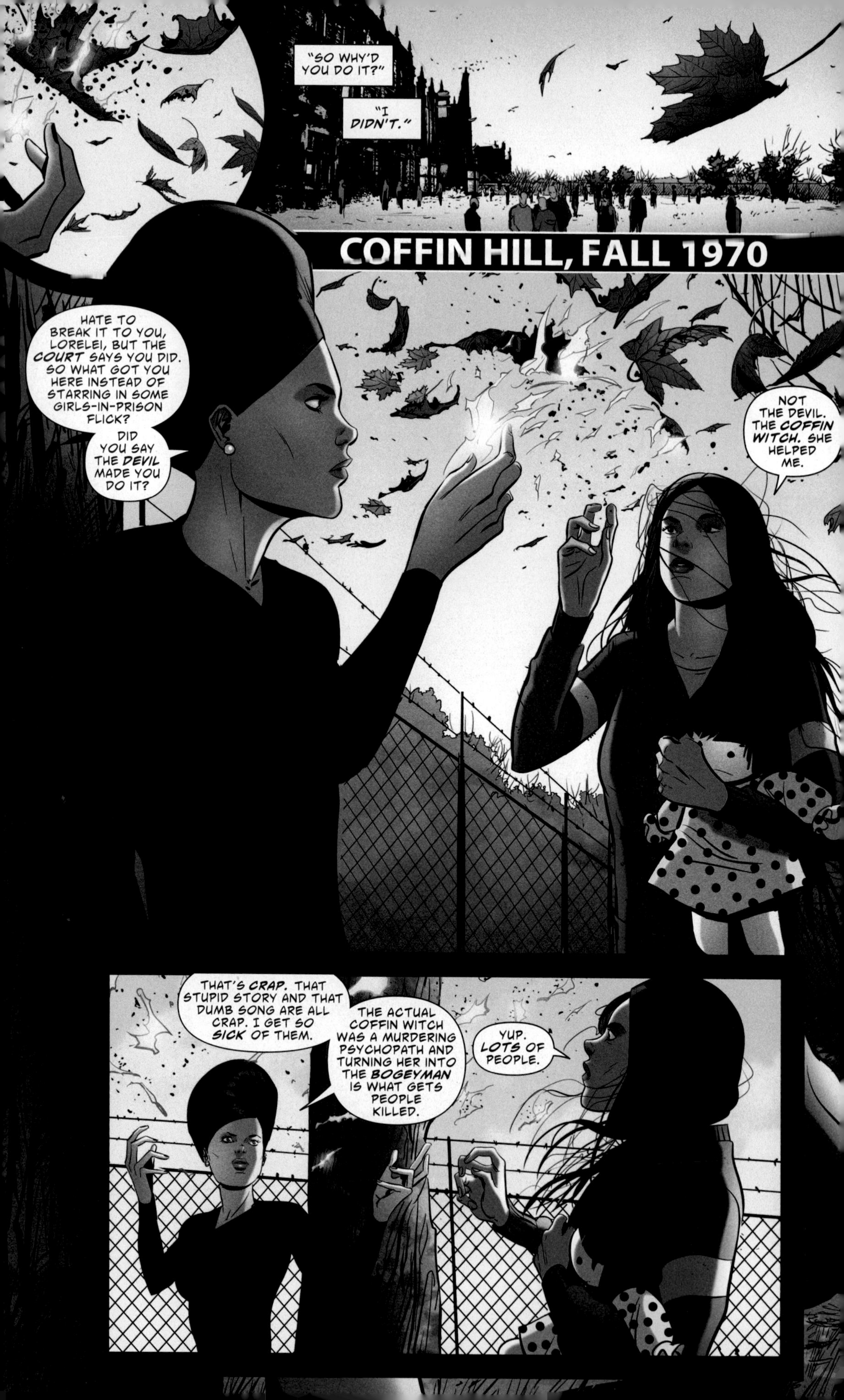
"SO WHY'D YOU DO IT?"
"I DIDN'T."
COFFIN HILL, FALL 1970
HATE TO BREAK IT TO YOU, LORELEI, BUT THE COURT SAYS YOU DID. SO WHAT GOT YOU HERE INSTEAD OF STARRING IN SOME GIRLS-IN-PRISON FLICK?
DID YOU SAY THE DEVIL MADE YOU DO IT?
NOT THE DEVIL. THE COFFIN WITCH. SHE HELPED ME.
THAT'S CRAP. THAT STUPID STORY AND THAT DUMB SONG ARE ALL CRAP. I GET SO SICK OF THEM.
THE ACTUAL COFFIN WITCH WAS A MURDERING PSYCHOPATH AND TURNING HER INTO THE BOGEYMAN IS WHAT GETS PEOPLE KILLED.
YUP. LOTS OF PEOPLE.

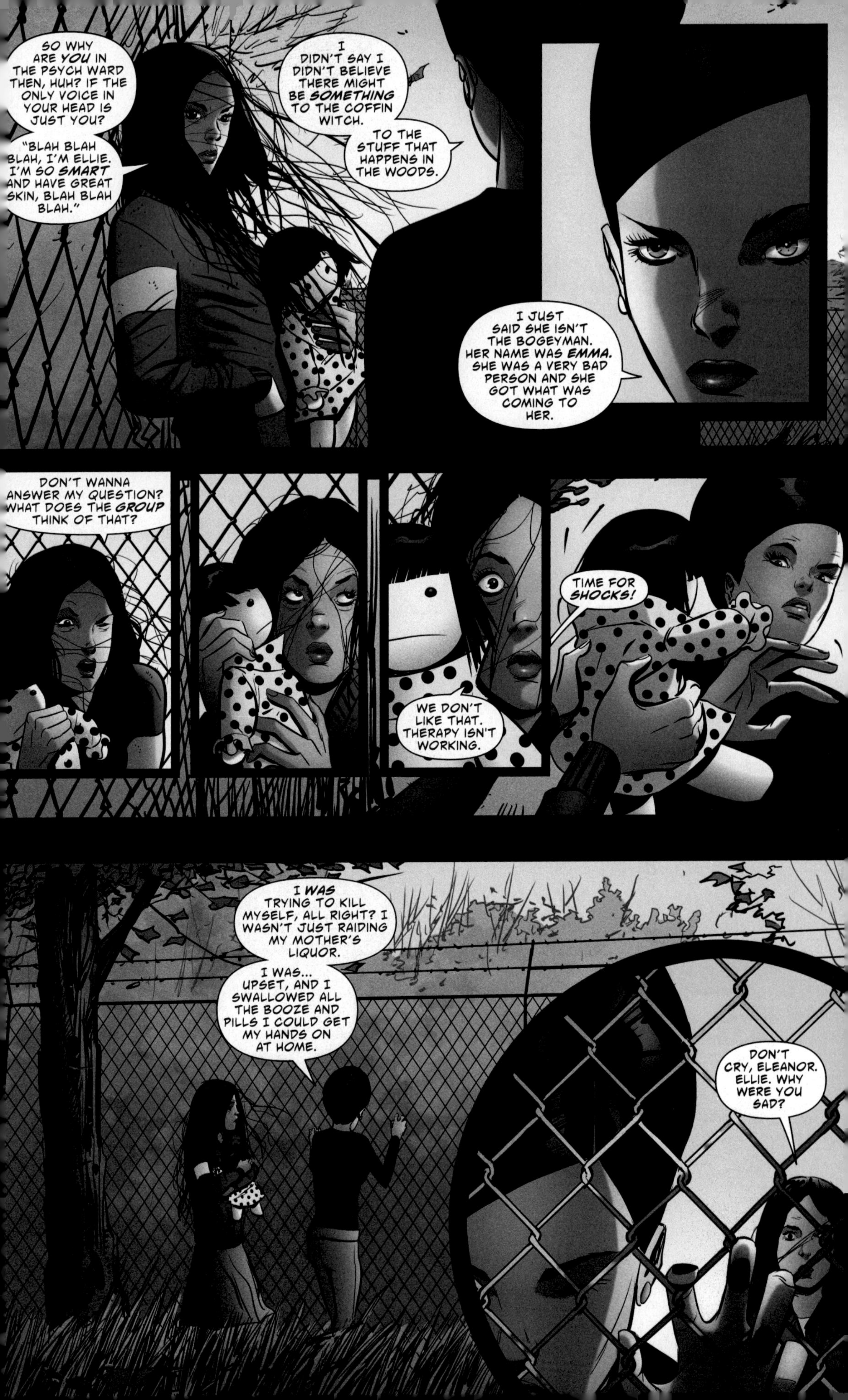

SO WHY ARE YOU IN THE PSYCH WARD THEN, HUH? IF THE ONLY VOICE IN YOUR HEAD IS JUST YOU?
"BLAH BLAH BLAH, I'M ELLIE. I'M SO SMART AND HAVE GREAT SKIN, BLAH BLAH BLAH."
I DIDN'T SAY I DIDN'T BELIEVE THERE MIGHT BE SOMETHING TO THE COFFIN WITCH.
TO THE STUFF THAT HAPPENS IN THE WOODS.
I JUST SAID SHE ISN'T THE BOGEYMAN. HER NAME WAS EMMA. SHE WAS A VERY BAD PERSON AND SHE GOT WHAT WAS COMING TO HER.
DON'T WANNA ANSWER MY QUESTION? WHAT DOES THE GROUP THINK OF THAT?
TIME FOR SHOCKS!
WE DON'T LIKE THAT. THERAPY ISN'T WORKING.
I WAS TRYING TO KILL MYSELF, ALL RIGHT? I WASN'T JUST RAIDING MY MOTHER'S LIQUOR.
I WAS... UPSET, AND I SWALLOWED ALL THE BOOZE AND PILLS I COULD GET MY HANDS ON AT HOME.
DON'T CRY, ELEANOR. ELLIE. WHY WERE YOU SAD?

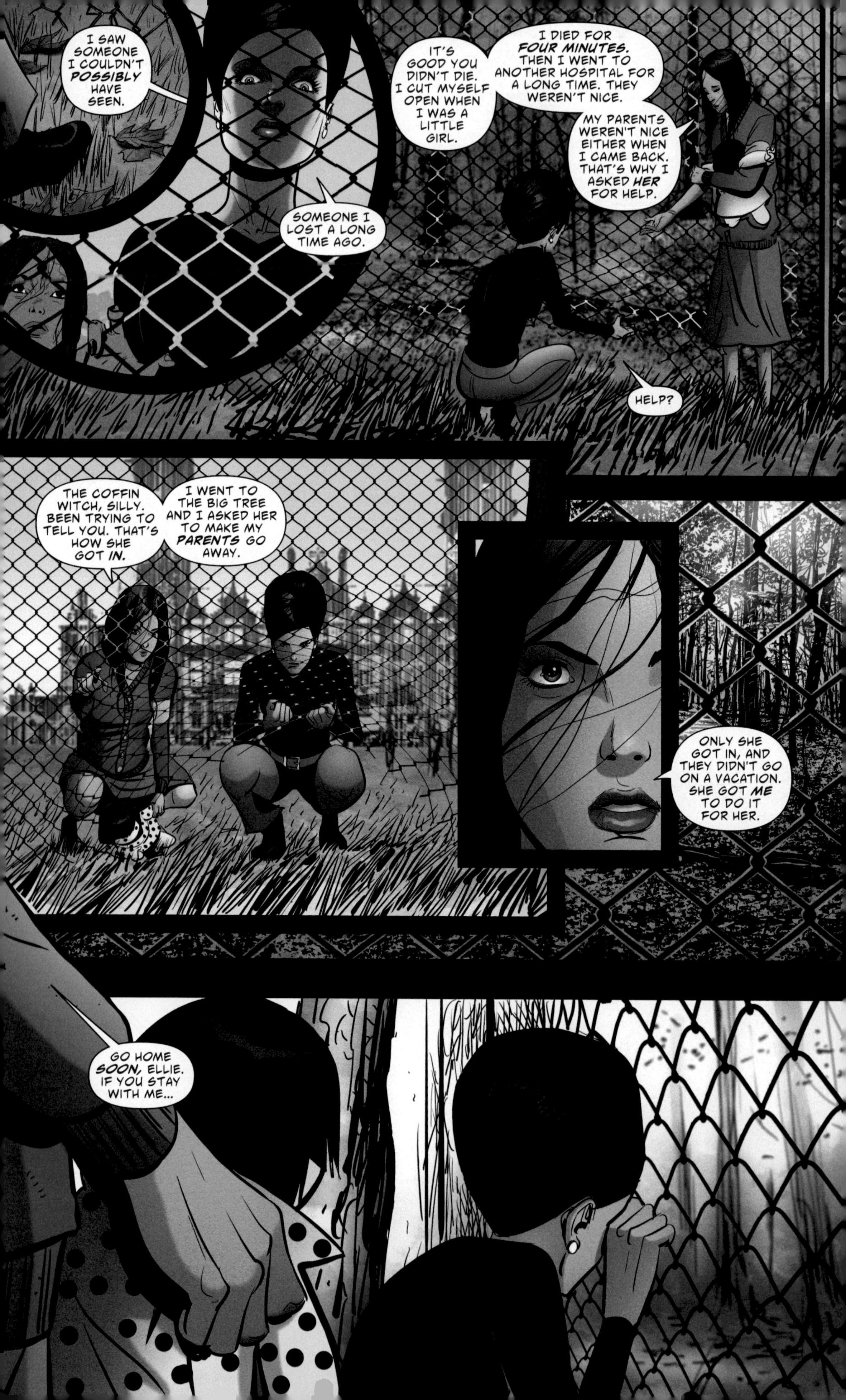
I SAW SOMEONE I COULDN'T POSSIBLY HAVE SEEN.
SOMEONE I LOST A LONG TIME AGO.
IT'S GOOD YOU DIDN'T DIE. I CUT MYSELF OPEN WHEN I WAS A LITTLE GIRL.
I DIED FOR FOUR MINUTES. THEN I WENT TO ANOTHER HOSPITAL FOR A LONG TIME. THEY WEREN'T NICE.
MY PARENTS WEREN'T NICE EITHER WHEN I CAME BACK. THAT'S WHY I ASKED HER FOR HELP.
HELP?
THE COFFIN WITCH, SILLY. BEEN TRYING TO TELL YOU. THAT'S HOW SHE GOT IN.
I WENT TO THE BIG TREE AND I ASKED HER TO MAKE MY PARENTS GO AWAY.
ONLY SHE GOT IN, AND THEY DIDN'T GO ON A VACATION. SHE GOT ME TO DO IT FOR HER.
GO HOME SOON, ELLIE. IF YOU STAY WITH ME...

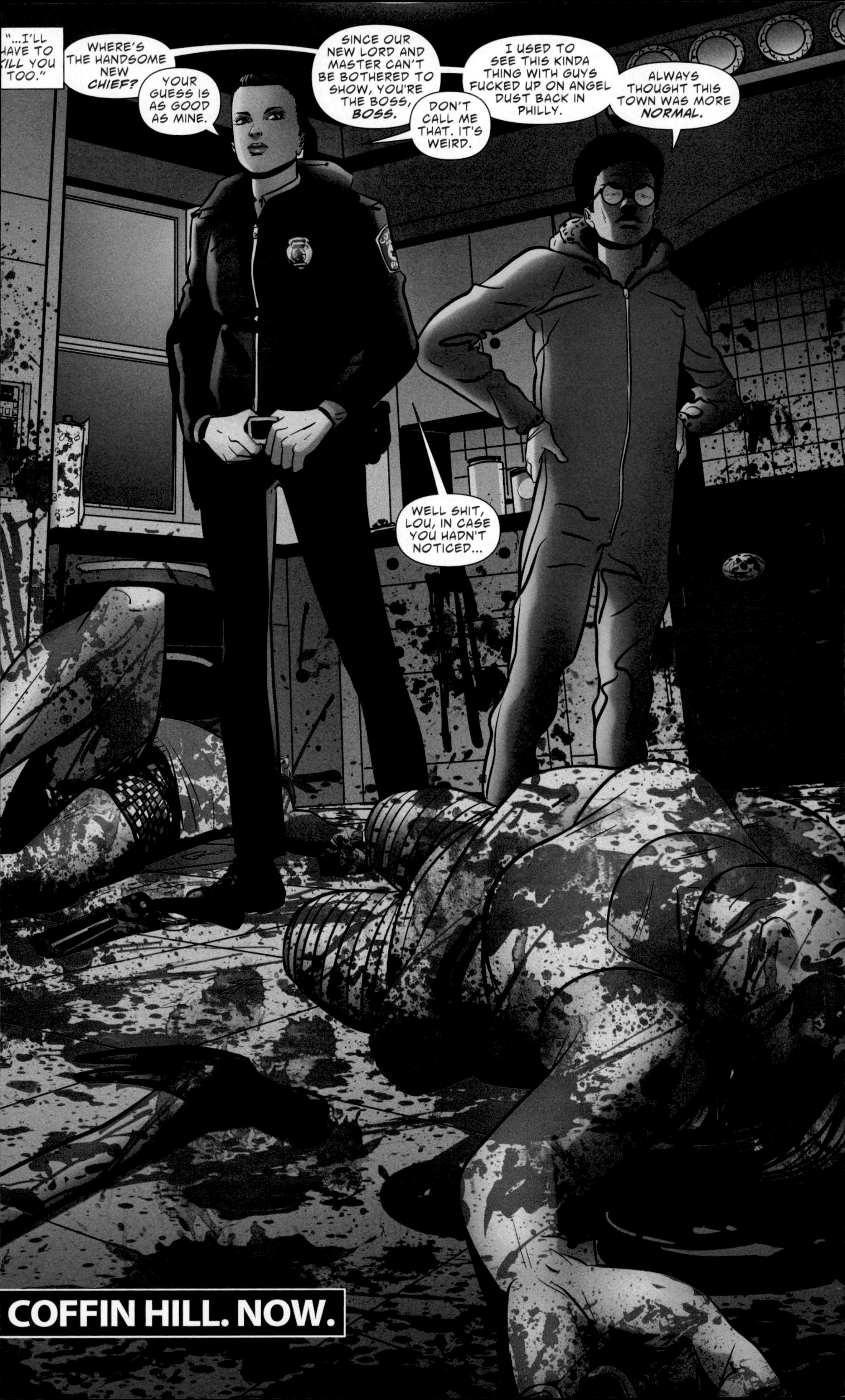
"...I'LL HAVE TO KILL YOU TOO."
WHERE'S THE HANDSOME NEW CHIEF?
YOUR GUESS IS AS GOOD AS MINE.
SINCE OUR NEW LORD AND MASTER CAN'T BE BOTHERED TO SHOW, YOU'RE THE BOSS, BOSS.
DON'T CALL ME THAT. IT'S WEIRD.
I USED TO SEE THIS KINDA THING WITH GUYS FUCKED UP ON ANGEL DUST BACK IN PHILLY.
ALWAYS THOUGHT THIS TOWN WAS MORE NORMAL.
WELL SHIT, LOU, IN CASE YOU HADN'T NOTICED...
COFFIN HILL. NOW.

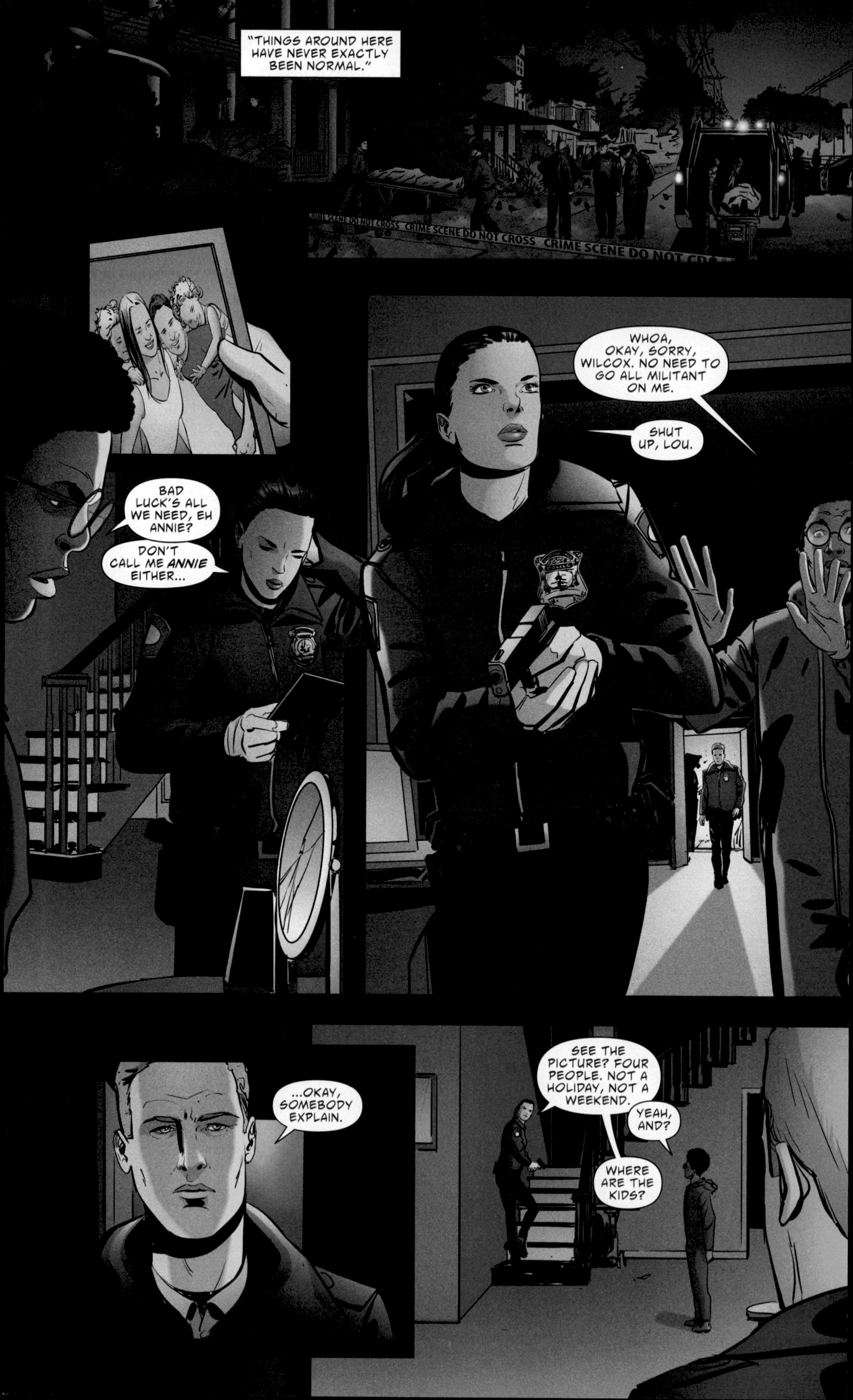
"THINGS AROUND HERE HAVE NEVER EXACTLY BEEN NORMAL."
CRIME SCENE DO NOT CROSS
WHOA, OKAY, SORRY, WILCOX. NO NEED TO GO ALL MILITANT ON ME.
SHUT UP, LOU.
BAD LUCK'S ALL WE NEED, EH ANNIE?
DON'T CALL ME ANNIE EITHER...
...OKAY, SOMEBODY EXPLAIN.
SEE THE PICTURE? FOUR PEOPLE. NOT A HOLIDAY, NOT A WEEKEND.
YEAH, AND?
WHERE ARE THE KIDS?

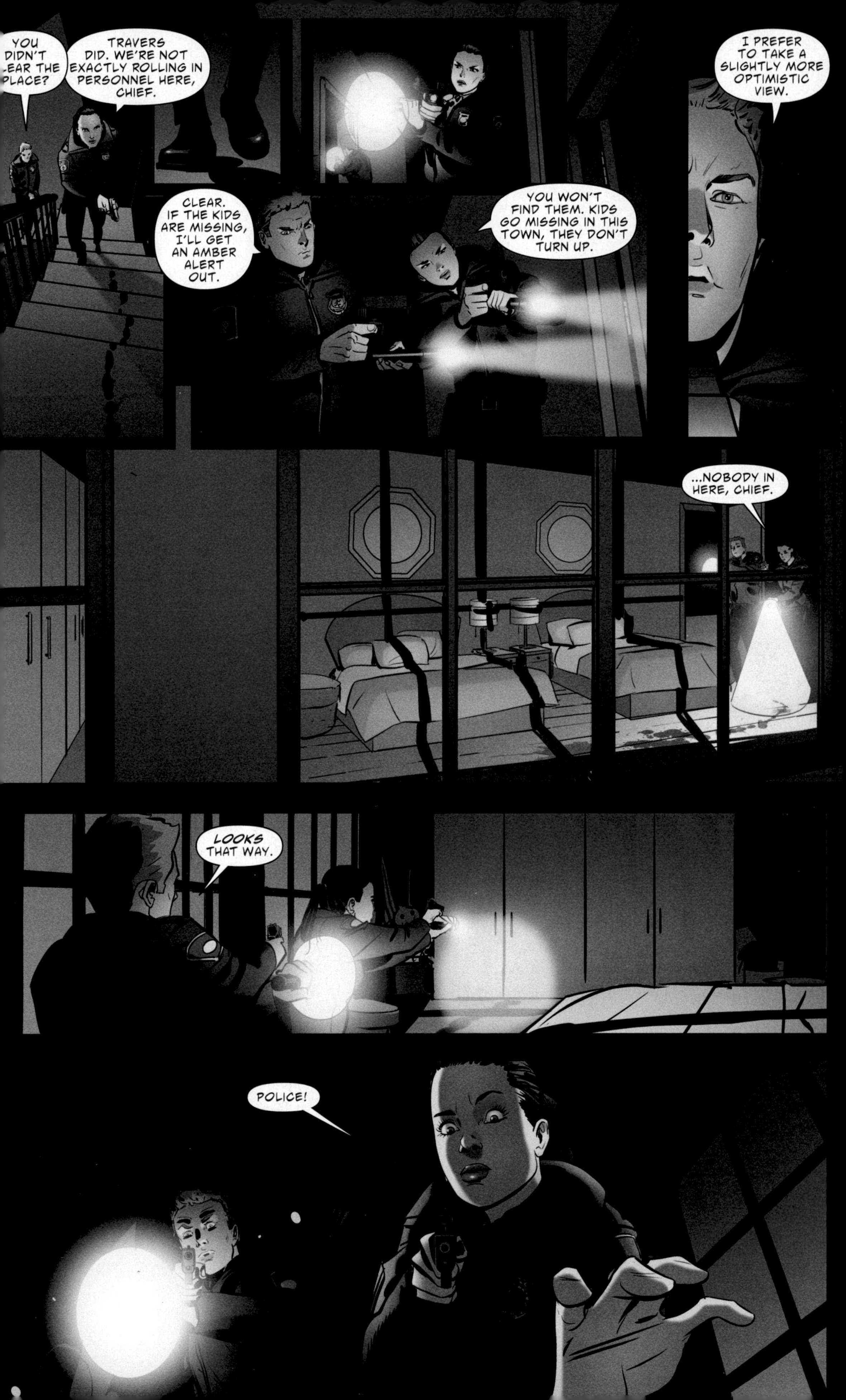
YOU DIDN'T CLEAR THE PLACE?
TRAVERS DID. WE'RE NOT EXACTLY ROLLING IN PERSONNEL HERE, CHIEF.
CLEAR. IF THE KIDS ARE MISSING, I'LL GET AN AMBER ALERT OUT.
YOU WON'T FIND THEM. KIDS GO MISSING IN THIS TOWN, THEY DON'T TURN UP.
I PREFER TO TAKE A SLIGHTLY MORE OPTIMISTIC VIEW.
...NOBODY IN HERE, CHIEF.
LOOKS THAT WAY.
POLICE!

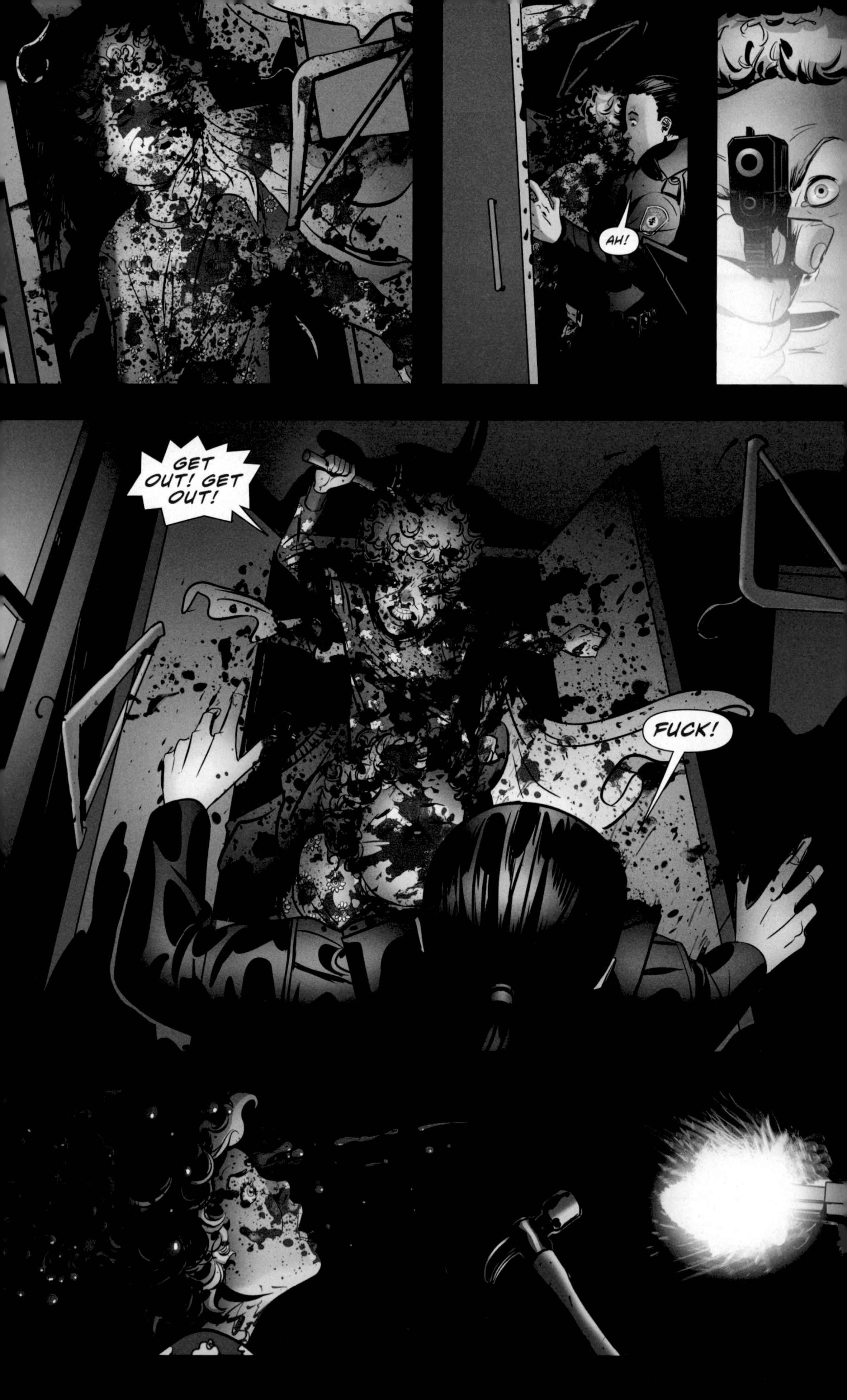
AH!
GET OUT! GET OUT!
FUCK!

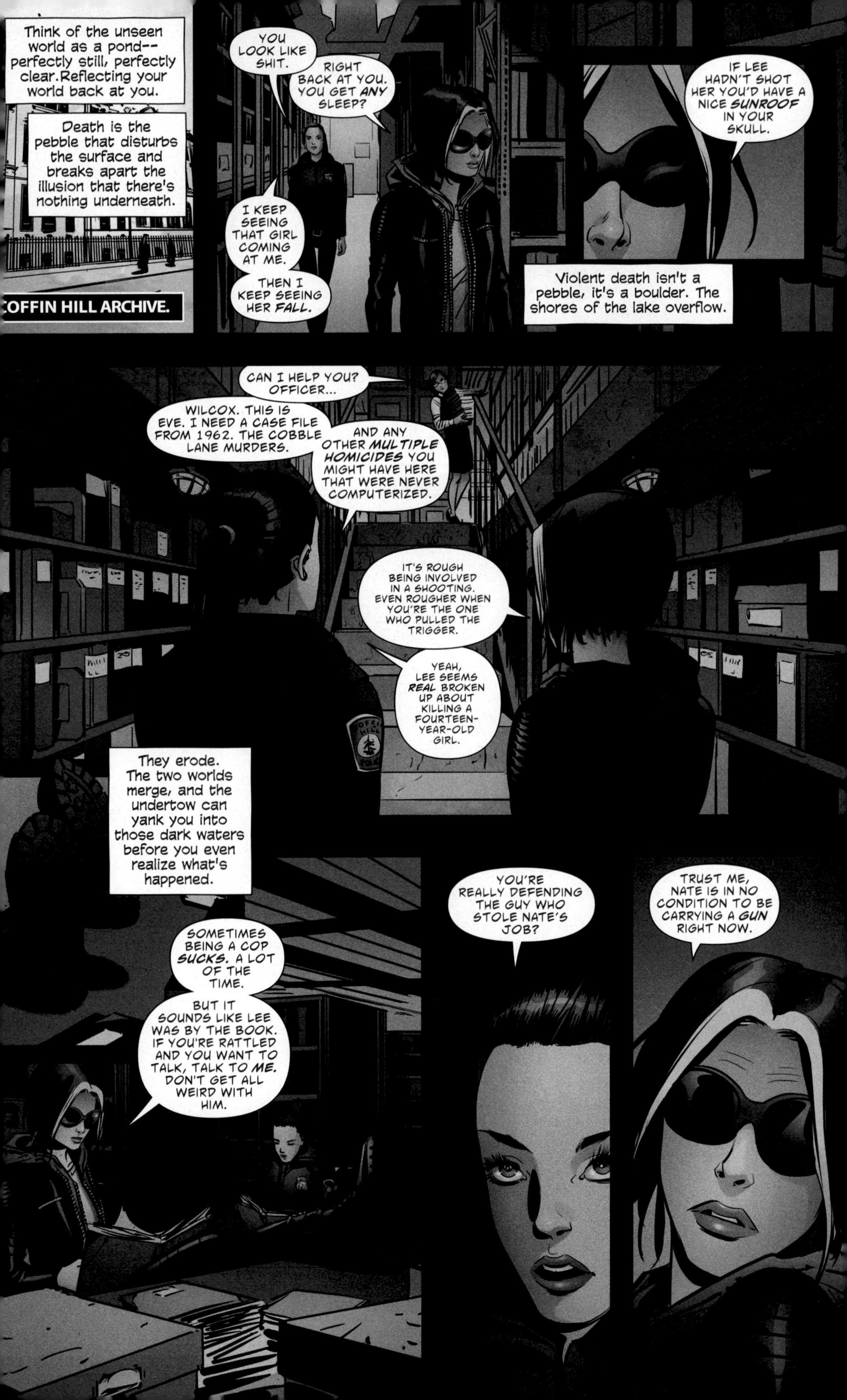
Think of the unseen world as a pond--perfectly still, perfectly clear. Reflecting your world back at you.
Death is the pebble that disturbs the surface and breaks apart the illusion that there's nothing underneath.
COFFIN HILL ARCHIVE.
YOU LOOK LIKE SHIT.
RIGHT BACK AT YOU. YOU GET ANY SLEEP?
I KEEP SEEING THAT GIRL COMING AT ME.
THEN I KEEP SEEING HER FALL.
IF LEE HADN'T SHOT HER YOU'D HAVE A NICE SUNROOF IN YOUR SKULL.
Violent death isn't a pebble, it's a boulder. The shores of the lake overflow.
CAN I HELP YOU? OFFICER...
WILCOX. THIS IS EVE. I NEED A CASE FILE FROM 1962. THE COBBLE LANE MURDERS.
AND ANY OTHER MULTIPLE HOMICIDES YOU MIGHT HAVE HERE THAT WERE NEVER COMPUTERIZED.
IT'S ROUGH BEING INVOLVED IN A SHOOTING. EVEN ROUGHER WHEN YOU'RE THE ONE WHO PULLED THE TRIGGER.
YEAH, LEE SEEMS REAL BROKEN UP ABOUT KILLING A FOURTEEN-YEAR-OLD GIRL.
They erode. The two worlds merge, and the undertow can yank you into those dark waters before you even realize what's happened.
SOMETIMES BEING A COP SUCKS. A LOT OF THE TIME.
BUT IT SOUNDS LIKE LEE WAS BY THE BOOK. IF YOU'RE RATTLED AND YOU WANT TO TALK, TALK TO ME. DON'T GET ALL WEIRD WITH HIM.
YOU'RE REALLY DEFENDING THE GUY WHO STOLE NATE'S JOB?
TRUST ME, NATE IS IN NO CONDITION TO BE CARRYING A GUN RIGHT NOW.

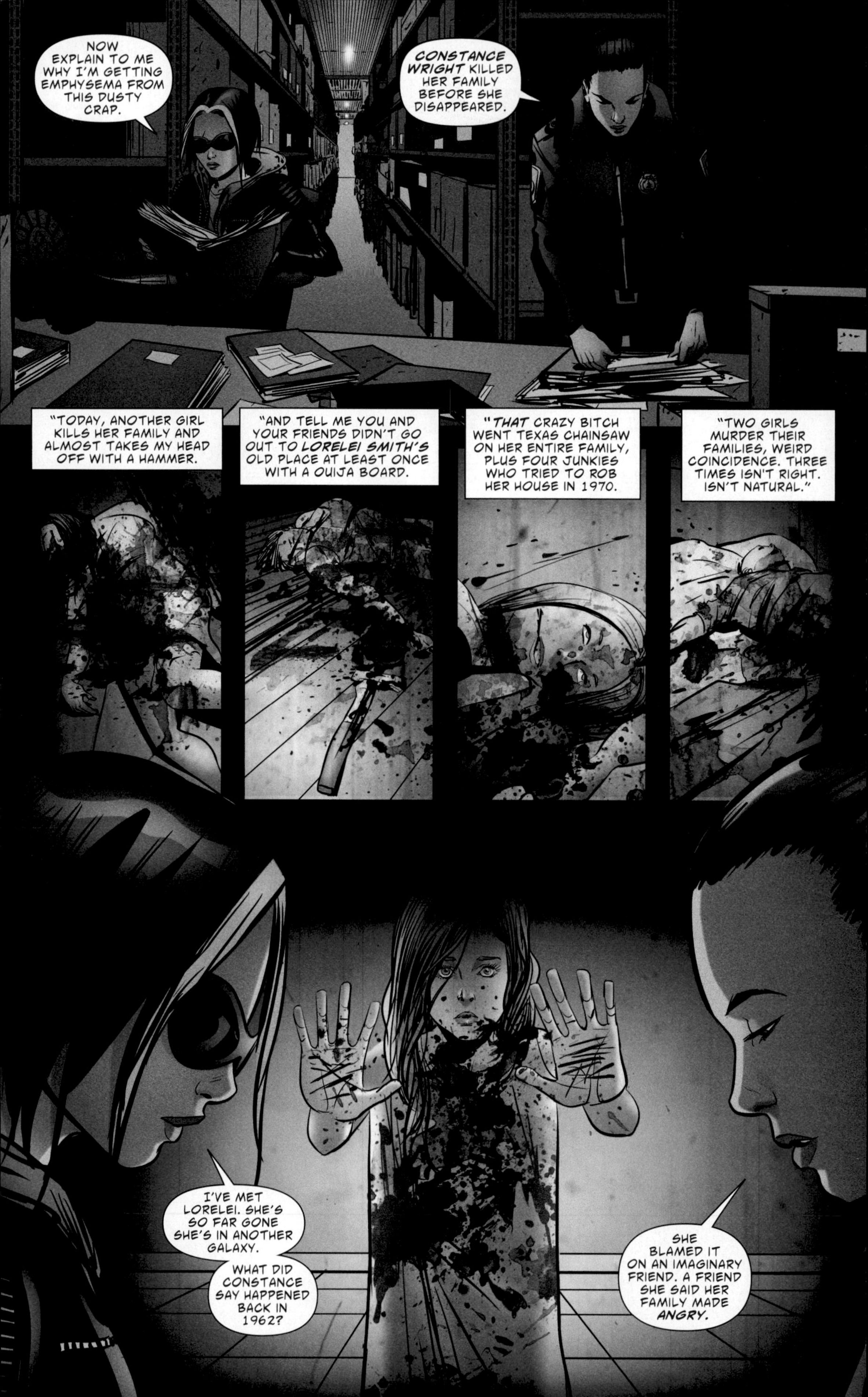
NOW EXPLAIN TO ME WHY I'M GETTING EMPHYSEMA FROM THIS DUSTY CRAP.
CONSTANCE WRIGHT KILLED HER FAMILY BEFORE SHE DISAPPEARED.
"TODAY, ANOTHER GIRL KILLS HER FAMILY AND ALMOST TAKES MY HEAD OFF WITH A HAMMER.
"AND TELL ME YOU AND YOUR FRIENDS DIDN'T GO OUT TO LORELEI SMITH'S OLD PLACE AT LEAST ONCE WITH A OUIJA BOARD.
"THAT CRAZY BITCH WENT TEXAS CHAINSAW ON HER ENTIRE FAMILY, PLUS FOUR JUNKIES WHO TRIED TO ROB HER HOUSE IN 1970.
"TWO GIRLS MURDER THEIR FAMILIES, WEIRD COINCIDENCE. THREE TIMES ISN'T RIGHT. ISN'T NATURAL."
I'VE MET LORELEI. SHE'S SO FAR GONE SHE'S IN ANOTHER GALAXY.
WHAT DID CONSTANCE SAY HAPPENED BACK IN 1962?
SHE BLAMED IT ON AN IMAGINARY FRIEND. A FRIEND SHE SAID HER FAMILY MADE ANGRY.

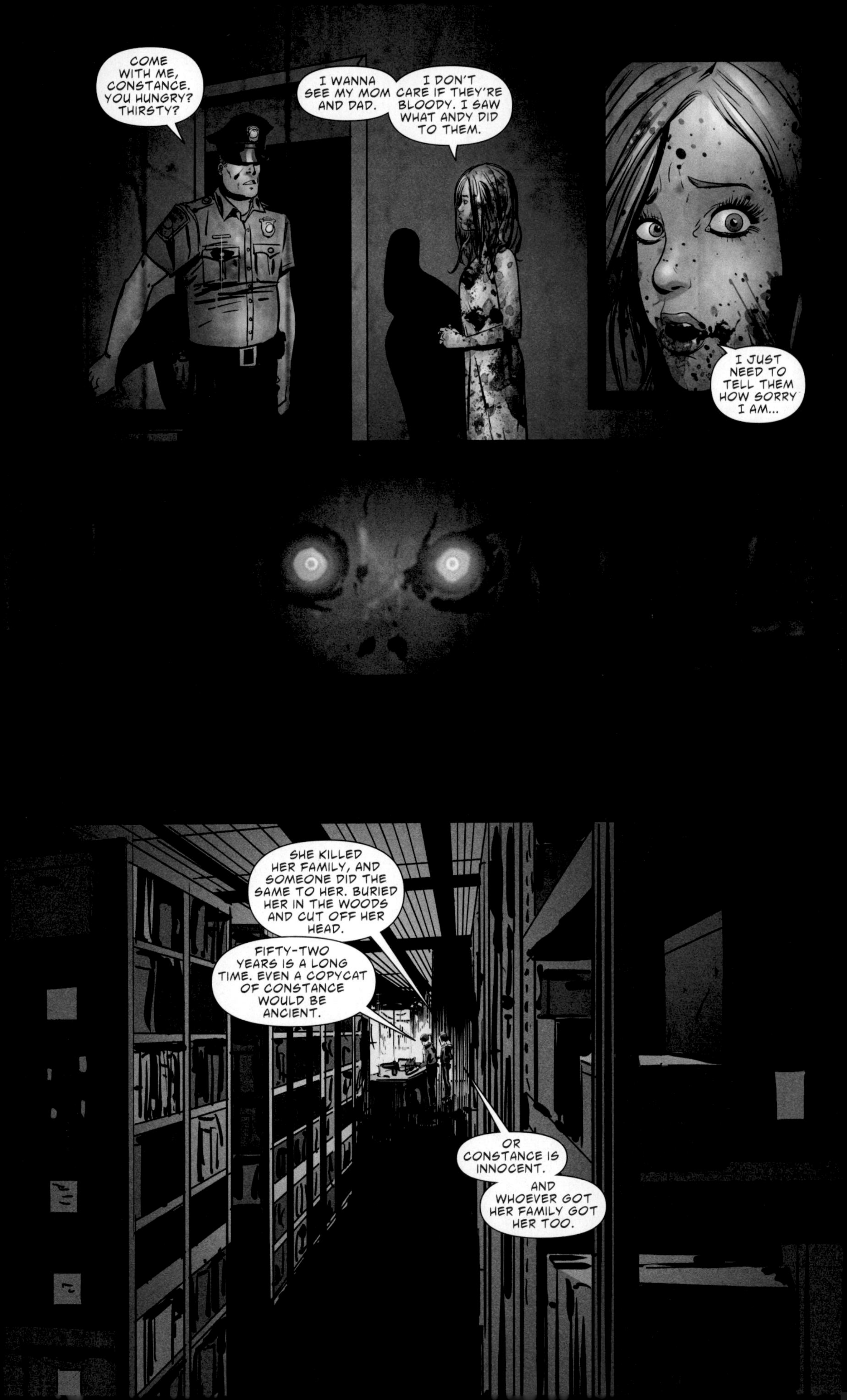
COME WITH ME, CONSTANCE. YOU HUNGRY? THIRSTY?
I WANNA SEE MY MOM AND DAD.
I DON'T CARE IF THEY'RE BLOODY. I SAW WHAT ANDY DID TO THEM.
I JUST NEED TO TELL THEM HOW SORRY I AM...
SHE KILLED HER FAMILY, AND SOMEONE DID THE SAME TO HER. BURIED HER IN THE WOODS AND CUT OFF HER HEAD.
FIFTY-TWO YEARS IS A LONG TIME. EVEN A COPYCAT OF CONSTANCE WOULD BE ANCIENT.
OR CONSTANCE IS INNOCENT.
AND WHOEVER GOT HER FAMILY GOT HER TOO.

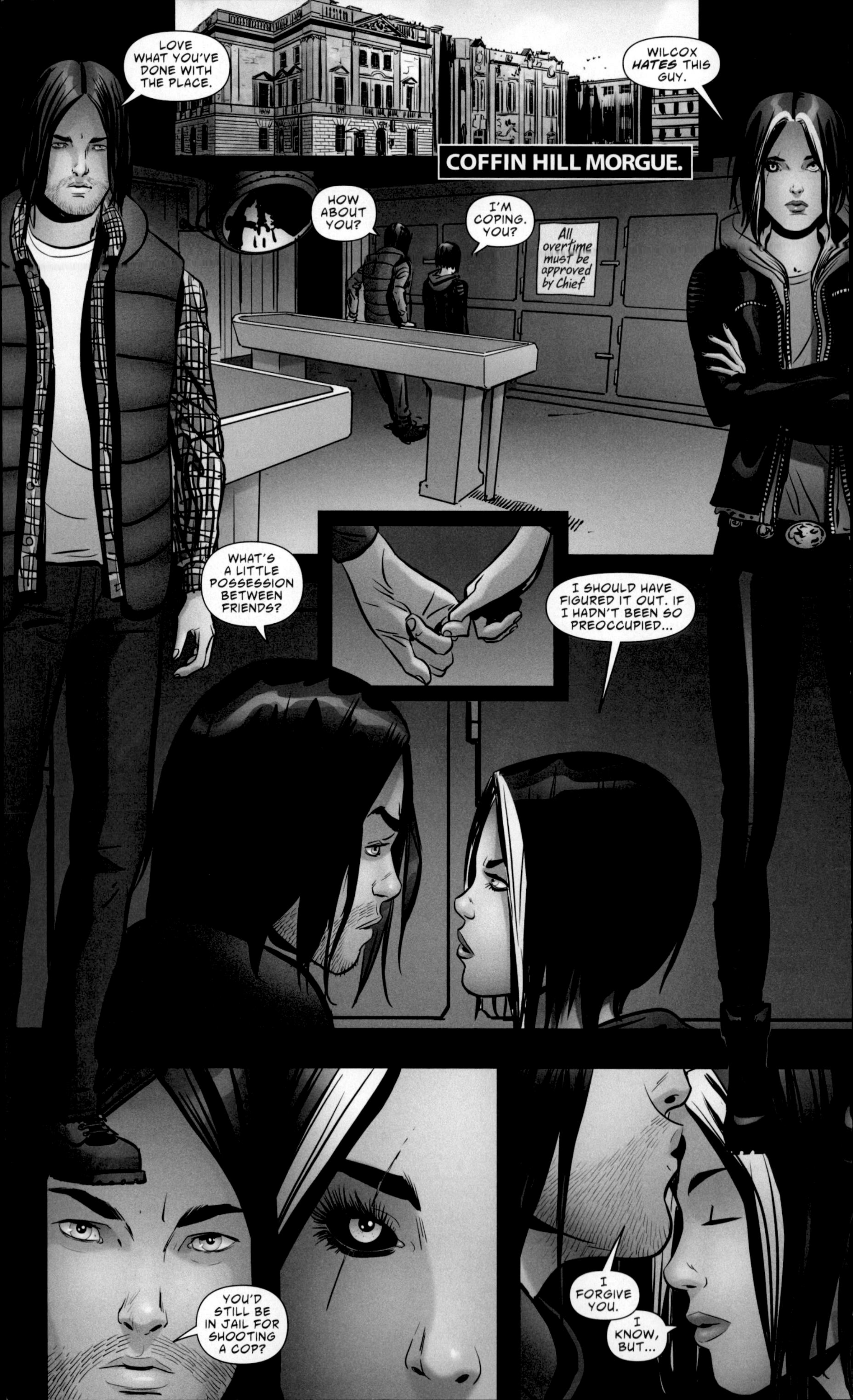
LOVE WHAT YOU'VE DONE WITH THE PLACE.
WILCOX HATES THIS GUY.
COFFIN HILL MORGUE.
HOW ABOUT YOU?
I'M COPING. YOU?
All overtime must be approved by Chief
WHAT'S A LITTLE POSSESSION BETWEEN FRIENDS?
I SHOULD HAVE FIGURED IT OUT. IF I HADN'T BEEN SO PREOCCUPIED...
YOU'D STILL BE IN JAIL FOR SHOOTING A COP?
I FORGIVE YOU.
I KNOW, BUT...

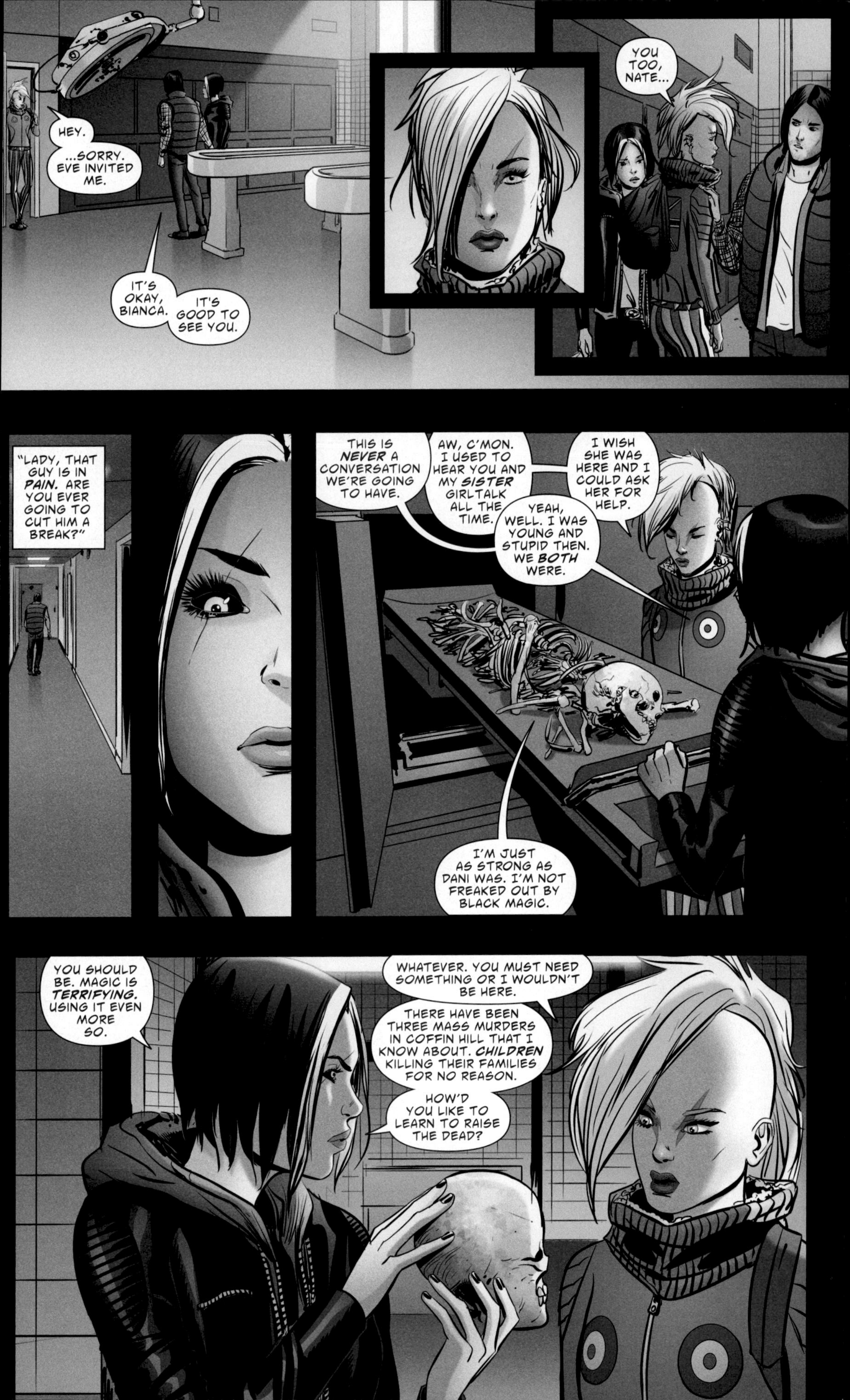
HEY.
...SORRY. EVE INVITED ME.
IT'S OKAY, BIANCA.
IT'S GOOD TO SEE YOU.
YOU TOO, NATE...
"LADY, THAT GUY IS IN PAIN. ARE YOU EVER GOING TO CUT HIM A BREAK?"
THIS IS NEVER A CONVERSATION WE'RE GOING TO HAVE.
AW, C'MON. I USED TO HEAR YOU AND MY SISTER GIRLTALK ALL THE TIME.
I WISH SHE WAS HERE AND I COULD ASK HER FOR HELP.
YEAH, WELL. I WAS YOUNG AND STUPID THEN. WE BOTH WERE.
I'M JUST AS STRONG AS DANI WAS. I'M NOT FREAKED OUT BY BLACK MAGIC.
YOU SHOULD BE. MAGIC IS TERRIFYING. USING IT EVEN MORE SO.
WHATEVER. YOU MUST NEED SOMETHING OR I WOULDN'T BE HERE.
THERE HAVE BEEN THREE MASS MURDERS IN COFFIN HILL THAT I KNOW ABOUT. CHILDREN KILLING THEIR FAMILIES FOR NO REASON.
HOW'D YOU LIKE TO LEARN TO RAISE THE DEAD?

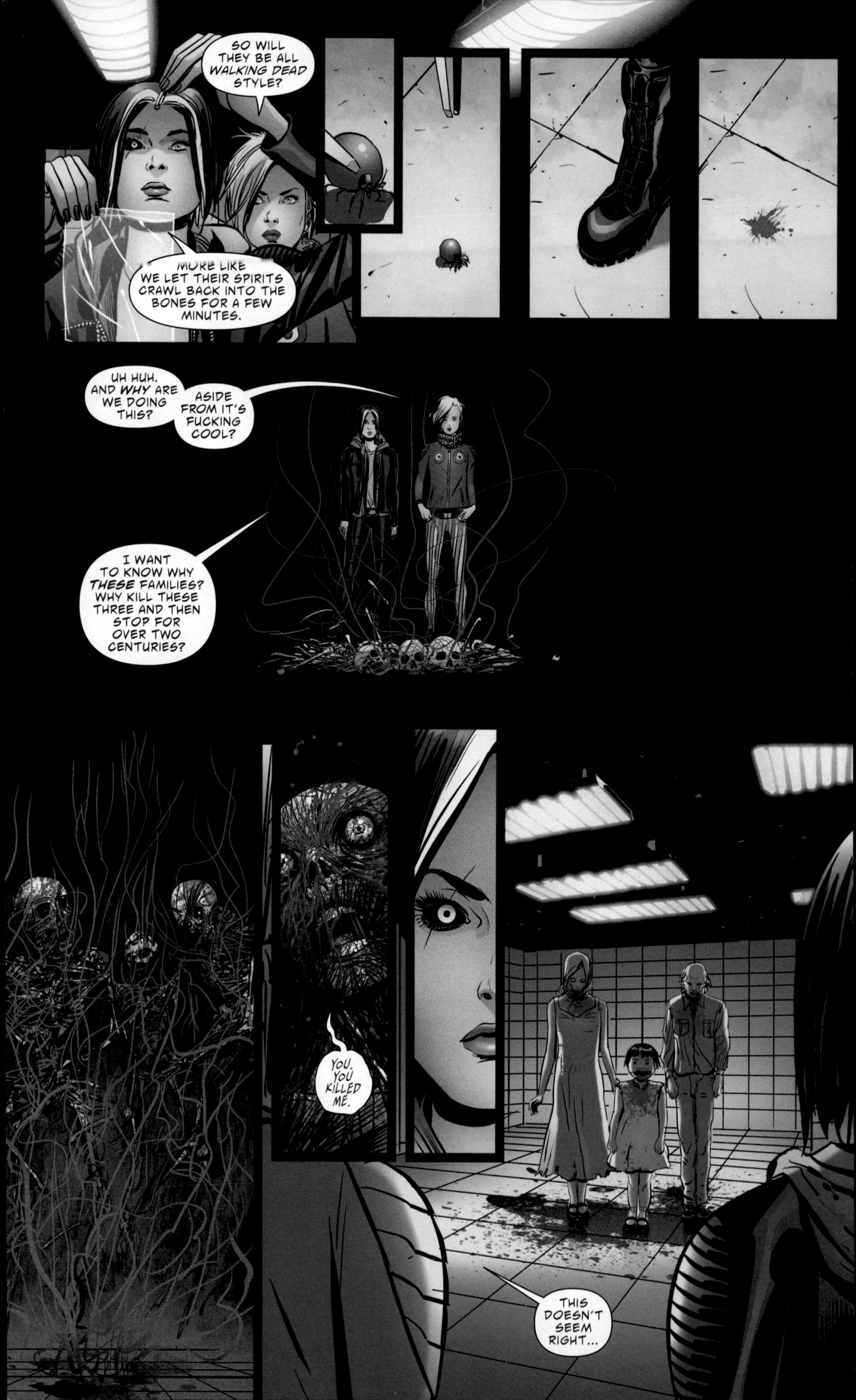
SO WILL THEY BE ALL WALKING DEAD STYLE?
MORE LIKE WE LET THEIR SPIRITS CRAWL BACK INTO THE BONES FOR A FEW MINUTES.
UH HUH. AND WHY ARE WE DOING THIS?
ASIDE FROM IT'S FUCKING COOL?
I WANT TO KNOW WHY THESE FAMILIES? WHY KILL THESE THREE AND THEN STOP FOR OVER TWO CENTURIES?
YOU. YOU KILLED ME.
THIS DOESN'T SEEM RIGHT...

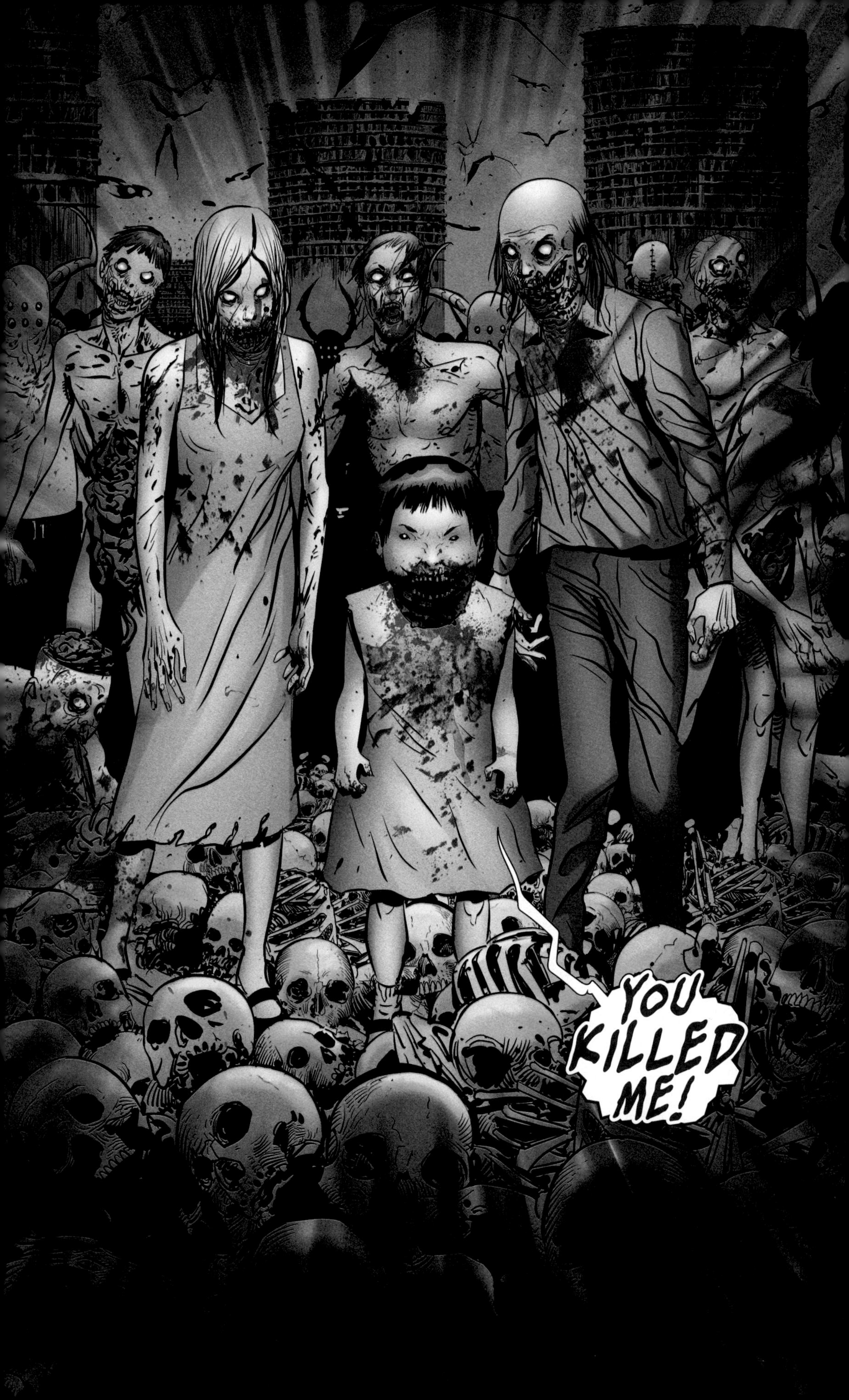
YOU KILLED ME!

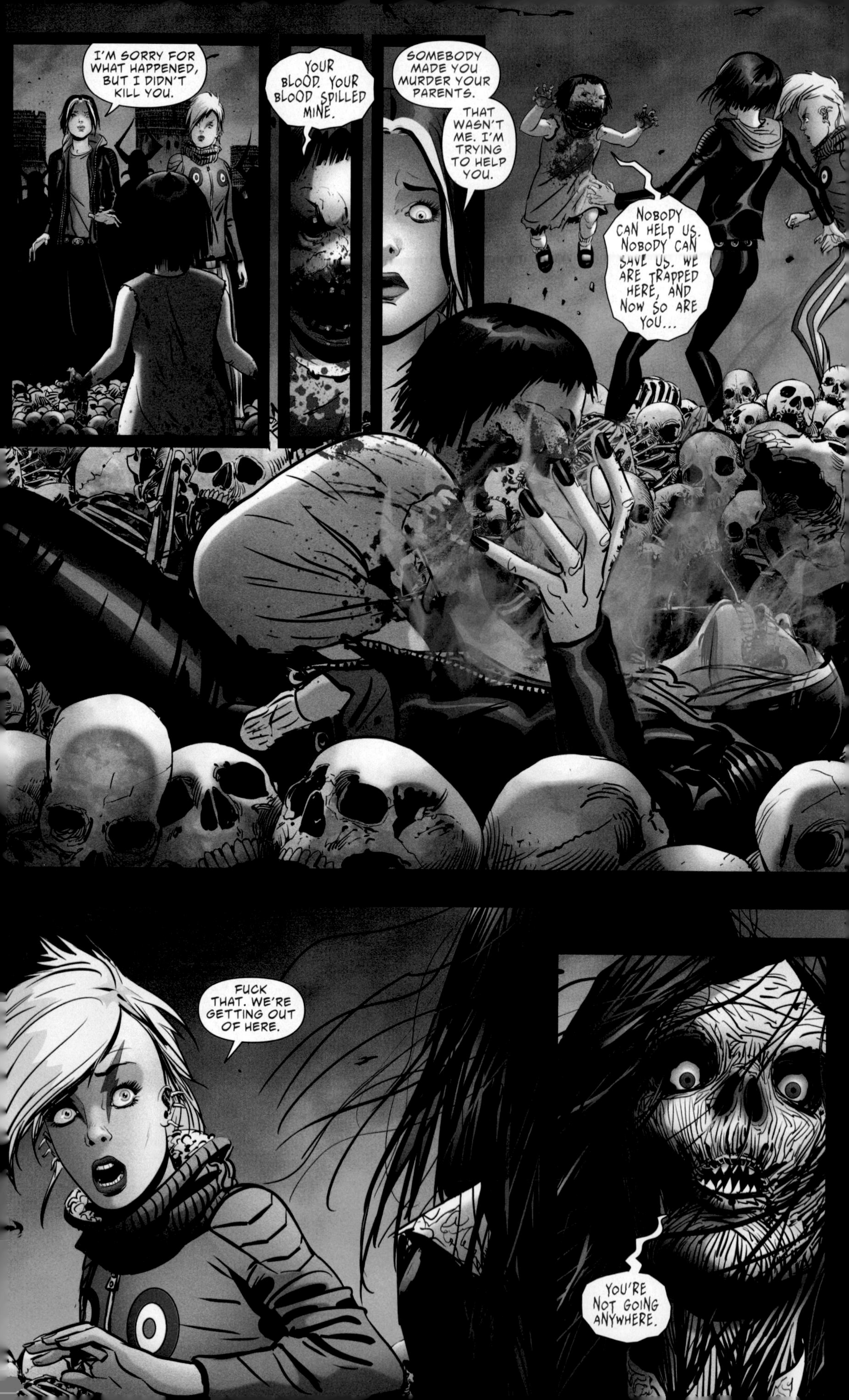

I'M SORRY FOR WHAT HAPPENED, BUT I DIDN'T KILL YOU.
YOUR BLOOD. YOUR BLOOD SPILLED MINE.
SOMEBODY MADE YOU MURDER YOUR PARENTS.
THAT WASN'T ME. I'M TRYING TO HELP YOU.
NOBODY CAN HELP US. NOBODY CAN SAVE US. WE ARE TRAPPED HERE, AND NOW SO ARE YOU...
FUCK THAT. WE'RE GETTING OUT OF HERE.
YOU'RE NOT GOING ANYWHERE.

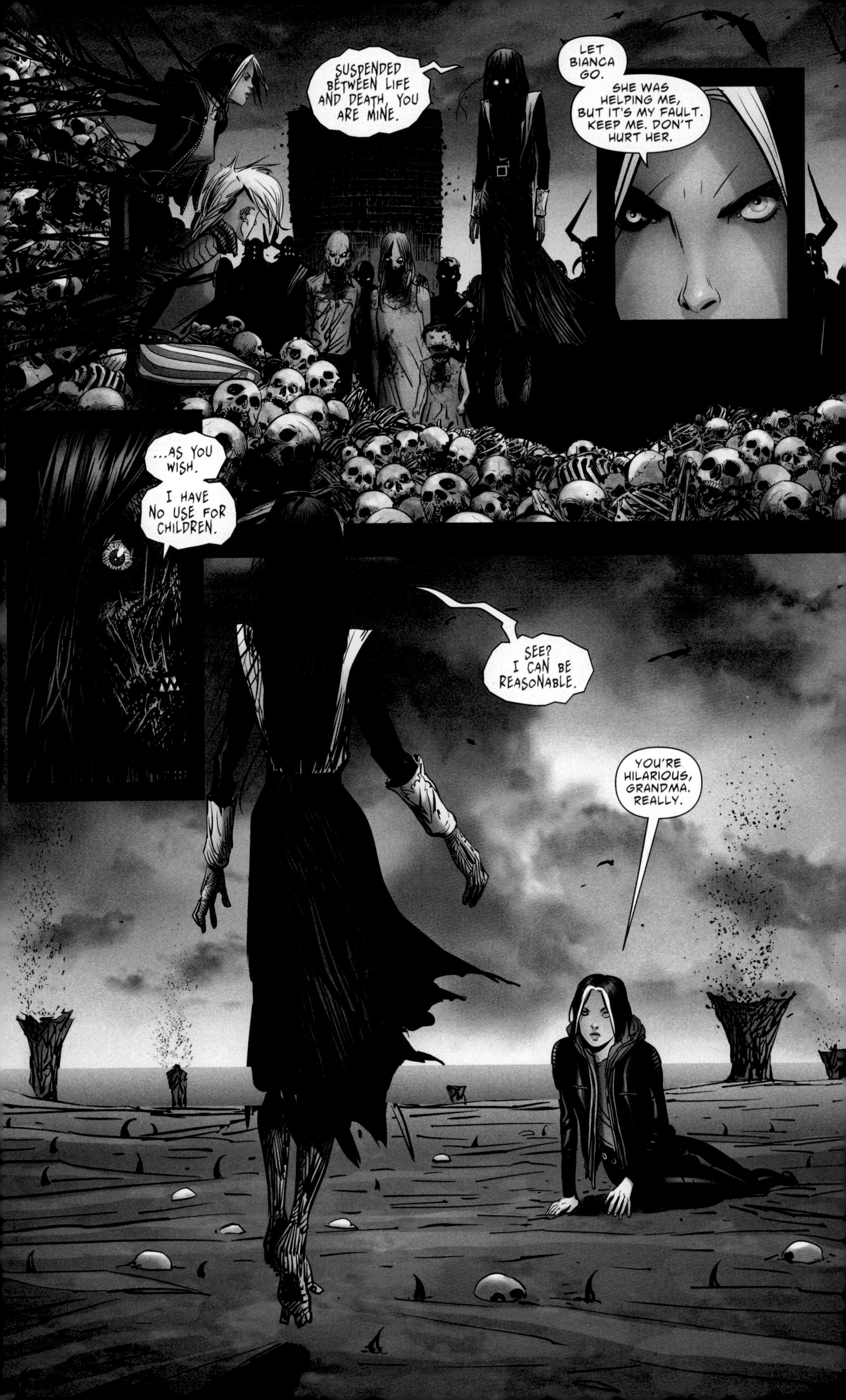
SUSPENDED BETWEEN LIFE AND DEATH, YOU ARE MINE.
LET BIANCA GO.
SHE WAS HELPING ME, BUT IT'S MY FAULT. KEEP ME. DON'T HURT HER.
...AS YOU WISH.
I HAVE NO USE FOR CHILDREN.
SEE? I CAN BE REASONABLE.
YOU'RE HILARIOUS, GRANDMA. REALLY.

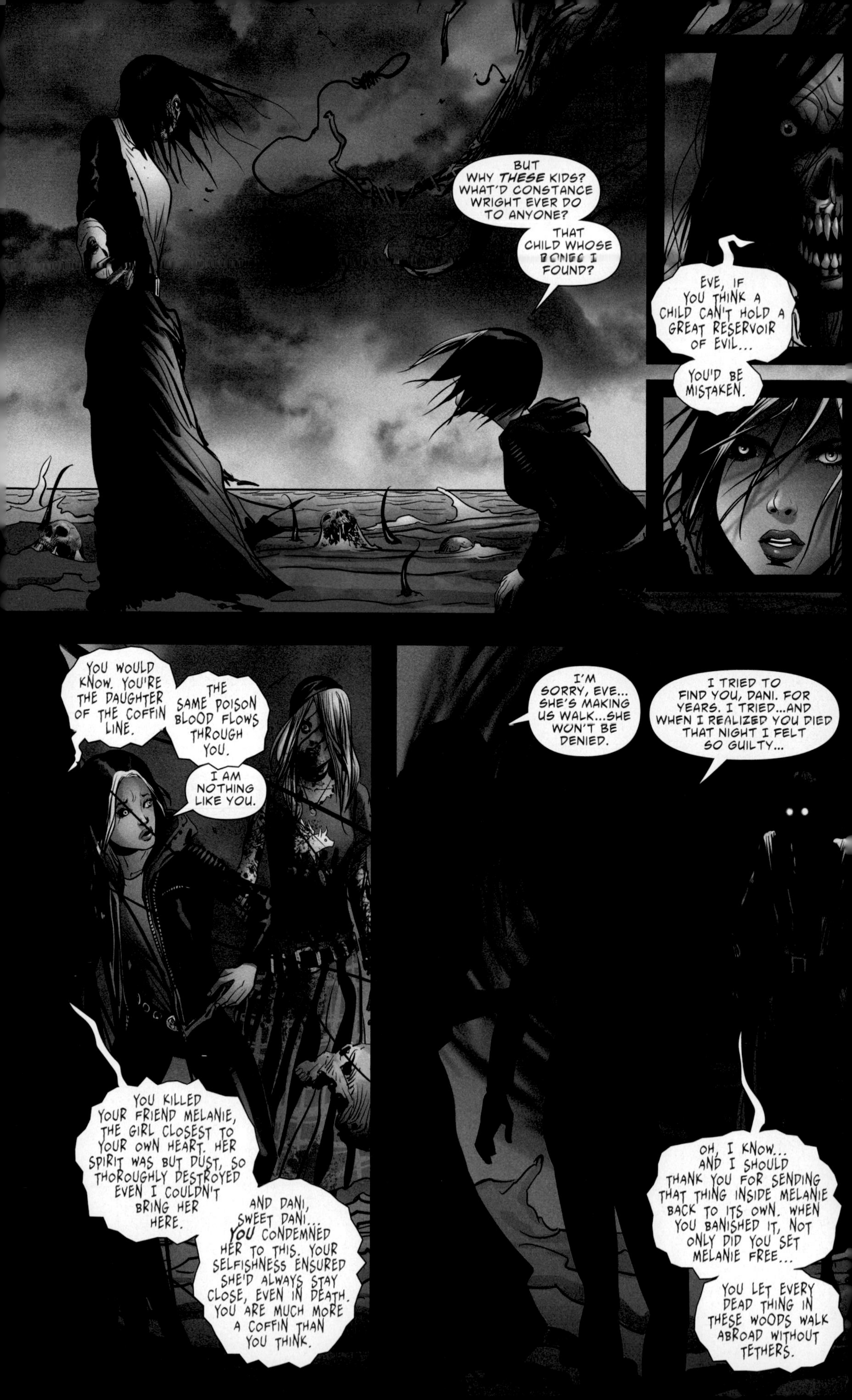

BUT WHY *THESE* KIDS? WHAT'D CONSTANCE WRIGHT EVER DO TO ANYONE?
THAT CHILD WHOSE BONES I FOUND?
EVE, IF YOU THINK A CHILD CAN'T HOLD A GREAT RESERVOIR OF EVIL...
YOU'D BE MISTAKEN.
YOU WOULD KNOW. YOU'RE THE DAUGHTER OF THE COFFIN LINE.
THE SAME POISON BLOOD FLOWS THROUGH YOU.
I AM NOTHING LIKE YOU.
YOU KILLED YOUR FRIEND MELANIE, THE GIRL CLOSEST TO YOUR OWN HEART. HER SPIRIT WAS BUT DUST, SO THOROUGHLY DESTROYED EVEN I COULDN'T BRING HER HERE.
AND DANI, SWEET DANI... *YOU* CONDEMNED HER TO THIS. YOUR SELFISHNESS ENSURED SHE'D ALWAYS STAY CLOSE, EVEN IN DEATH. YOU ARE MUCH MORE A COFFIN THAN YOU THINK.
I'M SORRY, EVE... SHE'S MAKING US WALK...SHE WON'T BE DENIED.
I TRIED TO FIND YOU, DANI. FOR YEARS. I TRIED...AND WHEN I REALIZED YOU DIED THAT NIGHT I FELT SO GUILTY...
OH, I KNOW... AND I SHOULD THANK YOU FOR SENDING THAT THING INSIDE MELANIE BACK TO ITS OWN. WHEN YOU BANISHED IT, NOT ONLY DID YOU SET MELANIE FREE...
YOU LET EVERY DEAD THING IN THESE WOODS WALK ABROAD WITHOUT TETHERS.

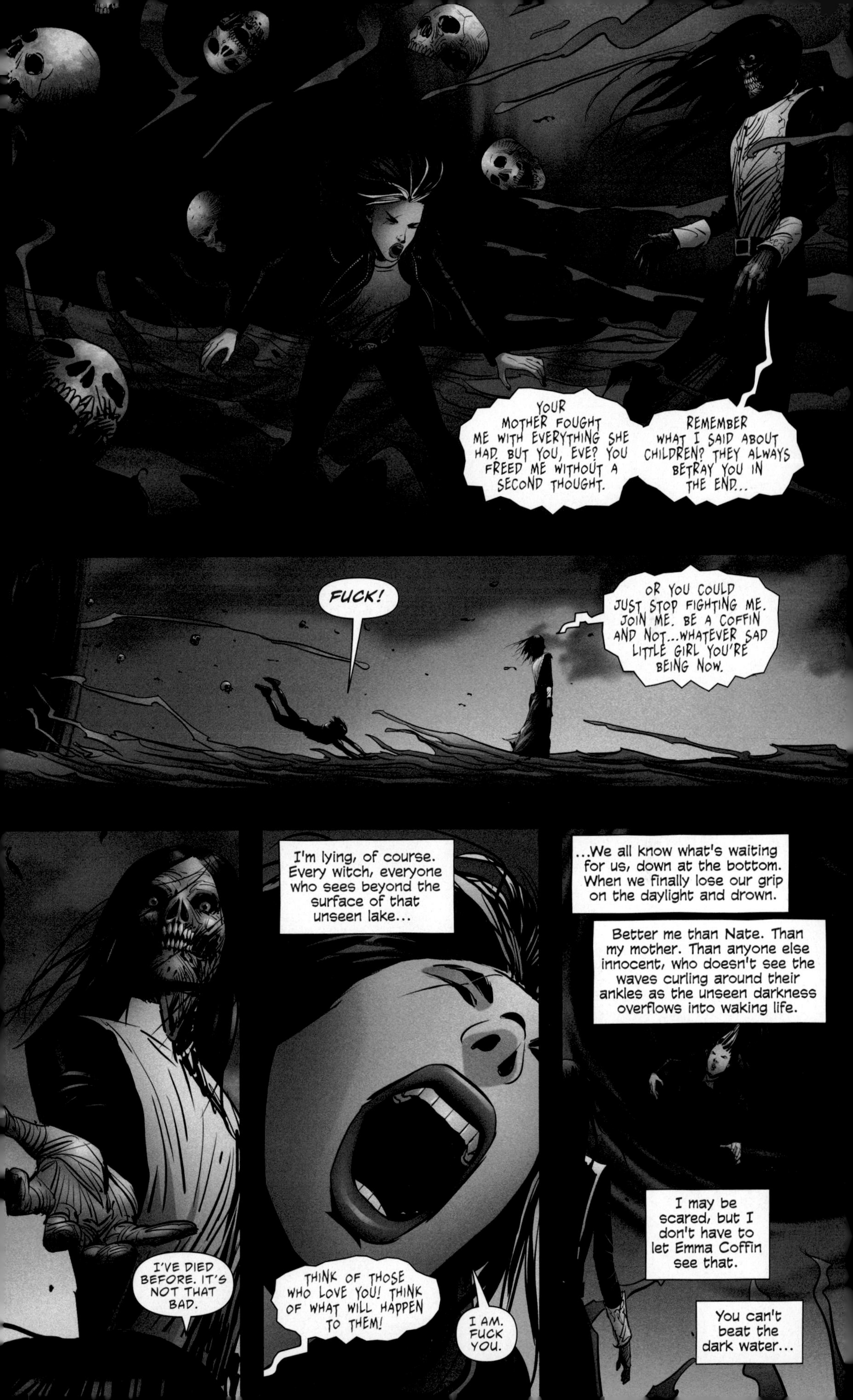
YOUR MOTHER FOUGHT ME WITH EVERYTHING SHE HAD. BUT YOU, EVE? YOU FREED ME WITHOUT A SECOND THOUGHT.
REMEMBER WHAT I SAID ABOUT CHILDREN? THEY ALWAYS BETRAY YOU IN THE END...
FUCK!
OR YOU COULD JUST STOP FIGHTING ME. JOIN ME. BE A COFFIN AND NOT...WHATEVER SAD LITTLE GIRL YOU'RE BEING NOW.
I'VE DIED BEFORE. IT'S NOT THAT BAD.
I'm lying, of course. Every witch, everyone who sees beyond the surface of that unseen lake...
THINK OF THOSE WHO LOVE YOU! THINK OF WHAT WILL HAPPEN TO THEM!
I AM. FUCK YOU.
...We all know what's waiting for us, down at the bottom. When we finally lose our grip on the daylight and drown.
Better me than Nate. Than my mother. Than anyone else innocent, who doesn't see the waves curling around their ankles as the unseen darkness overflows into waking life.
I may be scared, but I don't have to let Emma Coffin see that.
You can't beat the dark water...

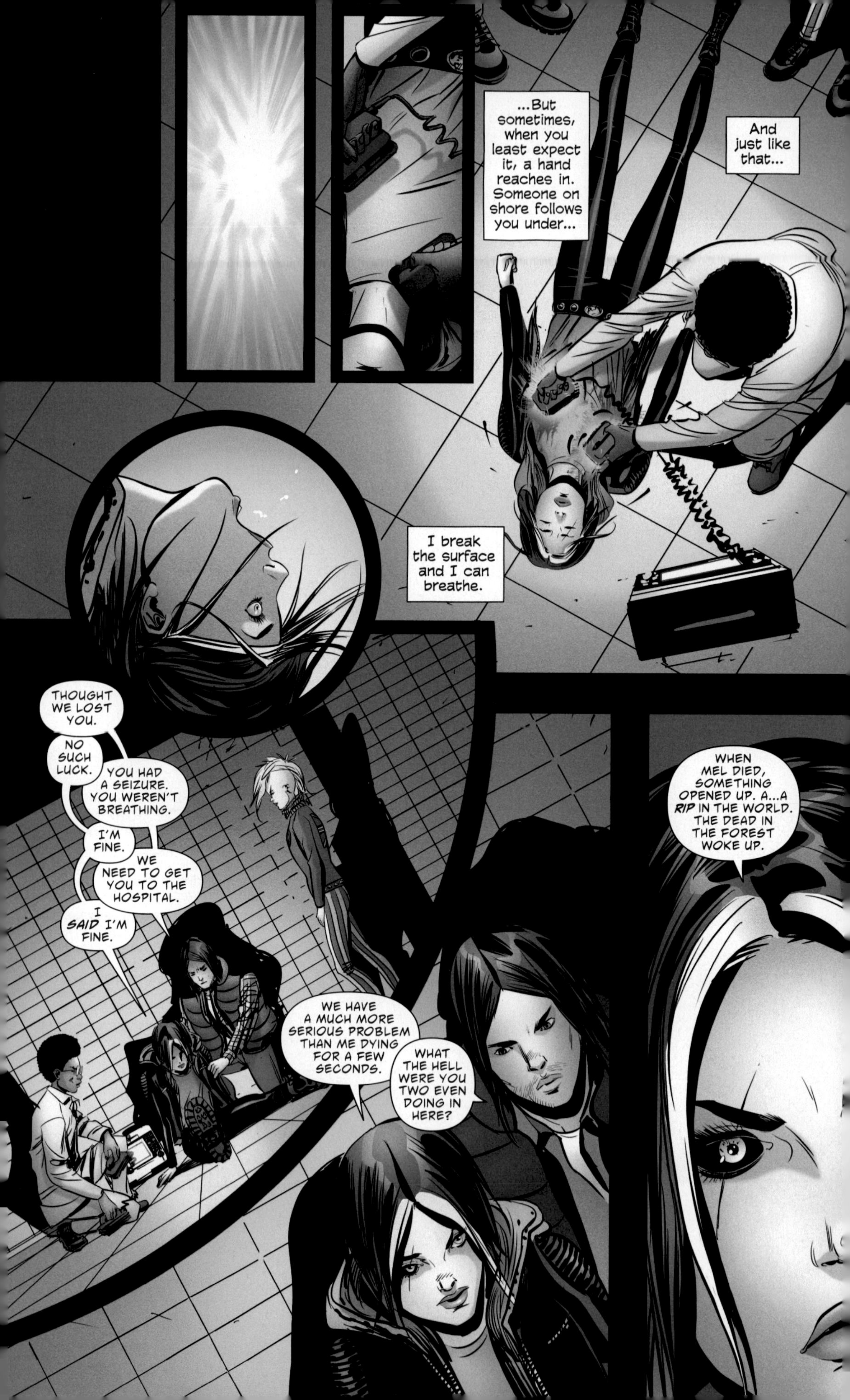
...But sometimes, when you least expect it, a hand reaches in. Someone on shore follows you under...
And just like that...
I break the surface and I can breathe.
THOUGHT WE LOST YOU.
NO SUCH LUCK.
YOU HAD A SEIZURE. YOU WEREN'T BREATHING.
I'M FINE.
WE NEED TO GET YOU TO THE HOSPITAL.
I *SAID* I'M FINE.
WE HAVE A MUCH MORE SERIOUS PROBLEM THAN ME DYING FOR A FEW SECONDS.
WHAT THE HELL WERE YOU TWO EVEN DOING IN HERE?
WHEN MEL DIED, SOMETHING OPENED UP. A...A *RIP* IN THE WORLD. THE DEAD IN THE FOREST WOKE UP.

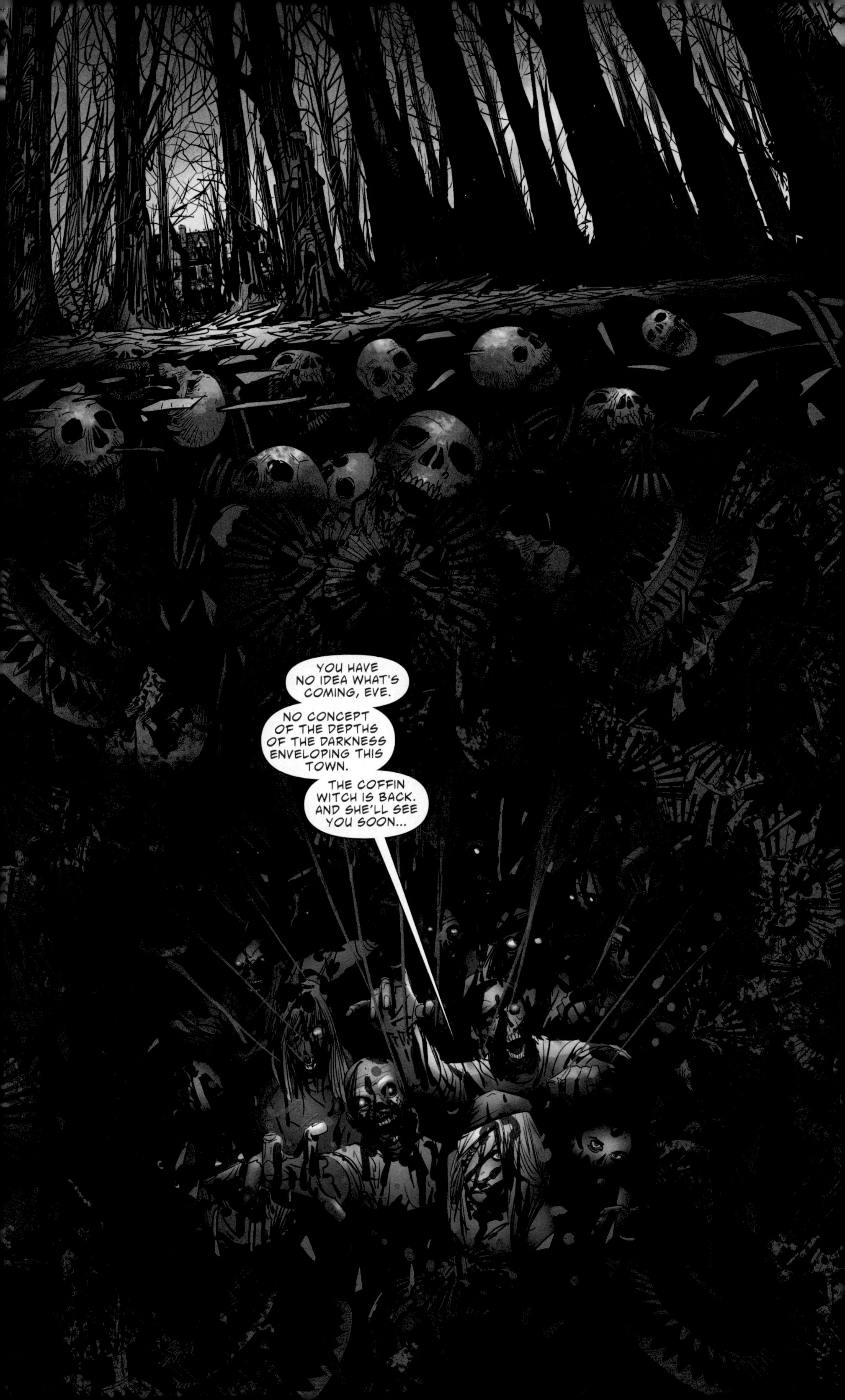
YOU HAVE NO IDEA WHAT'S COMING, EVE.
NO CONCEPT OF THE DEPTHS OF THE DARKNESS ENVELOPING THIS TOWN.
THE COFFIN WITCH IS BACK. AND SHE'LL SEE YOU SOON...

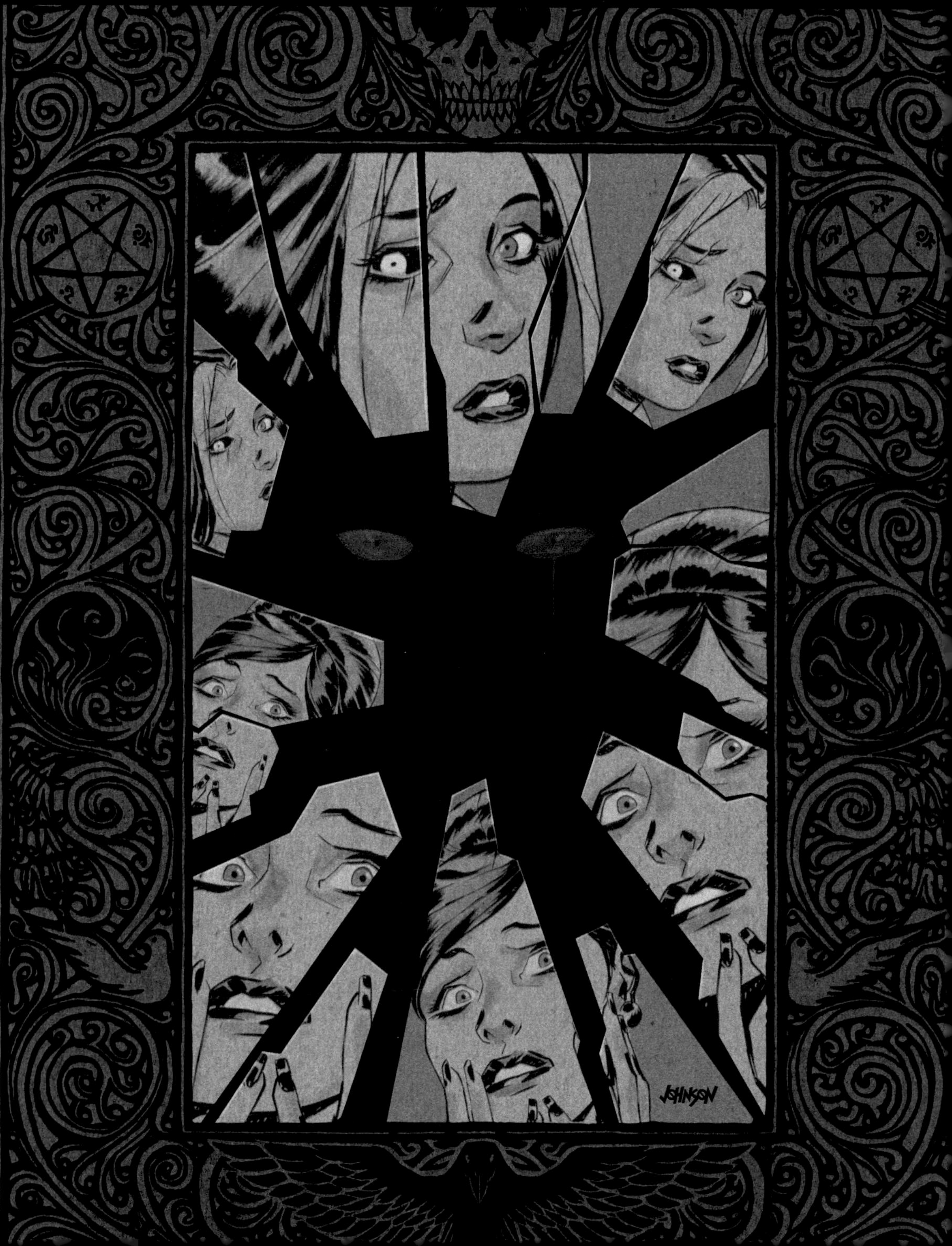
JOHNSON

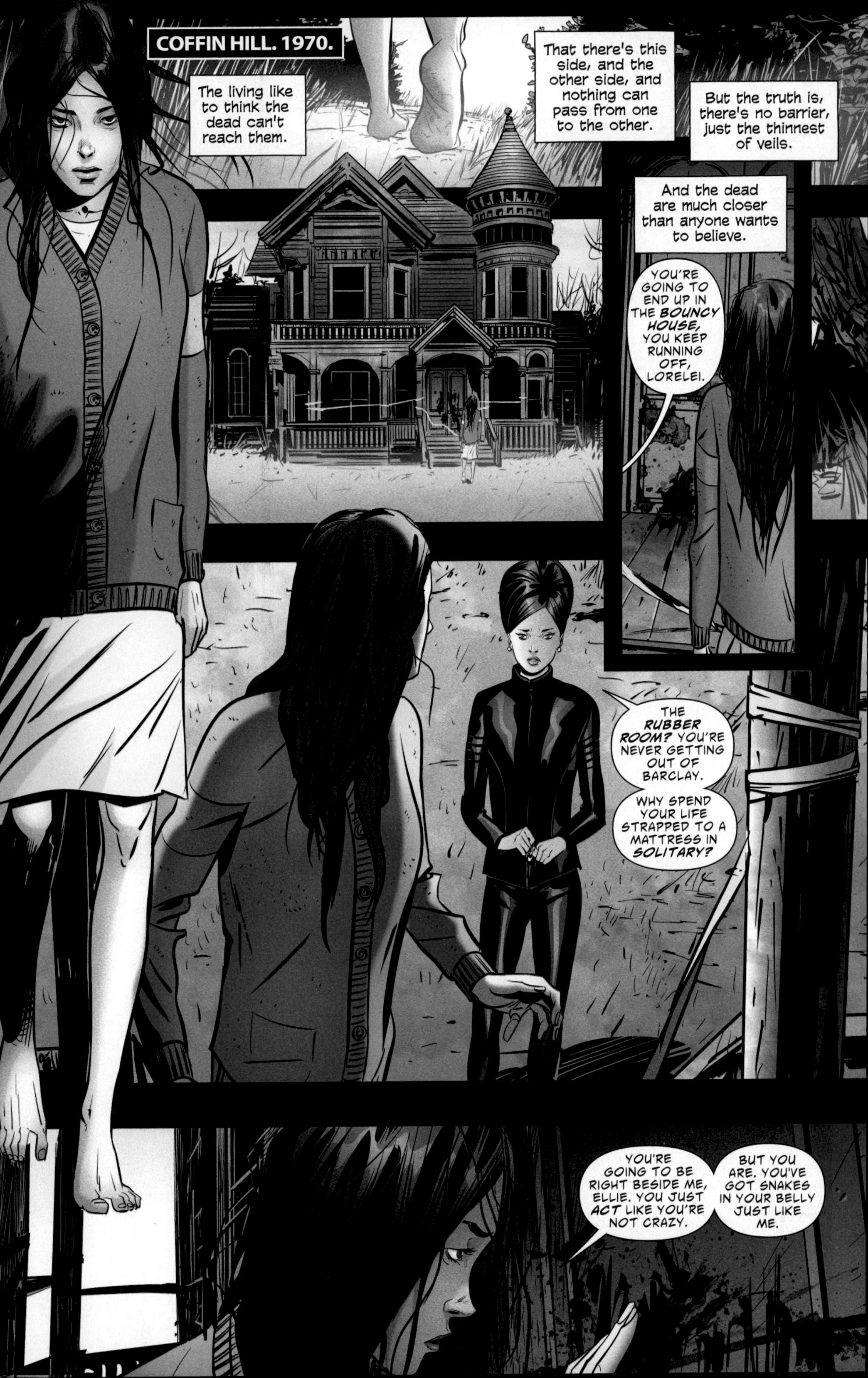
COFFIN HILL. 1970.
The living like to think the dead can't reach them.
That there's this side, and the other side, and nothing can pass from one to the other.
But the truth is, there's no barrier, just the thinnest of veils.
And the dead are much closer than anyone wants to believe.
YOU'RE GOING TO END UP IN THE BOUNCY HOUSE, YOU KEEP RUNNING OFF, LORELEI.
THE RUBBER ROOM? YOU'RE NEVER GETTING OUT OF BARCLAY.
WHY SPEND YOUR LIFE STRAPPED TO A MATTRESS IN SOLITARY?
YOU'RE GOING TO BE RIGHT BESIDE ME, ELLIE. YOU JUST ACT LIKE YOU'RE NOT CRAZY.
BUT YOU ARE. YOU'VE GOT SNAKES IN YOUR BELLY JUST LIKE ME.

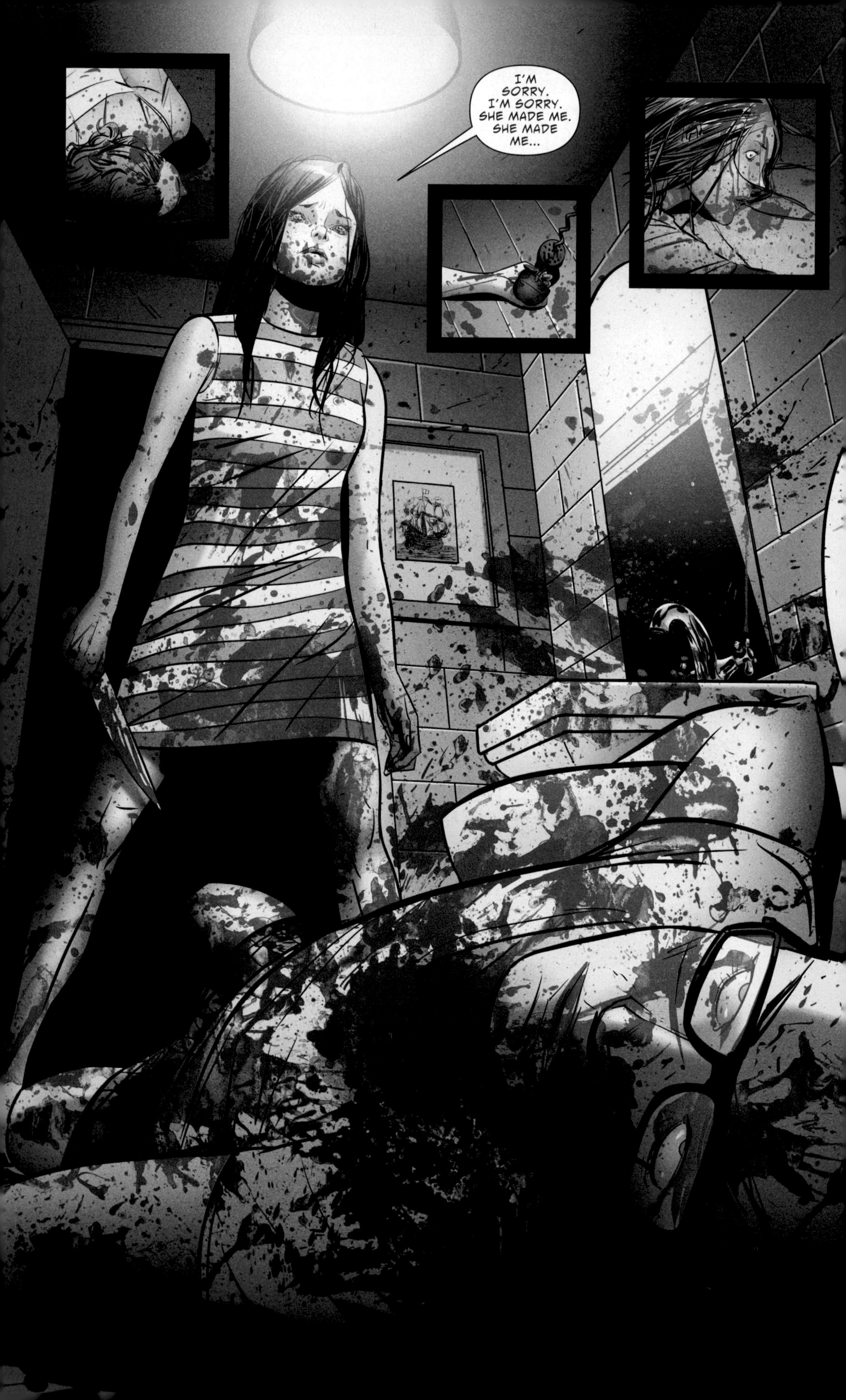
I'M SORRY. I'M SORRY. SHE MADE ME. SHE MADE ME...

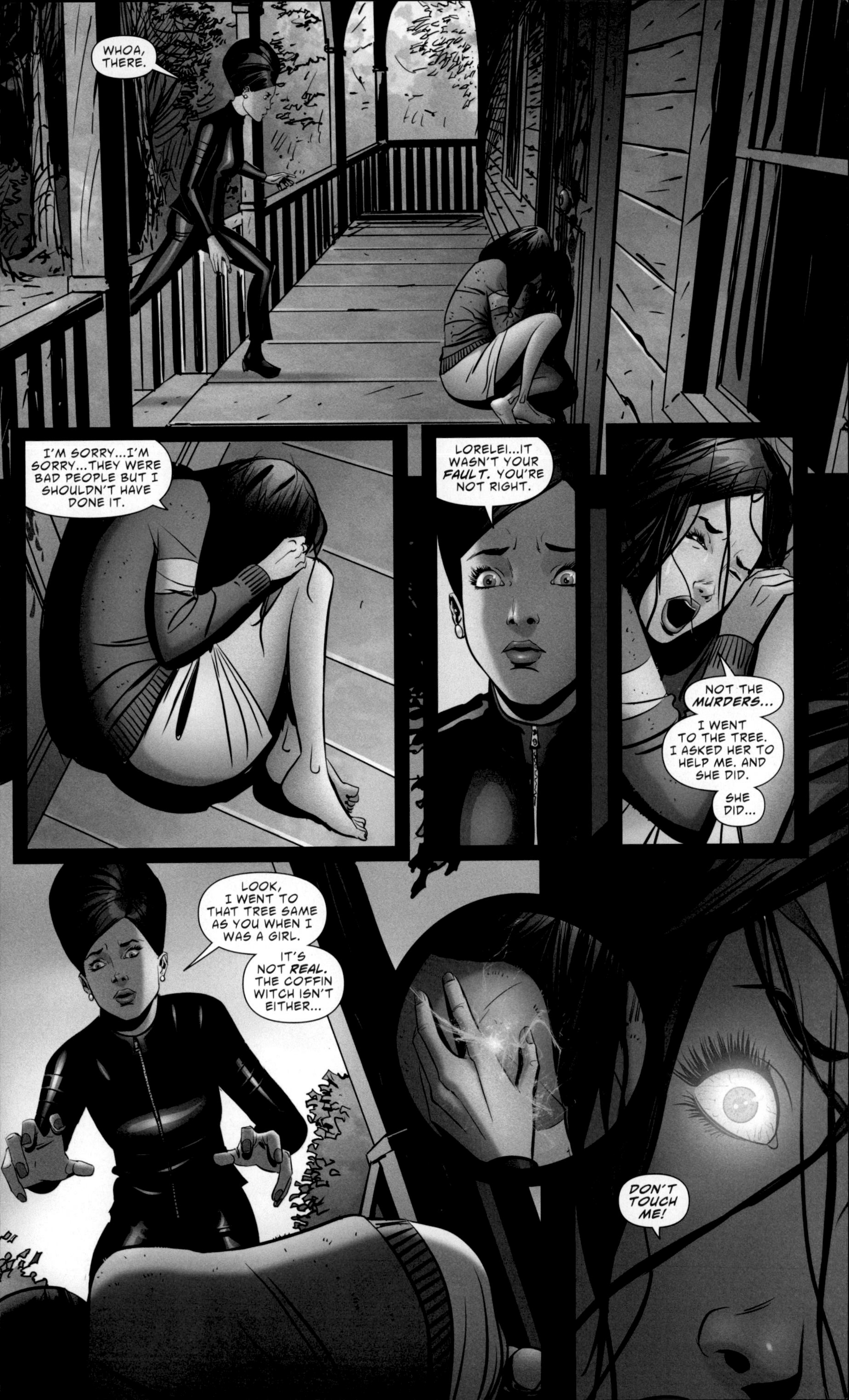
WHOA, THERE.
I'M SORRY...I'M SORRY...THEY WERE BAD PEOPLE BUT I SHOULDN'T HAVE DONE IT.
LORELEI...IT WASN'T YOUR FAULT. YOU'RE NOT RIGHT.
NOT THE MURDERS...
I WENT TO THE TREE. I ASKED HER TO HELP ME. AND SHE DID.
SHE DID...
LOOK, I WENT TO THAT TREE SAME AS YOU WHEN I WAS A GIRL.
IT'S NOT REAL. THE COFFIN WITCH ISN'T EITHER...
DON'T TOUCH ME!

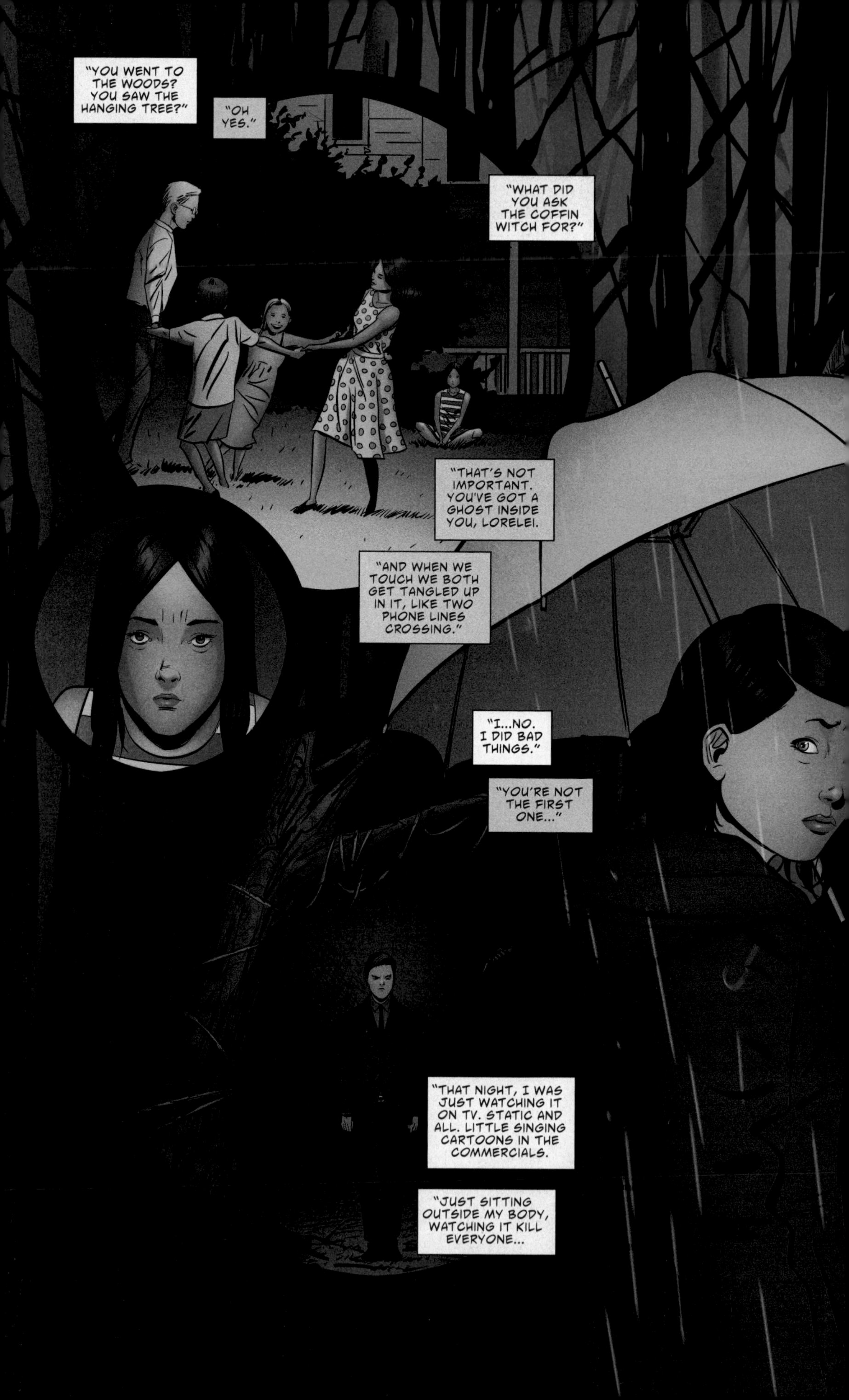
"YOU WENT TO THE WOODS? YOU SAW THE HANGING TREE?"
"OH YES."
"WHAT DID YOU ASK THE COFFIN WITCH FOR?"
"THAT'S NOT IMPORTANT. YOU'VE GOT A GHOST INSIDE YOU, LORELEI.
"AND WHEN WE TOUCH WE BOTH GET TANGLED UP IN IT, LIKE TWO PHONE LINES CROSSING."
"I...NO. I DID BAD THINGS."
"YOU'RE NOT THE FIRST ONE..."
"THAT NIGHT, I WAS JUST WATCHING IT ON TV. STATIC AND ALL. LITTLE SINGING CARTOONS IN THE COMMERCIALS.
"JUST SITTING OUTSIDE MY BODY, WATCHING IT KILL EVERYONE...

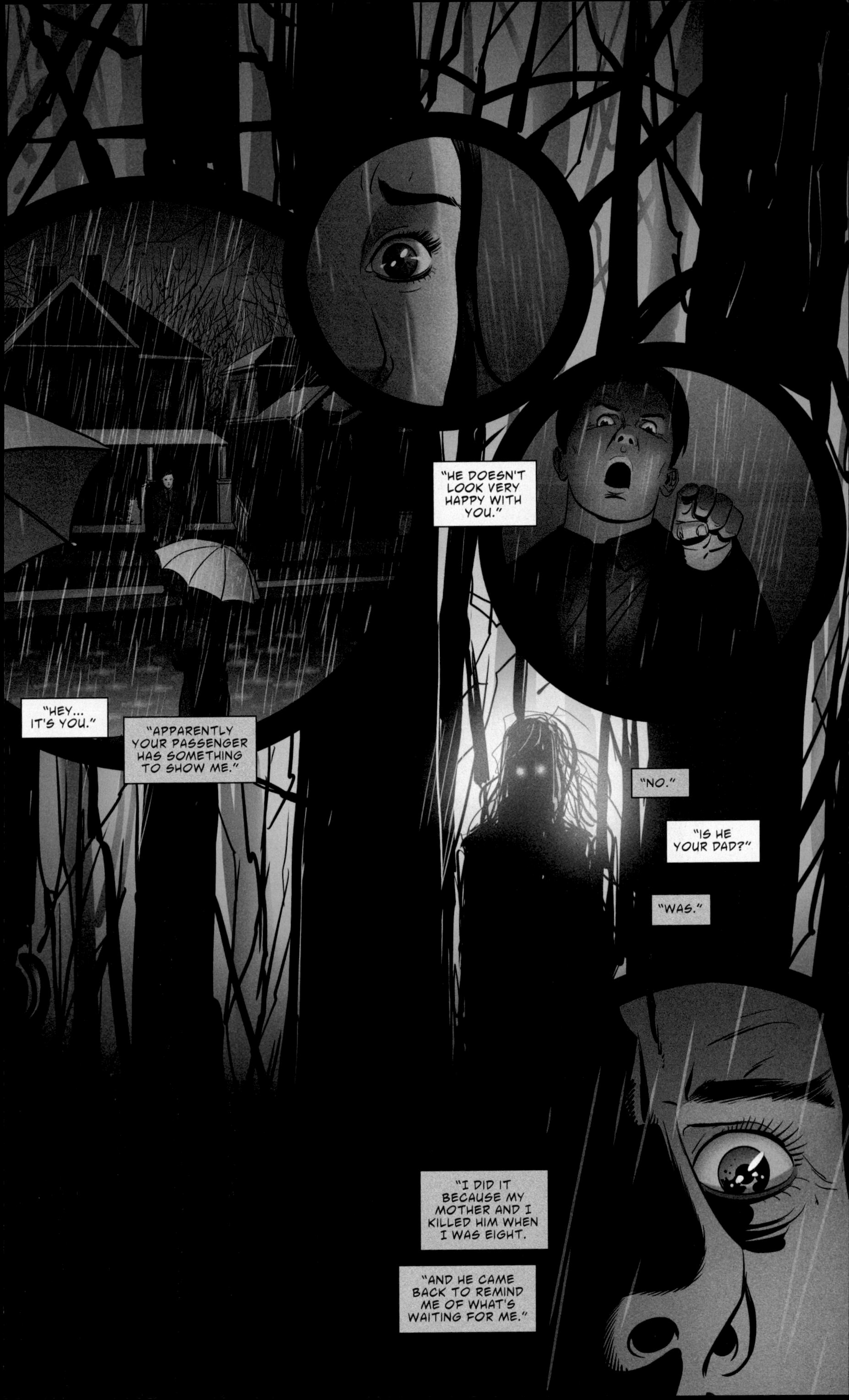
"HE DOESN'T LOOK VERY HAPPY WITH YOU."
"HEY... IT'S YOU."
"APPARENTLY YOUR PASSENGER HAS SOMETHING TO SHOW ME."
"NO."
"IS HE YOUR DAD?"
"WAS."
"I DID IT BECAUSE MY MOTHER AND I KILLED HIM WHEN I WAS EIGHT.
"AND HE CAME BACK TO REMIND ME OF WHAT'S WAITING FOR ME."

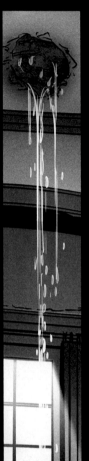

JUST PERFECT.

HI, CHIEF, IT'S WILCOX. I'M GOING TO BE LATE...LOOKS LIKE I HAVE A BUSTED PIPE.

YES, SIR. YES, I'LL FILE IT AS *PERSONAL TIME.* I UNDERSTAND I WON'T...

DICK.

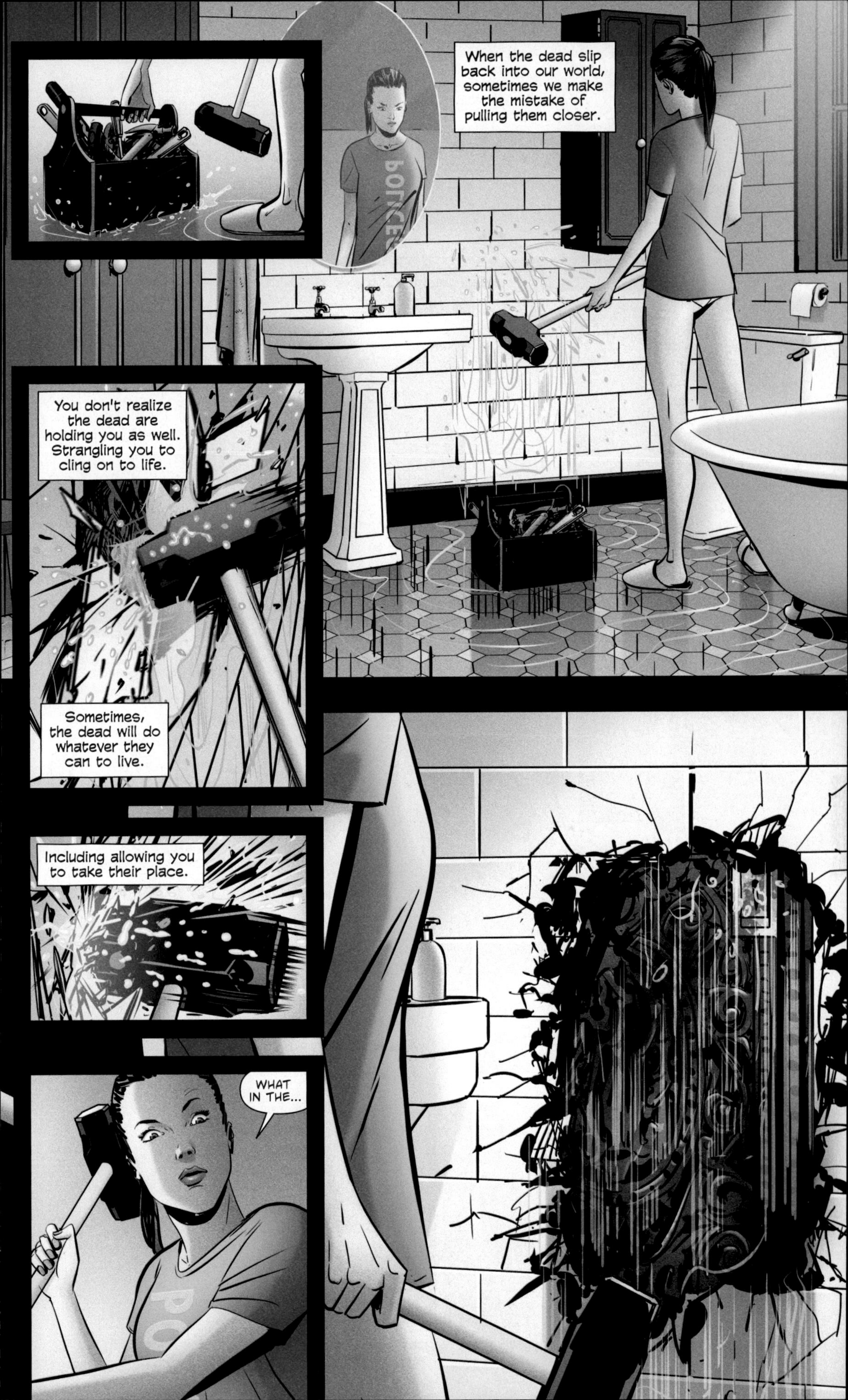
When the dead slip back into our world, sometimes we make the mistake of pulling them closer.
You don't realize the dead are holding you as well. Strangling you to cling on to life.
Sometimes, the dead will do whatever they can to live.
Including allowing you to take their place.
WHAT IN THE...

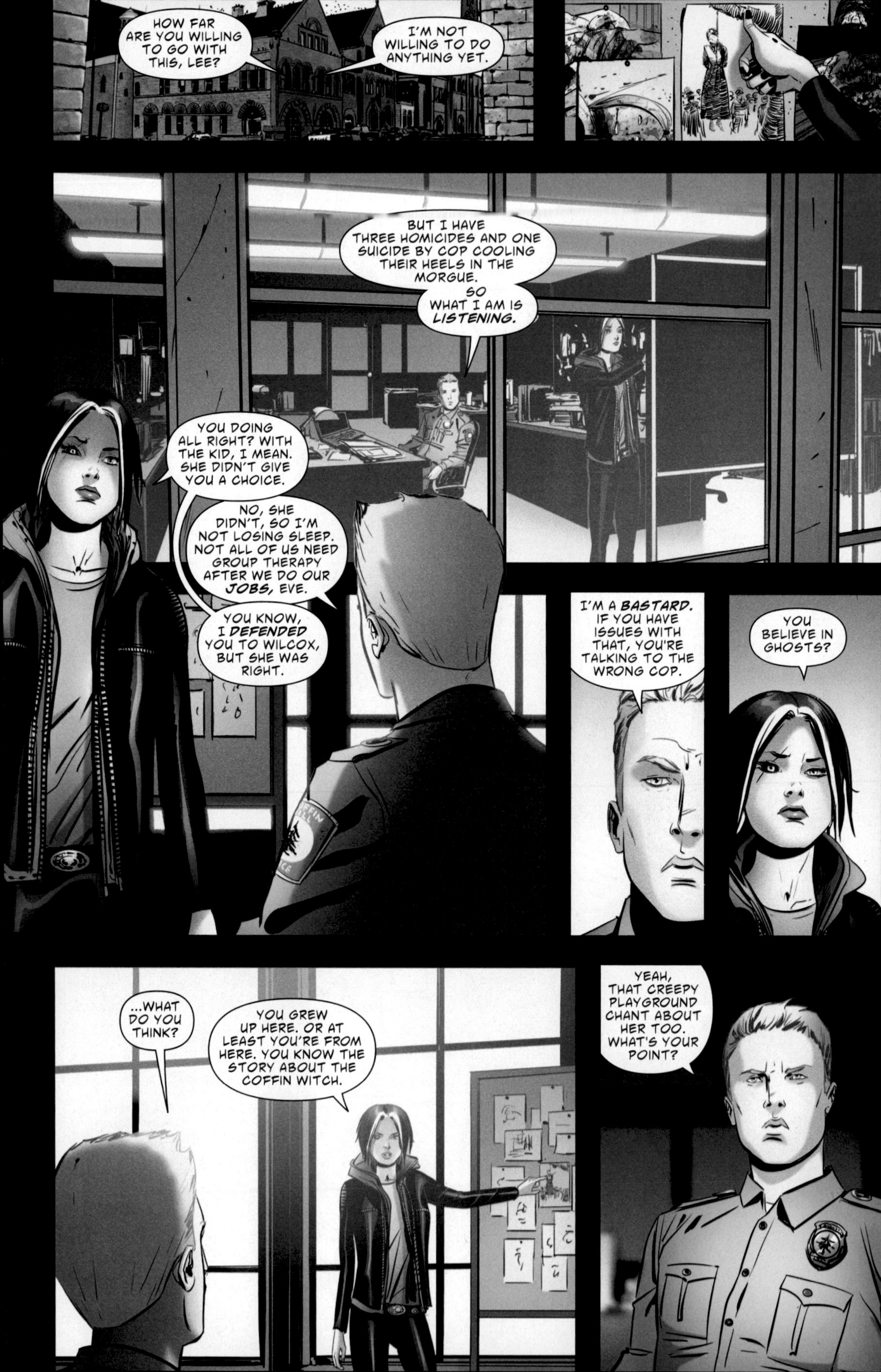
HOW FAR ARE YOU WILLING TO GO WITH THIS, LEE?
I'M NOT WILLING TO DO ANYTHING YET.
BUT I HAVE THREE HOMICIDES AND ONE SUICIDE BY COP COOLING THEIR HEELS IN THE MORGUE.
SO WHAT I AM IS *LISTENING.*
YOU DOING ALL RIGHT? WITH THE KID, I MEAN. SHE DIDN'T GIVE YOU A CHOICE.
NO, SHE DIDN'T, SO I'M NOT LOSING SLEEP. NOT ALL OF US NEED GROUP THERAPY AFTER WE DO OUR *JOBS,* EVE.
YOU KNOW, I *DEFENDED* YOU TO WILCOX, BUT SHE WAS RIGHT.
I'M A *BASTARD.* IF YOU HAVE ISSUES WITH THAT, YOU'RE TALKING TO THE WRONG COP.
YOU BELIEVE IN GHOSTS?
...WHAT DO YOU THINK?
YOU GREW UP HERE. OR AT LEAST YOU'RE FROM HERE. YOU KNOW THE STORY ABOUT THE COFFIN WITCH.
YEAH, THAT CREEPY PLAYGROUND CHANT ABOUT HER TOO. WHAT'S YOUR POINT?

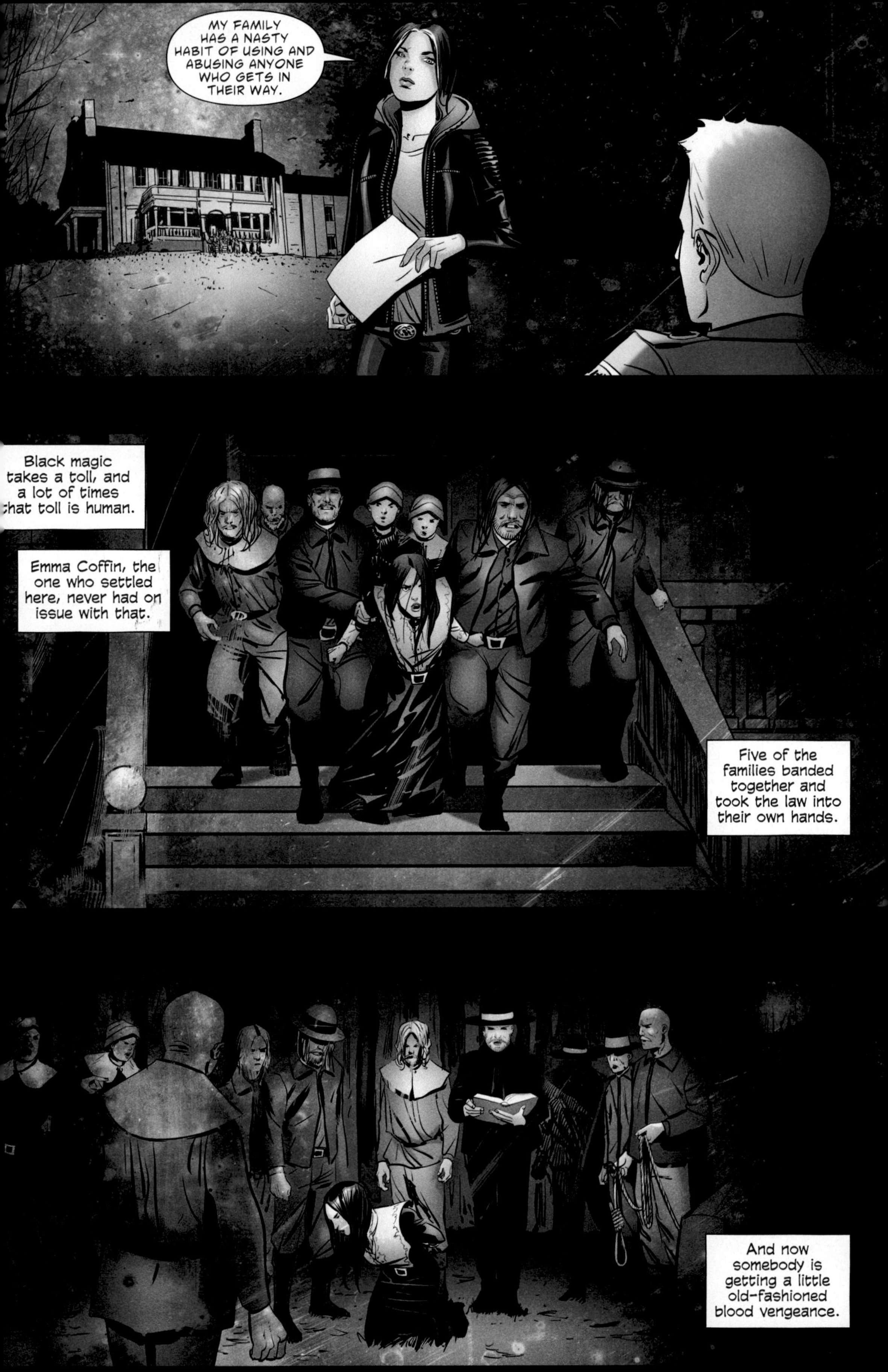
MY FAMILY HAS A NASTY HABIT OF USING AND ABUSING ANYONE WHO GETS IN THEIR WAY.
Black magic takes a toll, and a lot of times hat toll is human.
Emma Coffin, the one who settled here, never had an issue with that.
Five of the families banded together and took the law into their own hands.
And now somebody is getting a little old-fashioned blood vengeance.

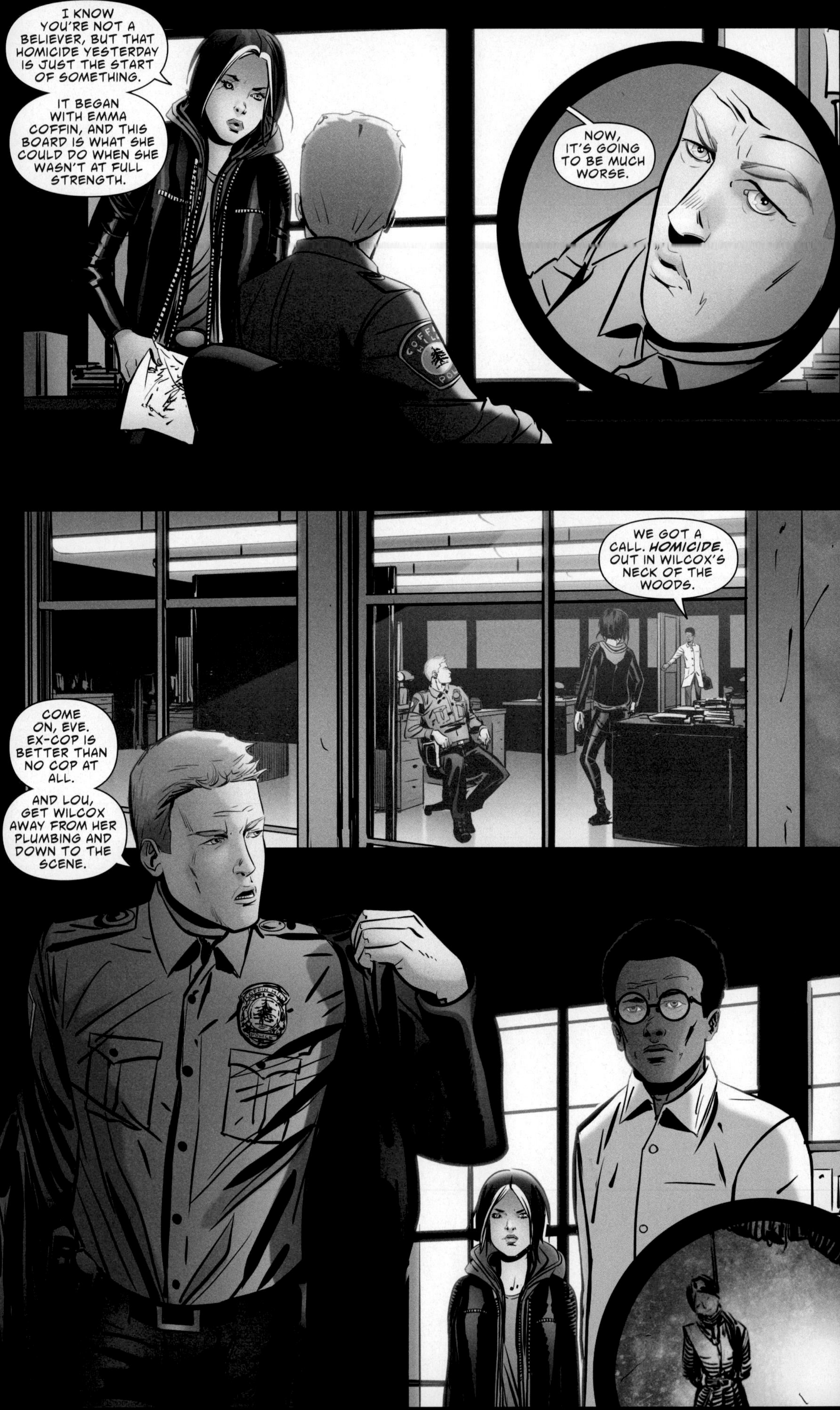

I KNOW YOU'RE NOT A BELIEVER, BUT THAT HOMICIDE YESTERDAY IS JUST THE START OF SOMETHING.
IT BEGAN WITH EMMA COFFIN, AND THIS BOARD IS WHAT SHE COULD DO WHEN SHE WASN'T AT FULL STRENGTH.
NOW, IT'S GOING TO BE MUCH WORSE.
WE GOT A CALL. ***HOMICIDE.*** OUT IN WILCOX'S NECK OF THE WOODS.
COME ON, EVE. EX-COP IS BETTER THAN NO COP AT ALL.
AND LOU, GET WILCOX AWAY FROM HER PLUMBING AND DOWN TO THE SCENE.

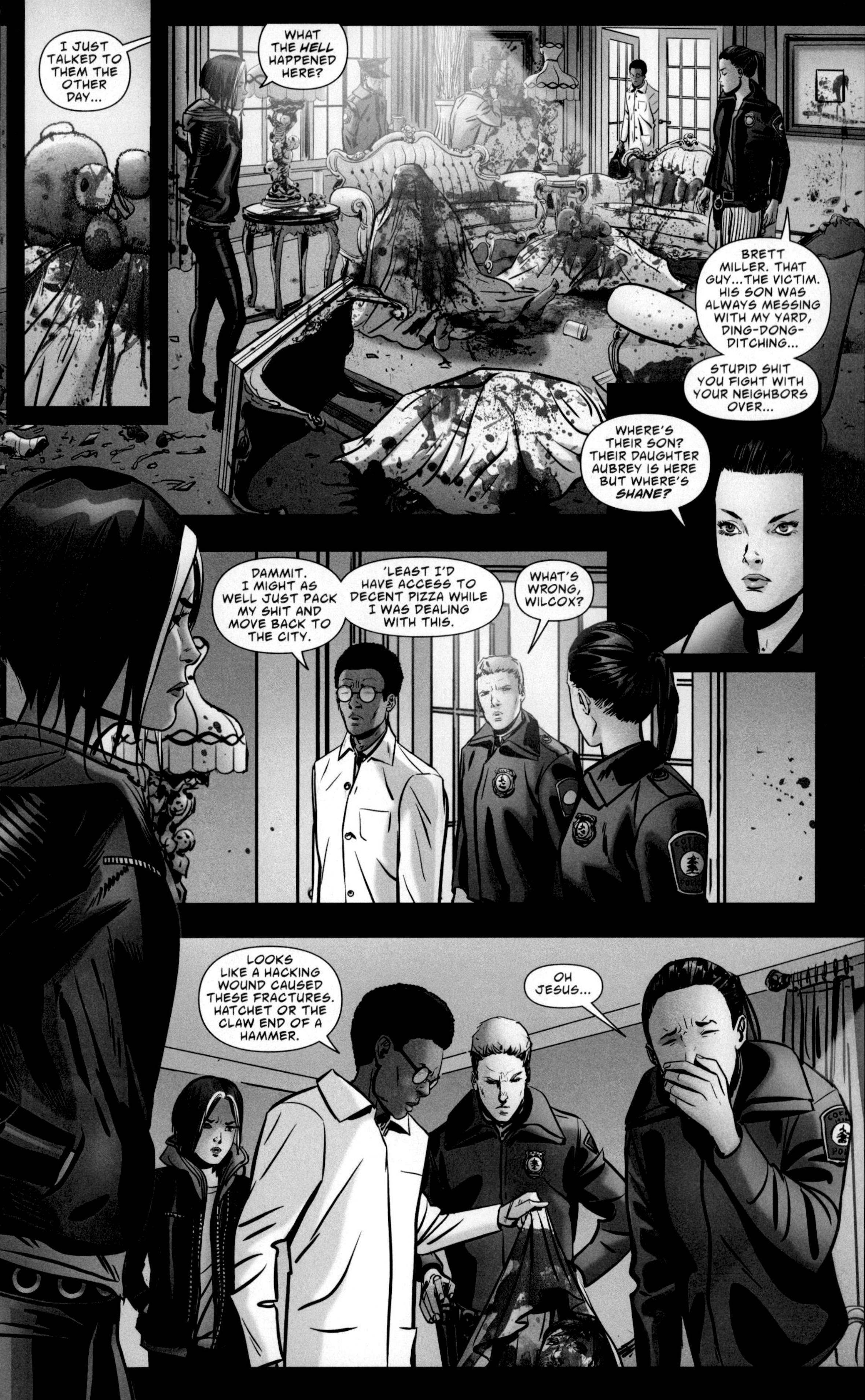
I JUST TALKED TO THEM THE OTHER DAY...
WHAT THE HELL HAPPENED HERE?
BRETT MILLER. THAT GUY...THE VICTIM. HIS SON WAS ALWAYS MESSING WITH MY YARD, DING-DONG-DITCHING...
STUPID SHIT YOU FIGHT WITH YOUR NEIGHBORS OVER...
WHERE'S THEIR SON? THEIR DAUGHTER AUBREY IS HERE BUT WHERE'S SHANE?
DAMMIT. I MIGHT AS WELL JUST PACK MY SHIT AND MOVE BACK TO THE CITY.
'LEAST I'D HAVE ACCESS TO DECENT PIZZA WHILE I WAS DEALING WITH THIS.
WHAT'S WRONG, WILCOX?
LOOKS LIKE A HACKING WOUND CAUSED THESE FRACTURES. HATCHET OR THE CLAW END OF A HAMMER.
OH JESUS...

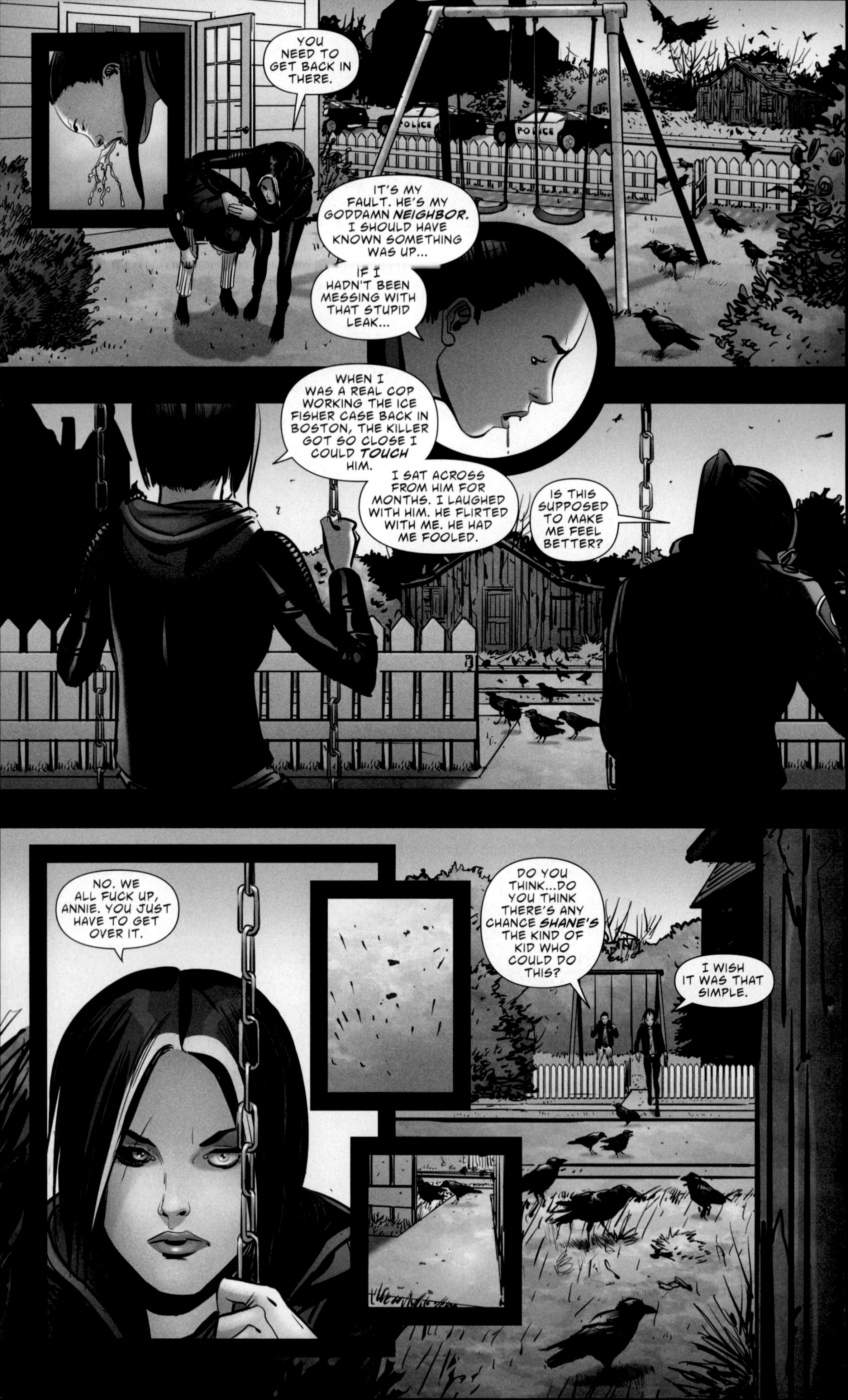
YOU NEED TO GET BACK IN THERE.
IT'S MY FAULT. HE'S MY GODDAMN NEIGHBOR. I SHOULD HAVE KNOWN SOMETHING WAS UP...
IF I HADN'T BEEN MESSING WITH THAT STUPID LEAK...
WHEN I WAS A REAL COP WORKING THE ICE FISHER CASE BACK IN BOSTON, THE KILLER GOT SO CLOSE I COULD TOUCH HIM.
I SAT ACROSS FROM HIM FOR MONTHS. I LAUGHED WITH HIM. HE FLIRTED WITH ME. HE HAD ME FOOLED.
IS THIS SUPPOSED TO MAKE ME FEEL BETTER?
NO. WE ALL FUCK UP, ANNIE. YOU JUST HAVE TO GET OVER IT.
DO YOU THINK...DO YOU THINK THERE'S ANY CHANCE SHANE'S THE KIND OF KID WHO COULD DO THIS?
I WISH IT WAS THAT SIMPLE.

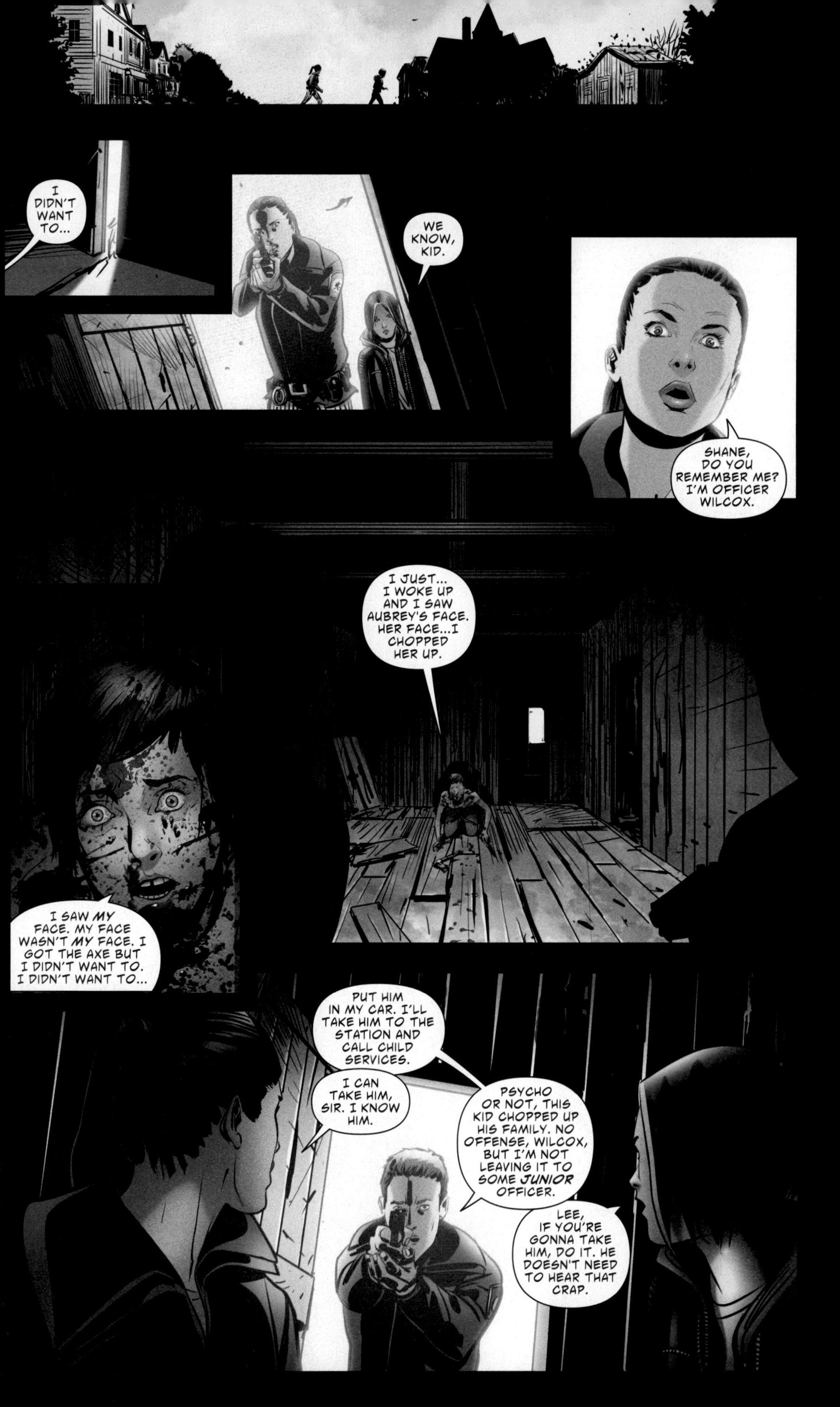
I DIDN'T WANT TO...
WE KNOW, KID.
SHANE, DO YOU REMEMBER ME? I'M OFFICER WILCOX.
I JUST... I WOKE UP AND I SAW AUBREY'S FACE. HER FACE...I CHOPPED HER UP.
I SAW MY FACE. MY FACE WASN'T MY FACE. I GOT THE AXE BUT I DIDN'T WANT TO. I DIDN'T WANT TO...
PUT HIM IN MY CAR. I'LL TAKE HIM TO THE STATION AND CALL CHILD SERVICES.
I CAN TAKE HIM, SIR. I KNOW HIM.
PSYCHO OR NOT, THIS KID CHOPPED UP HIS FAMILY. NO OFFENSE, WILCOX, BUT I'M NOT LEAVING IT TO SOME JUNIOR OFFICER.
LEE, IF YOU'RE GONNA TAKE HIM, DO IT. HE DOESN'T NEED TO HEAR THAT CRAP.

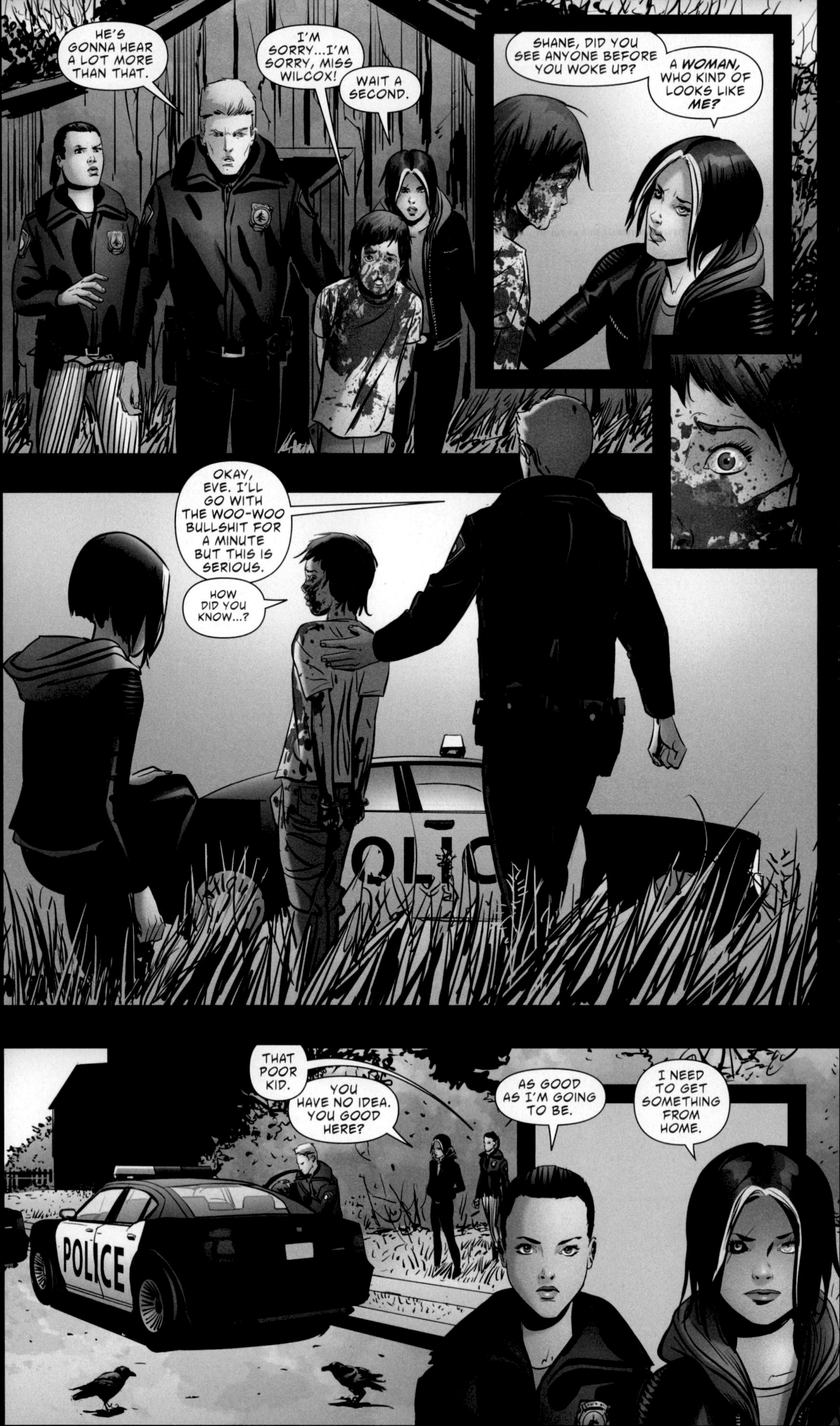
HE'S GONNA HEAR A LOT MORE THAN THAT.
I'M SORRY...I'M SORRY, MISS WILCOX!
WAIT A SECOND.
SHANE, DID YOU SEE ANYONE BEFORE YOU WOKE UP?
A WOMAN, WHO KIND OF LOOKS LIKE ME?
OKAY, EVE. I'LL GO WITH THE WOO-WOO BULLSHIT FOR A MINUTE BUT THIS IS SERIOUS.
HOW DID YOU KNOW...?
POLICE
THAT POOR KID.
YOU HAVE NO IDEA. YOU GOOD HERE?
AS GOOD AS I'M GOING TO BE.
I NEED TO GET SOMETHING FROM HOME.
POLICE

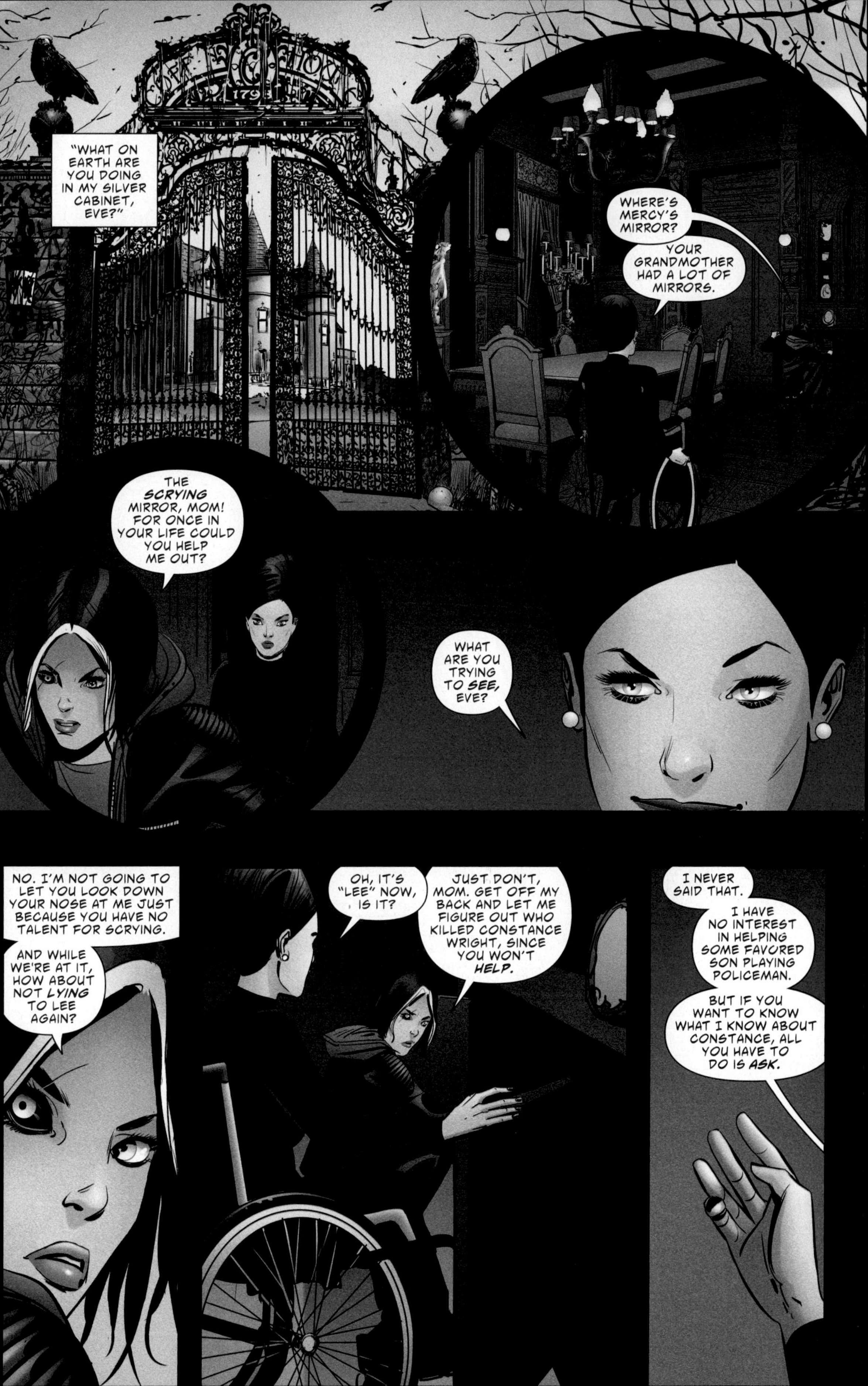
"WHAT ON EARTH ARE YOU DOING IN MY SILVER CABINET, EVE?"
WHERE'S MERCY'S MIRROR?
YOUR GRANDMOTHER HAD A LOT OF MIRRORS.
THE SCRYING MIRROR, MOM! FOR ONCE IN YOUR LIFE COULD YOU HELP ME OUT?
WHAT ARE YOU TRYING TO SEE, EVE?
NO. I'M NOT GOING TO LET YOU LOOK DOWN YOUR NOSE AT ME JUST BECAUSE YOU HAVE NO TALENT FOR SCRYING.
AND WHILE WE'RE AT IT, HOW ABOUT NOT LYING TO LEE AGAIN?
OH, IT'S "LEE" NOW, IS IT?
JUST DON'T, MOM. GET OFF MY BACK AND LET ME FIGURE OUT WHO KILLED CONSTANCE WRIGHT, SINCE YOU WON'T HELP.
I NEVER SAID THAT.
I HAVE NO INTEREST IN HELPING SOME FAVORED SON PLAYING POLICEMAN.
BUT IF YOU WANT TO KNOW WHAT I KNOW ABOUT CONSTANCE, ALL YOU HAVE TO DO IS ASK.

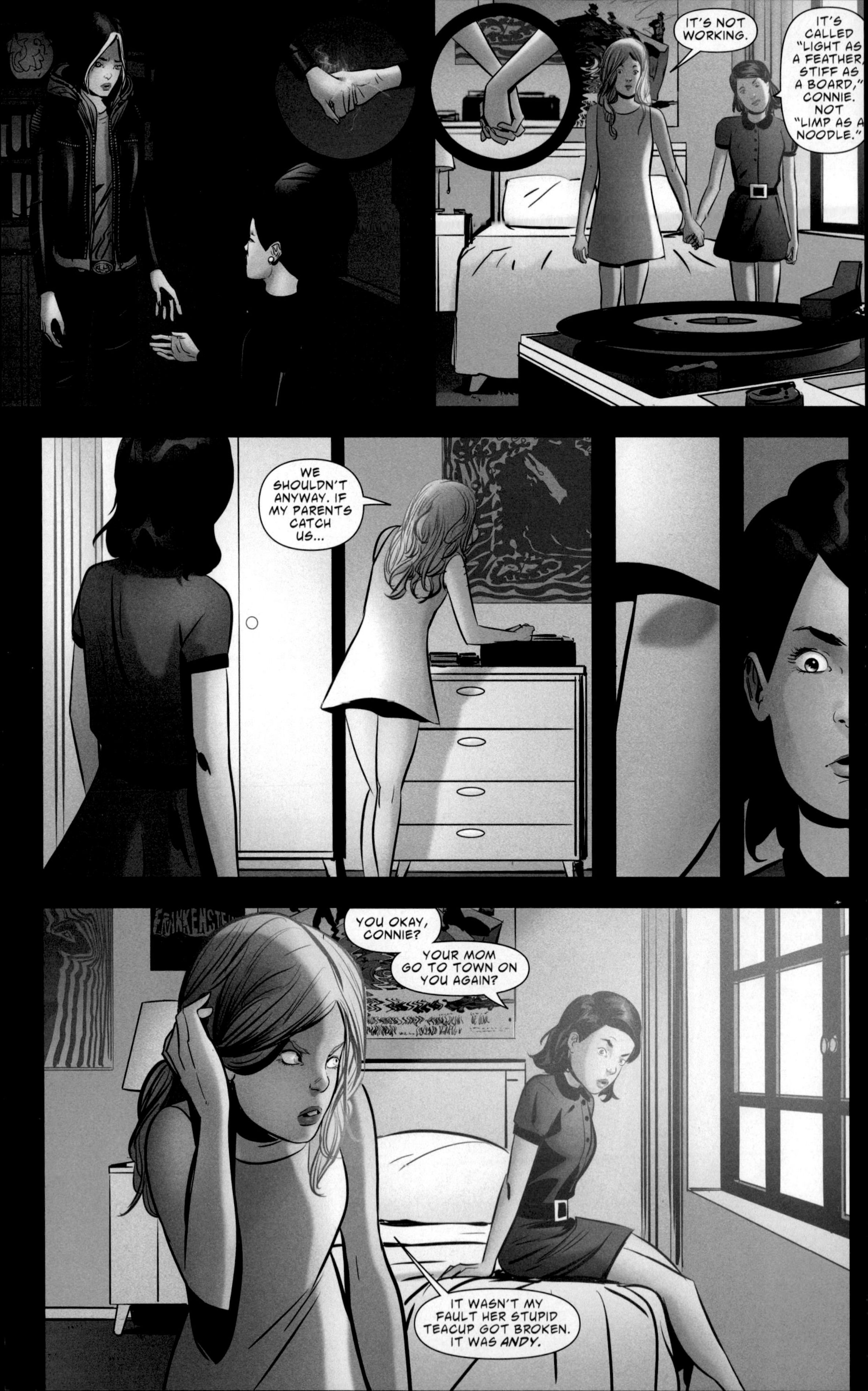
IT'S NOT WORKING.
IT'S CALLED "LIGHT AS A FEATHER, STIFF AS A BOARD," CONNIE. NOT "LIMP AS A NOODLE."
WE SHOULDN'T ANYWAY. IF MY PARENTS CATCH US...
YOU OKAY, CONNIE?
YOUR MOM GO TO TOWN ON YOU AGAIN?
IT WASN'T MY FAULT HER STUPID TEACUP GOT BROKEN. IT WAS *ANDY*.

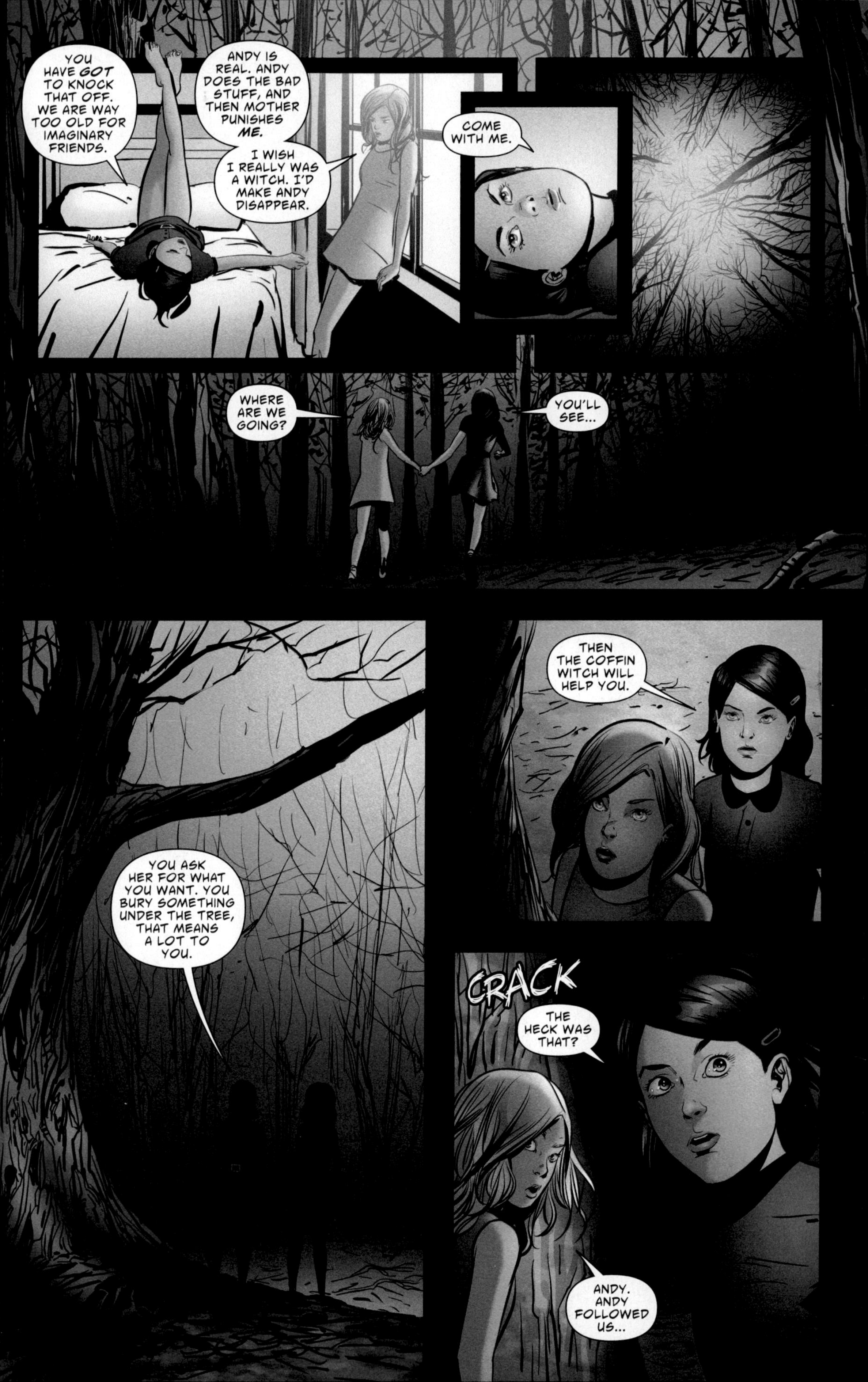
YOU HAVE GOT TO KNOCK THAT OFF. WE ARE WAY TOO OLD FOR IMAGINARY FRIENDS.
ANDY IS REAL. ANDY DOES THE BAD STUFF, AND THEN MOTHER PUNISHES ME.
I WISH I REALLY WAS A WITCH. I'D MAKE ANDY DISAPPEAR.
COME WITH ME.
WHERE ARE WE GOING?
YOU'LL SEE...
YOU ASK HER FOR WHAT YOU WANT. YOU BURY SOMETHING UNDER THE TREE, THAT MEANS A LOT TO YOU.
THEN THE COFFIN WITCH WILL HELP YOU.
CRACK
THE HECK WAS THAT?
ANDY. ANDY FOLLOWED US...

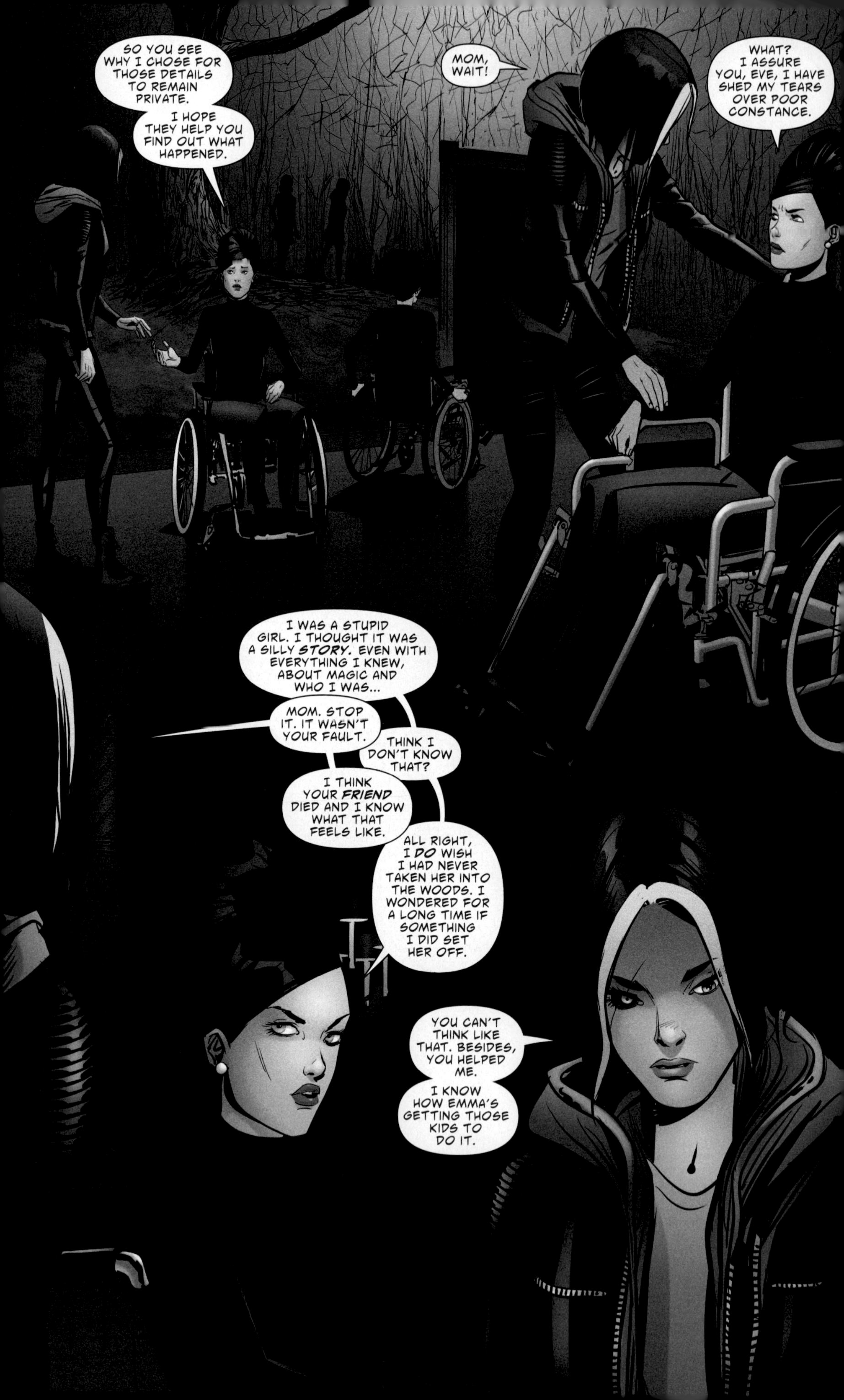
SO YOU SEE WHY I CHOSE FOR THOSE DETAILS TO REMAIN PRIVATE.
I HOPE THEY HELP YOU FIND OUT WHAT HAPPENED.
MOM, WAIT!
WHAT? I ASSURE YOU, EVE, I HAVE SHED MY TEARS OVER POOR CONSTANCE.
I WAS A STUPID GIRL. I THOUGHT IT WAS A SILLY STORY. EVEN WITH EVERYTHING I KNEW, ABOUT MAGIC AND WHO I WAS...
MOM. STOP IT. IT WASN'T YOUR FAULT.
THINK I DON'T KNOW THAT?
I THINK YOUR FRIEND DIED AND I KNOW WHAT THAT FEELS LIKE.
ALL RIGHT, I DO WISH I HAD NEVER TAKEN HER INTO THE WOODS. I WONDERED FOR A LONG TIME IF SOMETHING I DID SET HER OFF.
YOU CAN'T THINK LIKE THAT. BESIDES, YOU HELPED ME.
I KNOW HOW EMMA'S GETTING THOSE KIDS TO DO IT.

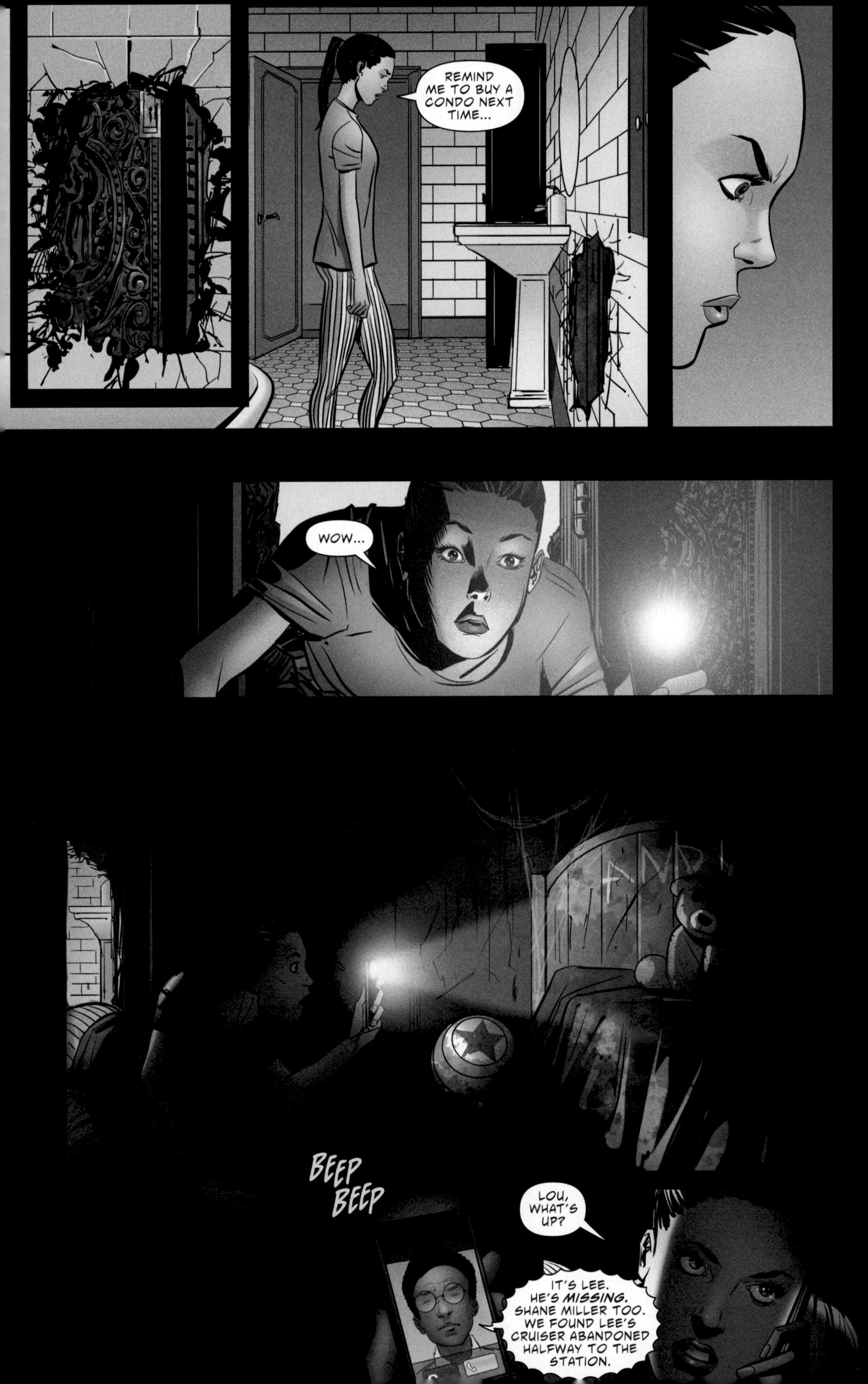
REMIND ME TO BUY A CONDO NEXT TIME...
WOW...
BEEP BEEP
LOU, WHAT'S UP?
IT'S LEE. HE'S *MISSING.* SHANE MILLER TOO. WE FOUND LEE'S CRUISER ABANDONED HALFWAY TO THE STATION.

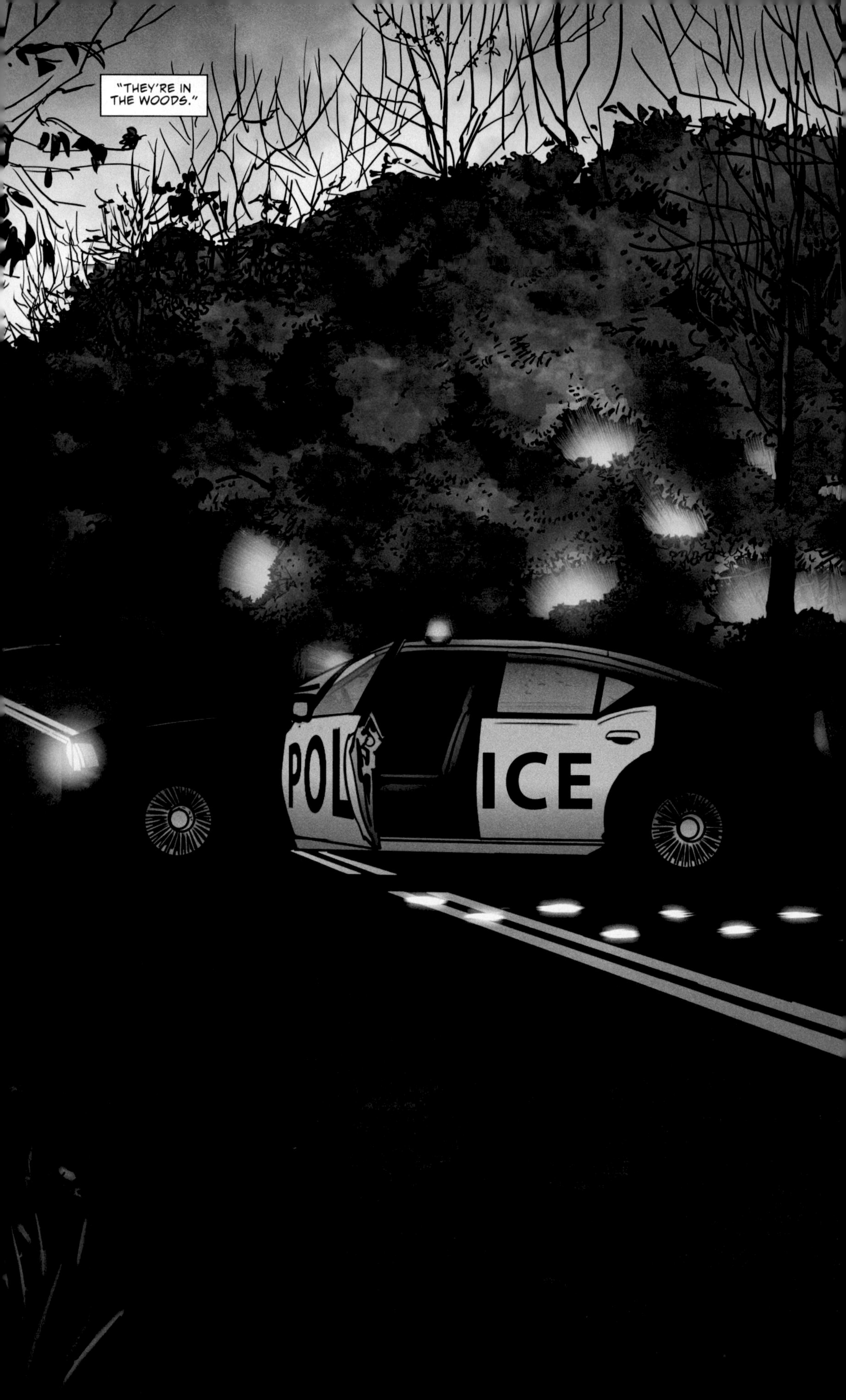
"THEY'RE IN THE WOODS."
POL ICE

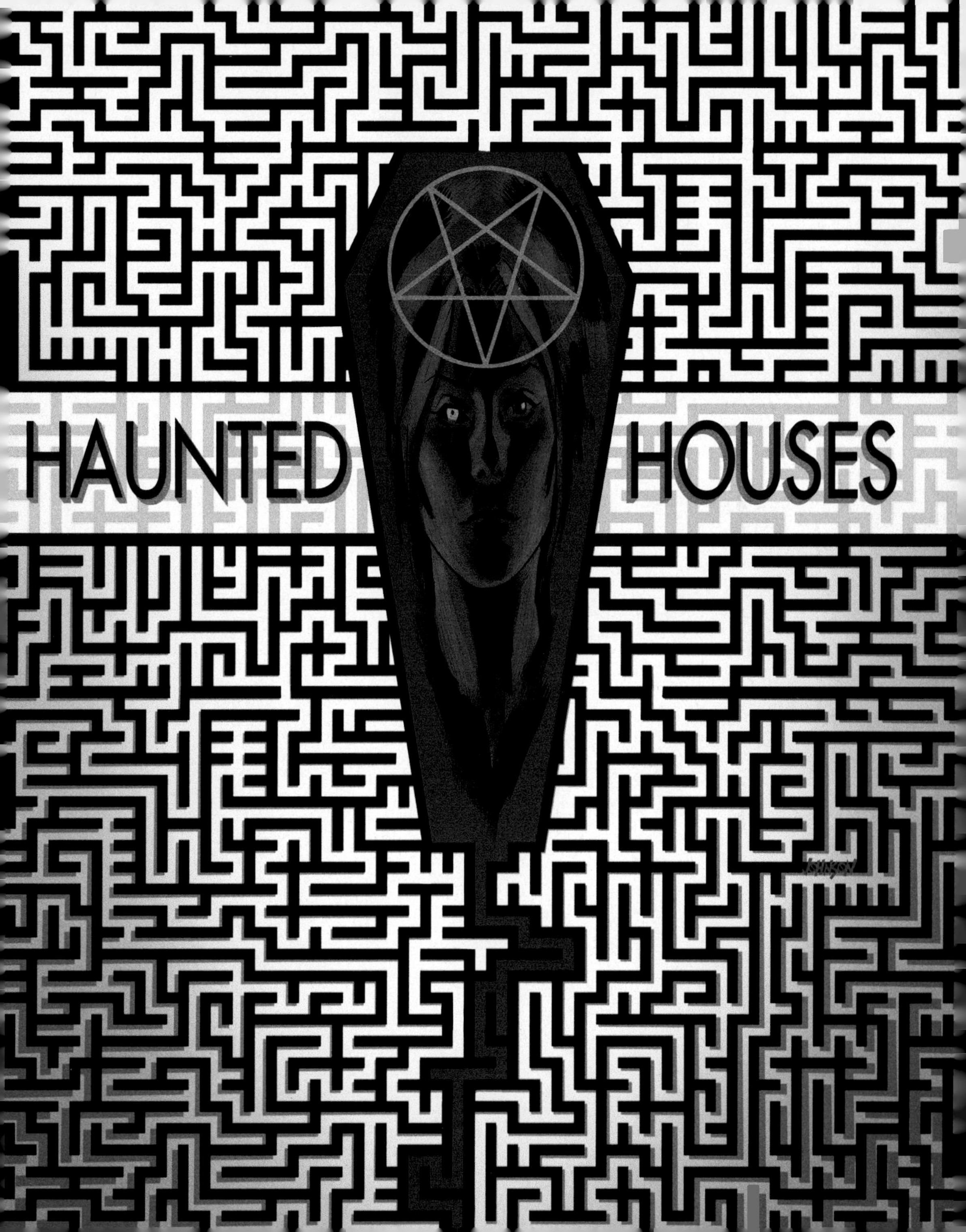

HAUNTED
HOUSES
JOHNSON

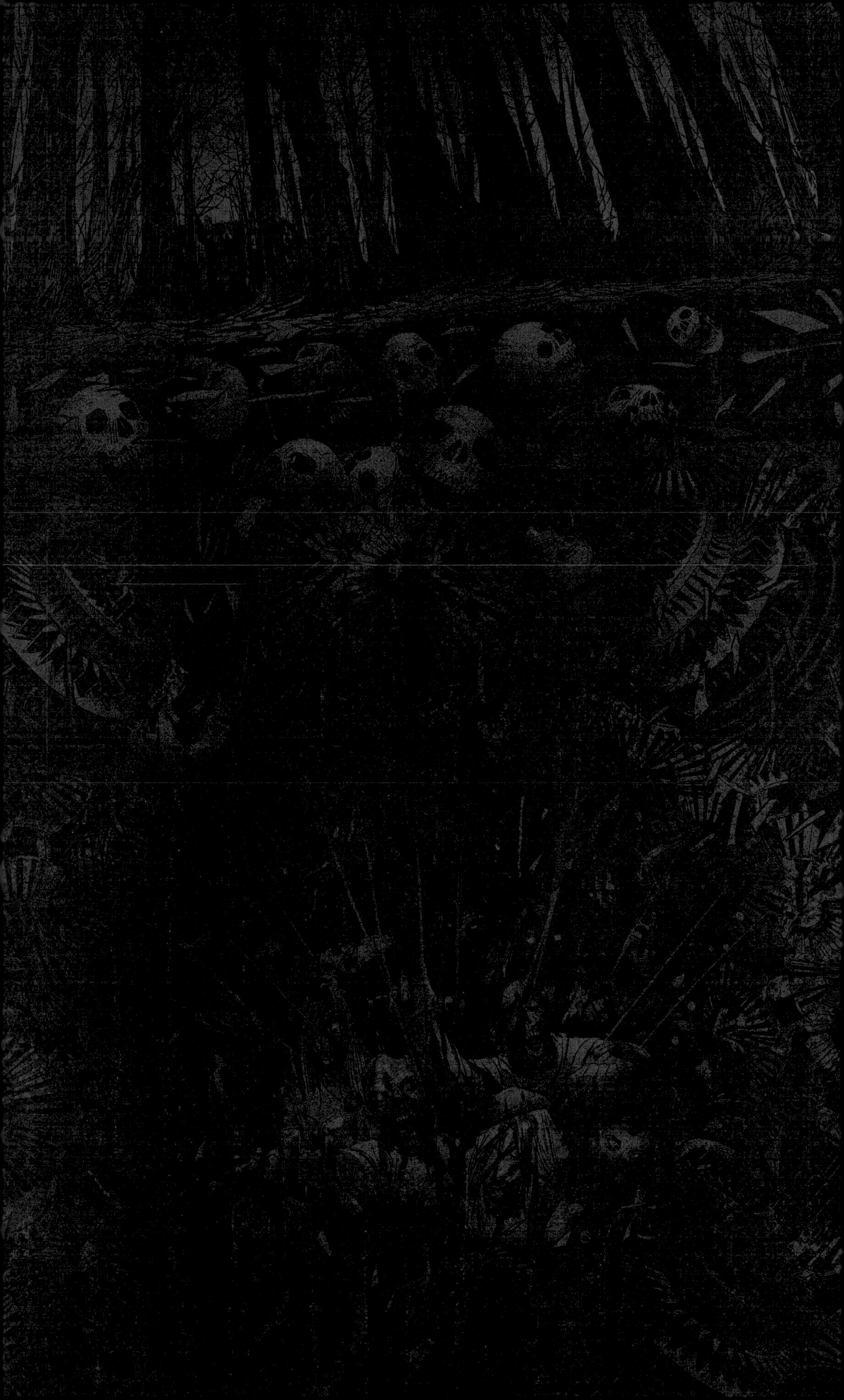

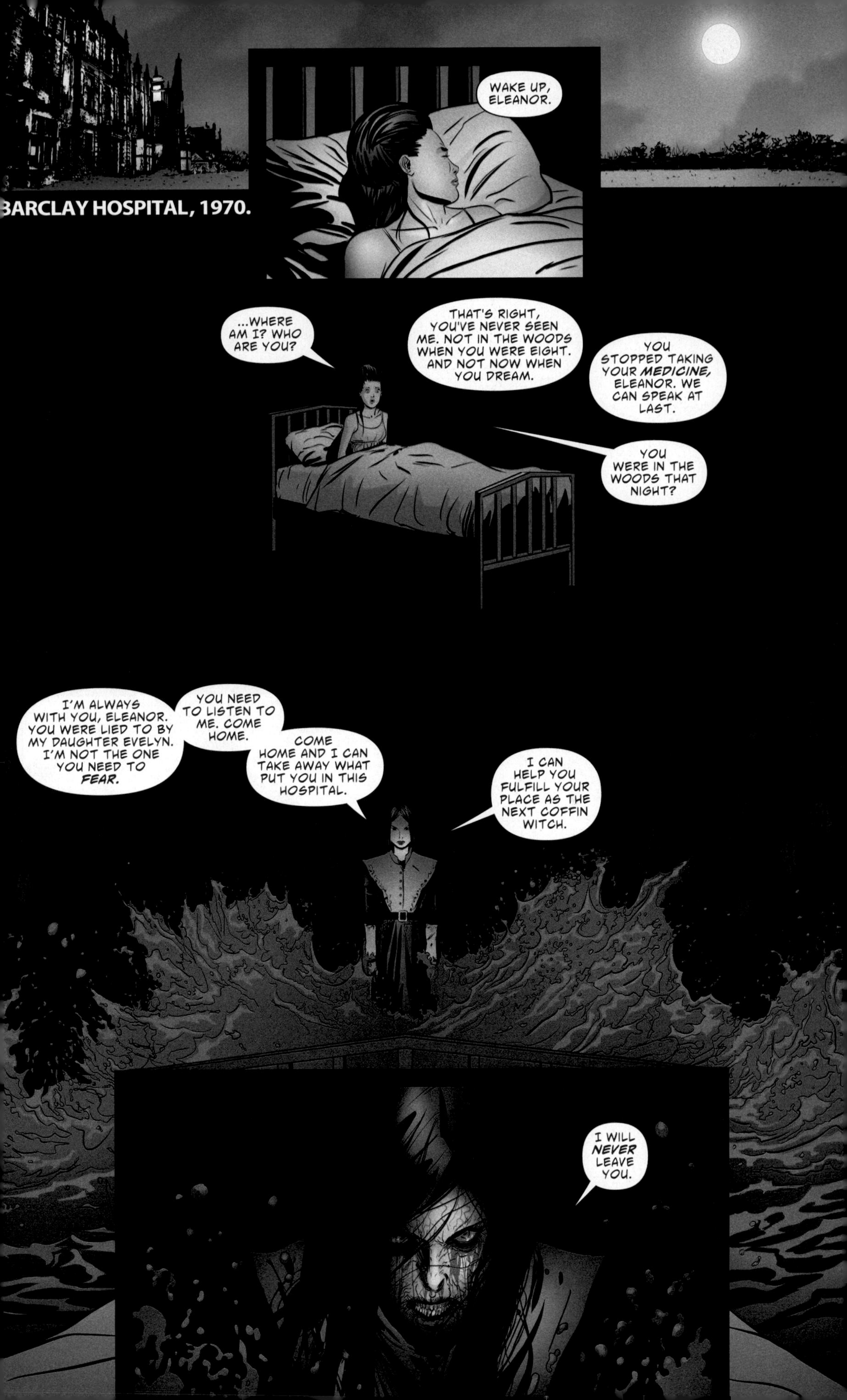
BARCLAY HOSPITAL, 1970.
WAKE UP, ELEANOR.
...WHERE AM I? WHO ARE YOU?
THAT'S RIGHT, YOU'VE NEVER SEEN ME. NOT IN THE WOODS WHEN YOU WERE EIGHT. AND NOT NOW WHEN YOU DREAM.
YOU STOPPED TAKING YOUR MEDICINE, ELEANOR. WE CAN SPEAK AT LAST.
YOU WERE IN THE WOODS THAT NIGHT?
I'M ALWAYS WITH YOU, ELEANOR. YOU WERE LIED TO BY MY DAUGHTER EVELYN. I'M NOT THE ONE YOU NEED TO FEAR.
YOU NEED TO LISTEN TO ME. COME HOME.
COME HOME AND I CAN TAKE AWAY WHAT PUT YOU IN THIS HOSPITAL.
I CAN HELP YOU FULFILL YOUR PLACE AS THE NEXT COFFIN WITCH.
I WILL NEVER LEAVE YOU.

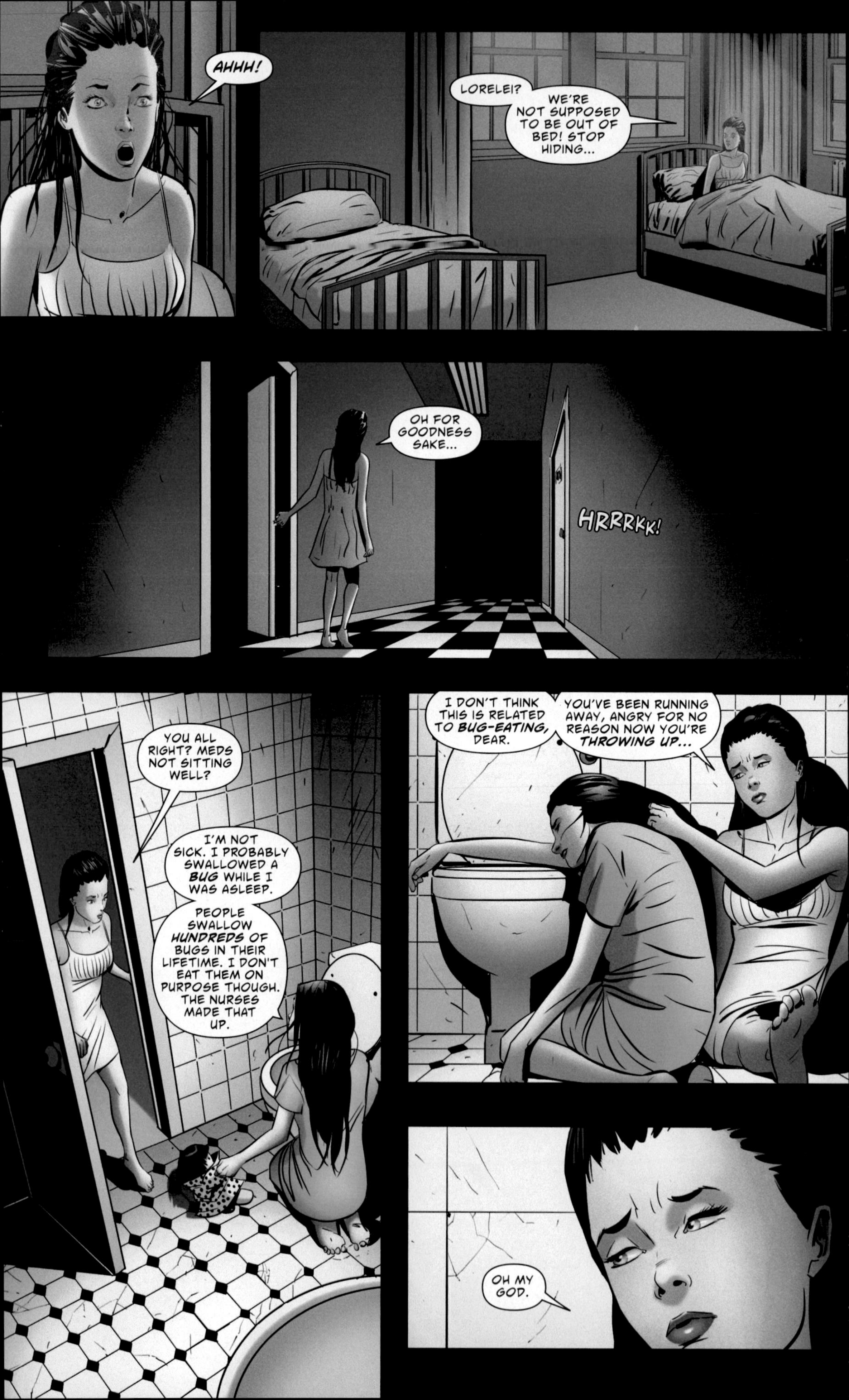
AHHH!
LORELEI?
WE'RE NOT SUPPOSED TO BE OUT OF BED! STOP HIDING...
OH FOR GOODNESS SAKE...
HRRRKK!
YOU ALL RIGHT? MEDS NOT SITTING WELL?
I'M NOT SICK. I PROBABLY SWALLOWED A BUG WHILE I WAS ASLEEP.
PEOPLE SWALLOW HUNDREDS OF BUGS IN THEIR LIFETIME. I DON'T EAT THEM ON PURPOSE THOUGH. THE NURSES MADE THAT UP.
YOU'VE BEEN RUNNING AWAY, ANGRY FOR NO REASON NOW YOU'RE THROWING UP...
I DON'T THINK THIS IS RELATED TO BUG-EATING, DEAR.
OH MY GOD.

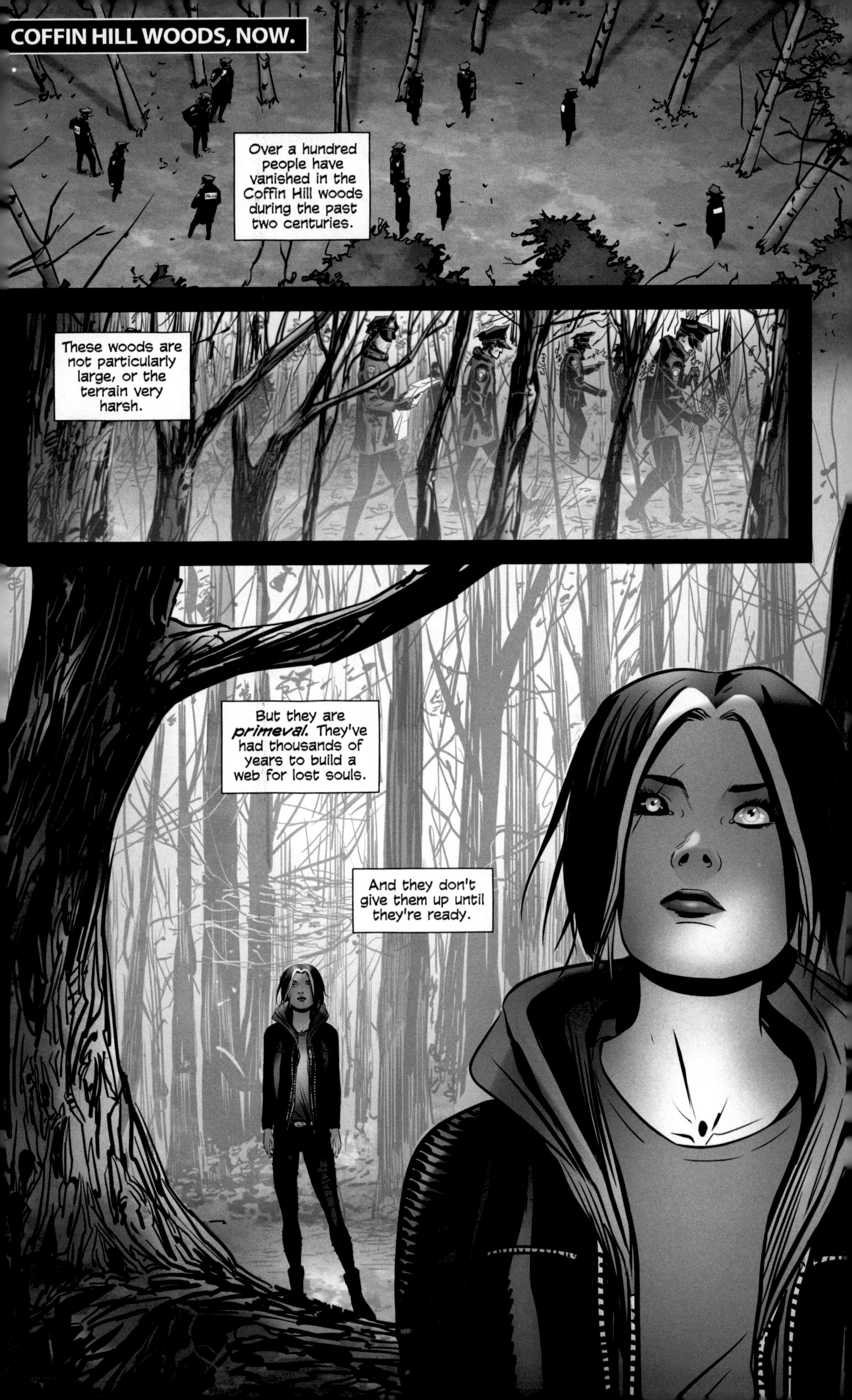
COFFIN HILL WOODS, NOW.
Over a hundred people have vanished in the Coffin Hill woods during the past two centuries.
These woods are not particularly large, or the terrain very harsh.
But they are *primeval.* They've had thousands of years to build a web for lost souls.
And they don't give them up until they're ready.

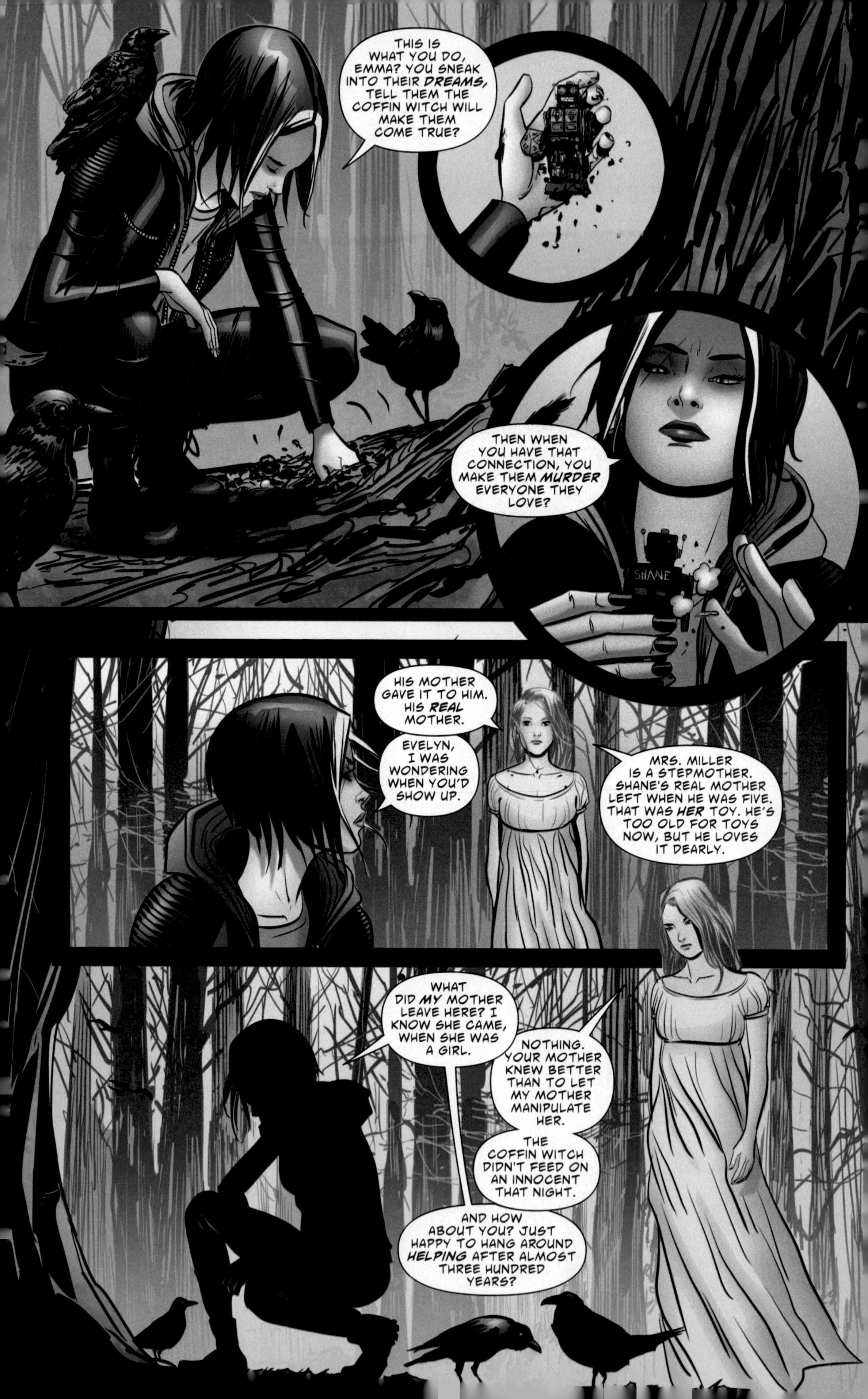
THIS IS WHAT YOU DO, EMMA? YOU SNEAK INTO THEIR DREAMS, TELL THEM THE COFFIN WITCH WILL MAKE THEM COME TRUE?
THEN WHEN YOU HAVE THAT CONNECTION, YOU MAKE THEM MURDER EVERYONE THEY LOVE?
SHANE
HIS MOTHER GAVE IT TO HIM. HIS REAL MOTHER.
EVELYN, I WAS WONDERING WHEN YOU'D SHOW UP.
MRS. MILLER IS A STEPMOTHER. SHANE'S REAL MOTHER LEFT WHEN HE WAS FIVE. THAT WAS HER TOY. HE'S TOO OLD FOR TOYS NOW, BUT HE LOVES IT DEARLY.
WHAT DID MY MOTHER LEAVE HERE? I KNOW SHE CAME, WHEN SHE WAS A GIRL.
NOTHING. YOUR MOTHER KNEW BETTER THAN TO LET MY MOTHER MANIPULATE HER.
THE COFFIN WITCH DIDN'T FEED ON AN INNOCENT THAT NIGHT.
AND HOW ABOUT YOU? JUST HAPPY TO HANG AROUND HELPING AFTER ALMOST THREE HUNDRED YEARS?

I DIED HERE TOO. I'M *BOUND* JUST LIKE MY MOTHER.

ALL THE GHOSTS IN COFFIN HILL ARE BOUND. I'VE SEEN A LOT OF FAMILIAR FACES.

NONE AS OLD AS YOU AND EMMA, THOUGH.

THIS LITTLE GIRL, CONSTANCE? BEEN DEAD ABOUT SIXTY YEARS. SHE CAN BARELY STRING A SENTENCE TOGETHER.

BUT YOU LOOK REALLY GOOD FOR A *DEAD* GIRL, EVELYN. SO DOES YOUR MOMMY.

LOOK, I'M STUCK HERE, BUT SHE'S NOT. SHE FOUND THE FIRST FAMILY WITHIN A FORTNIGHT. ONE OF THE ONES RESPONSIBLE.

THEIR BOY, DANIEL, HACKED HIS PARENTS HEADS OFF WITH A SPADE.

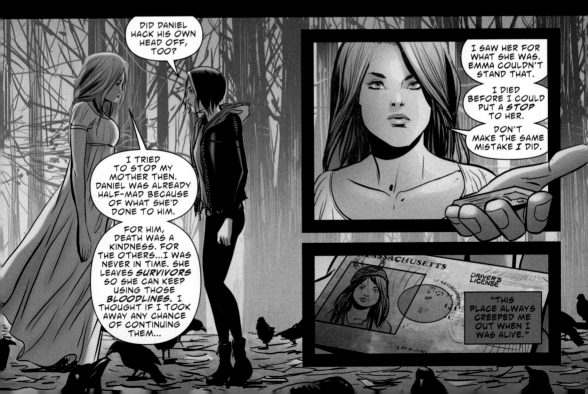

DID DANIEL HACK HIS OWN HEAD OFF, TOO?

I TRIED TO STOP MY MOTHER THEN. DANIEL WAS ALREADY HALF-MAD BECAUSE OF WHAT SHE'D DONE TO HIM.

FOR HIM, DEATH WAS A KINDNESS. FOR THE OTHERS...I WAS NEVER IN TIME. SHE LEAVES *SURVIVORS* SO SHE CAN KEEP USING THOSE *BLOODLINES.* I THOUGHT IF I TOOK AWAY ANY CHANCE OF CONTINUING THEM...

I SAW HER FOR WHAT SHE WAS. EMMA COULDN'T STAND THAT.

I DIED BEFORE I COULD PUT A *STOP* TO HER.

DON'T MAKE THE SAME MISTAKE *I* DID.

MASSACHUSETTS

DRIVER'S LICENSE

"THIS PLACE ALWAYS CREEPED ME OUT WHEN I WAS ALIVE."

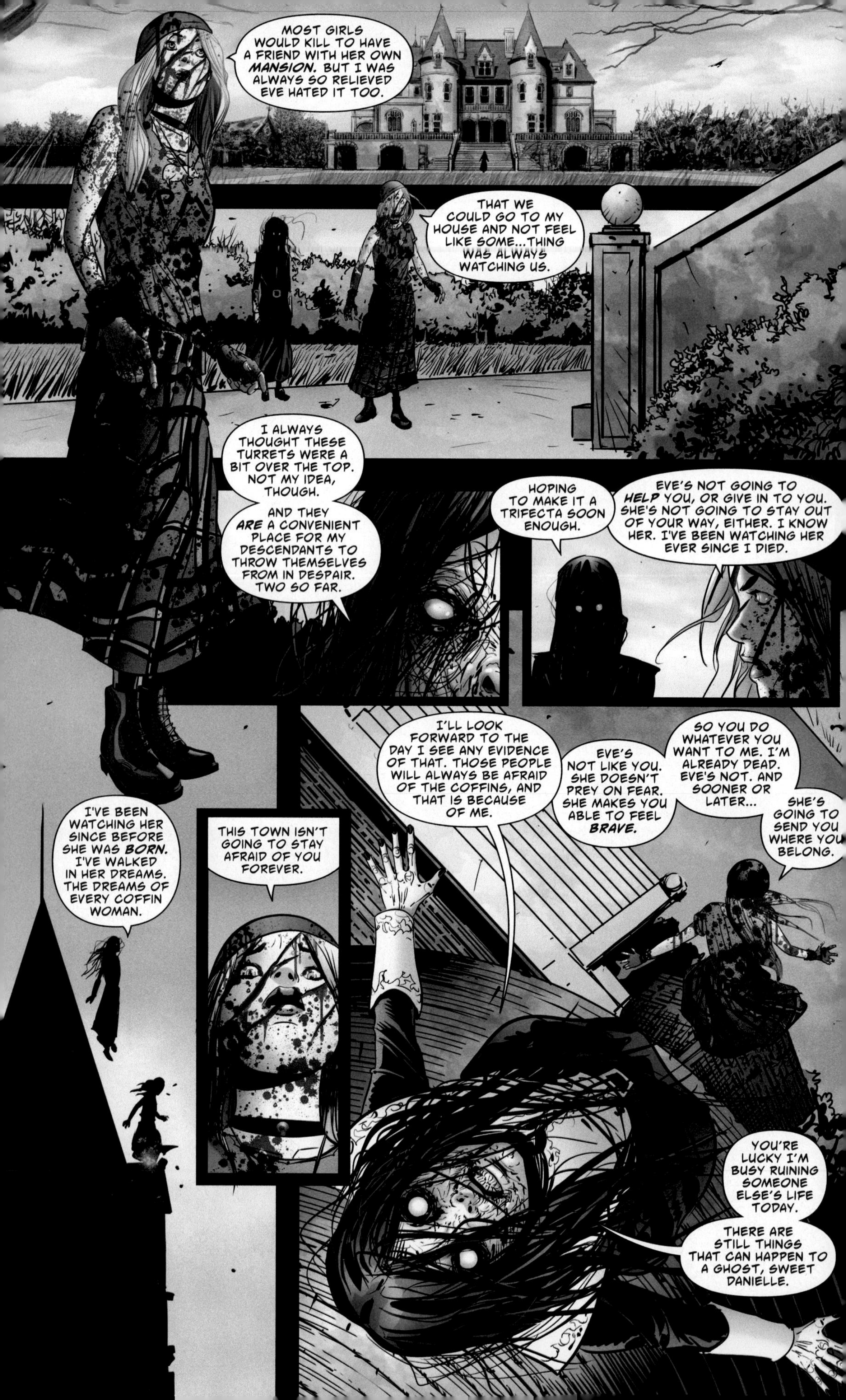
MOST GIRLS WOULD KILL TO HAVE A FRIEND WITH HER OWN MANSION. BUT I WAS ALWAYS SO RELIEVED EVE HATED IT TOO.
THAT WE COULD GO TO MY HOUSE AND NOT FEEL LIKE SOME...THING WAS ALWAYS WATCHING US.
I ALWAYS THOUGHT THESE TURRETS WERE A BIT OVER THE TOP. NOT MY IDEA, THOUGH.
AND THEY ARE A CONVENIENT PLACE FOR MY DESCENDANTS TO THROW THEMSELVES FROM IN DESPAIR. TWO SO FAR.
HOPING TO MAKE IT A TRIFECTA SOON ENOUGH.
EVE'S NOT GOING TO HELP YOU, OR GIVE IN TO YOU. SHE'S NOT GOING TO STAY OUT OF YOUR WAY, EITHER. I KNOW HER. I'VE BEEN WATCHING HER EVER SINCE I DIED.
I'VE BEEN WATCHING HER SINCE BEFORE SHE WAS BORN. I'VE WALKED IN HER DREAMS. THE DREAMS OF EVERY COFFIN WOMAN.
THIS TOWN ISN'T GOING TO STAY AFRAID OF YOU FOREVER.
I'LL LOOK FORWARD TO THE DAY I SEE ANY EVIDENCE OF THAT. THOSE PEOPLE WILL ALWAYS BE AFRAID OF THE COFFINS, AND THAT IS BECAUSE OF ME.
EVE'S NOT LIKE YOU. SHE DOESN'T PREY ON FEAR. SHE MAKES YOU ABLE TO FEEL BRAVE.
SO YOU DO WHATEVER YOU WANT TO ME. I'M ALREADY DEAD. EVE'S NOT. AND SOONER OR LATER...
SHE'S GOING TO SEND YOU WHERE YOU BELONG.
YOU'RE LUCKY I'M BUSY RUINING SOMEONE ELSE'S LIFE TODAY.
THERE ARE STILL THINGS THAT CAN HAPPEN TO A GHOST, SWEET DANIELLE.

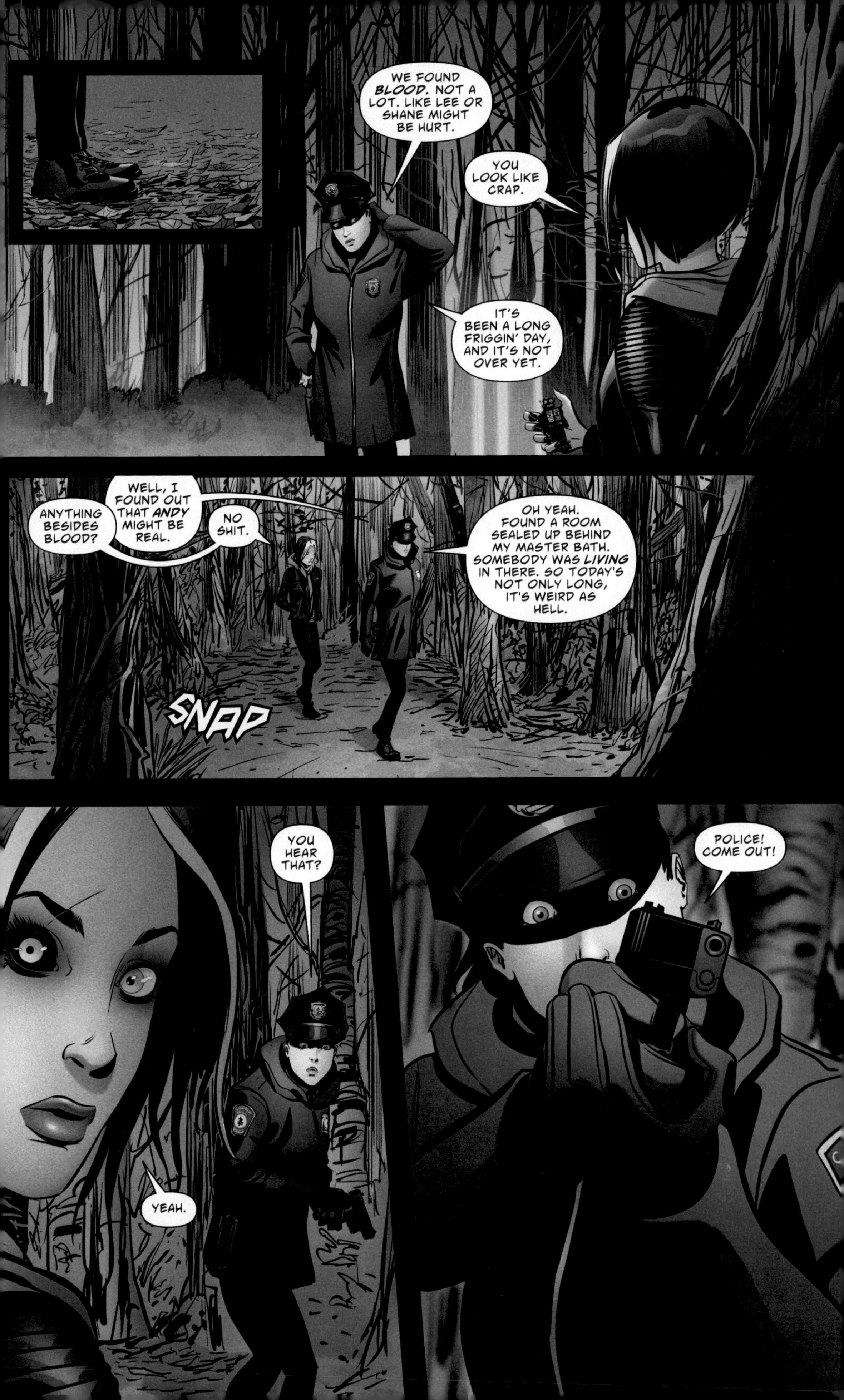
WE FOUND BLOOD. NOT A LOT. LIKE LEE OR SHANE MIGHT BE HURT.
YOU LOOK LIKE CRAP.
IT'S BEEN A LONG FRIGGIN' DAY, AND IT'S NOT OVER YET.
ANYTHING BESIDES BLOOD?
WELL, I FOUND OUT THAT ANDY MIGHT BE REAL.
NO SHIT.
OH YEAH. FOUND A ROOM SEALED UP BEHIND MY MASTER BATH. SOMEBODY WAS LIVING IN THERE. SO TODAY'S NOT ONLY LONG, IT'S WEIRD AS HELL.
SNAP
YOU HEAR THAT?
YEAH.
POLICE! COME OUT!

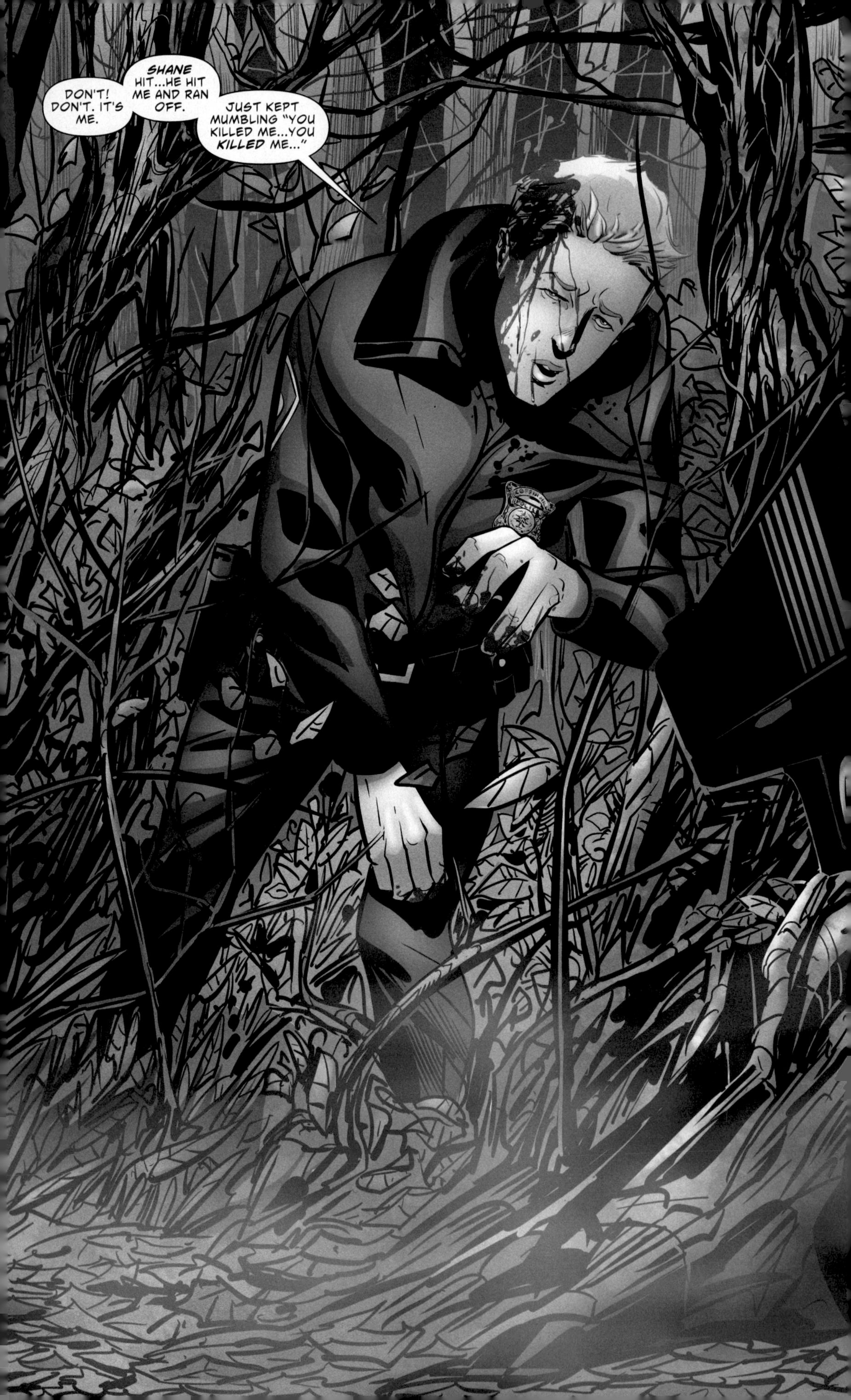
DON'T! DON'T. IT'S ME.
SHANE HIT...HE HIT ME AND RAN OFF.
JUST KEPT MUMBLING "YOU KILLED ME...YOU KILLED ME..."

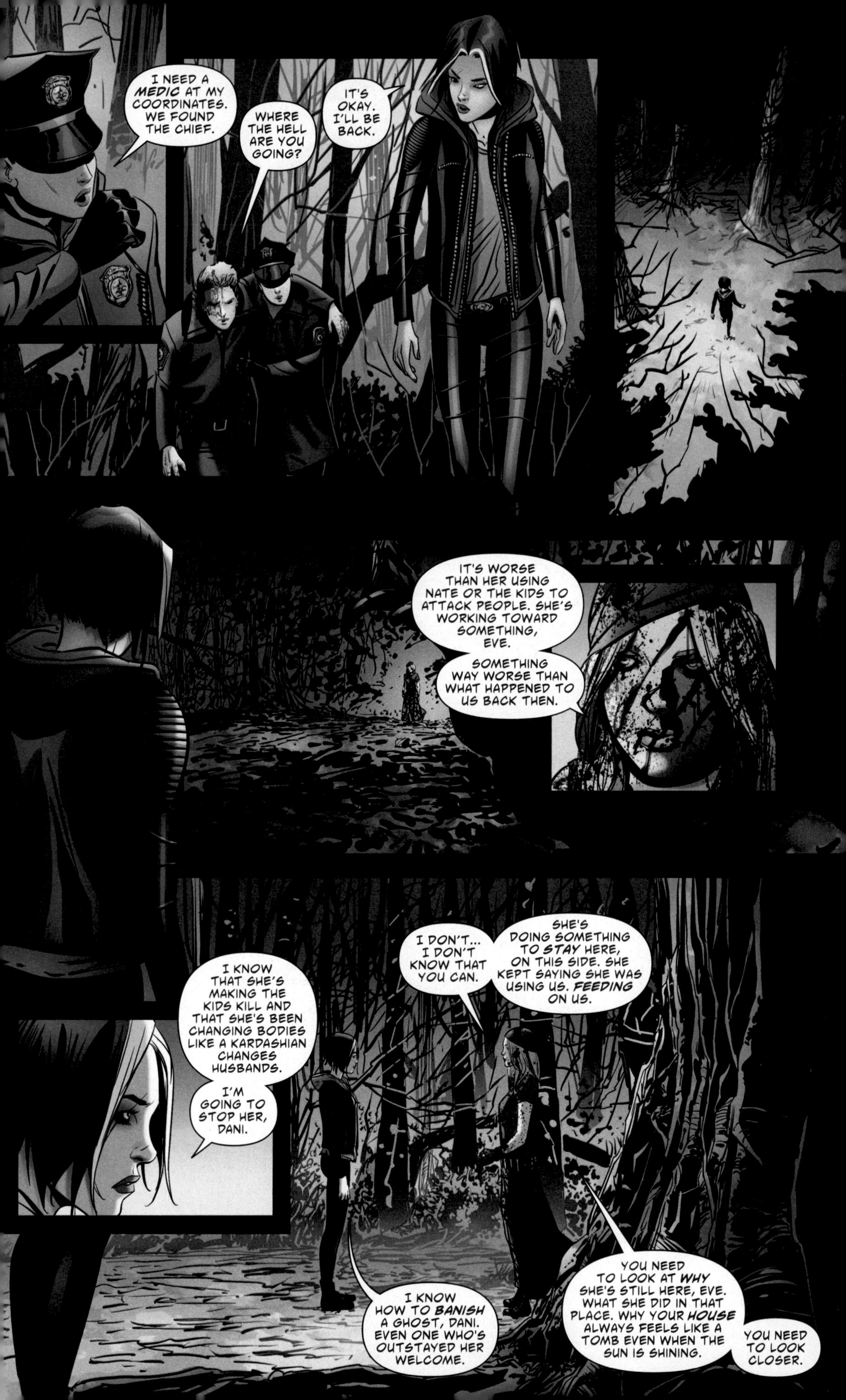
I NEED A *MEDIC* AT MY COORDINATES. WE FOUND THE CHIEF.
WHERE THE HELL ARE YOU GOING?
IT'S OKAY. I'LL BE BACK.
IT'S WORSE THAN HER USING NATE OR THE KIDS TO ATTACK PEOPLE. SHE'S WORKING TOWARD SOMETHING, EVE.
SOMETHING WAY WORSE THAN WHAT HAPPENED TO US BACK THEN.
I KNOW THAT SHE'S MAKING THE KIDS KILL AND THAT SHE'S BEEN CHANGING BODIES LIKE A KARDASHIAN CHANGES HUSBANDS.
I'M GOING TO STOP HER, DANI.
I DON'T... I DON'T KNOW THAT YOU CAN.
SHE'S DOING SOMETHING TO *STAY* HERE, ON THIS SIDE. SHE KEPT SAYING SHE WAS USING US. *FEEDING* ON US.
I KNOW HOW TO *BANISH* A GHOST, DANI. EVEN ONE WHO'S OUTSTAYED HER WELCOME.
YOU NEED TO LOOK AT *WHY* SHE'S STILL HERE, EVE. WHAT SHE DID IN THAT PLACE. WHY YOUR *HOUSE* ALWAYS FEELS LIKE A TOMB EVEN WHEN THE SUN IS SHINING.
YOU NEED TO LOOK CLOSER.

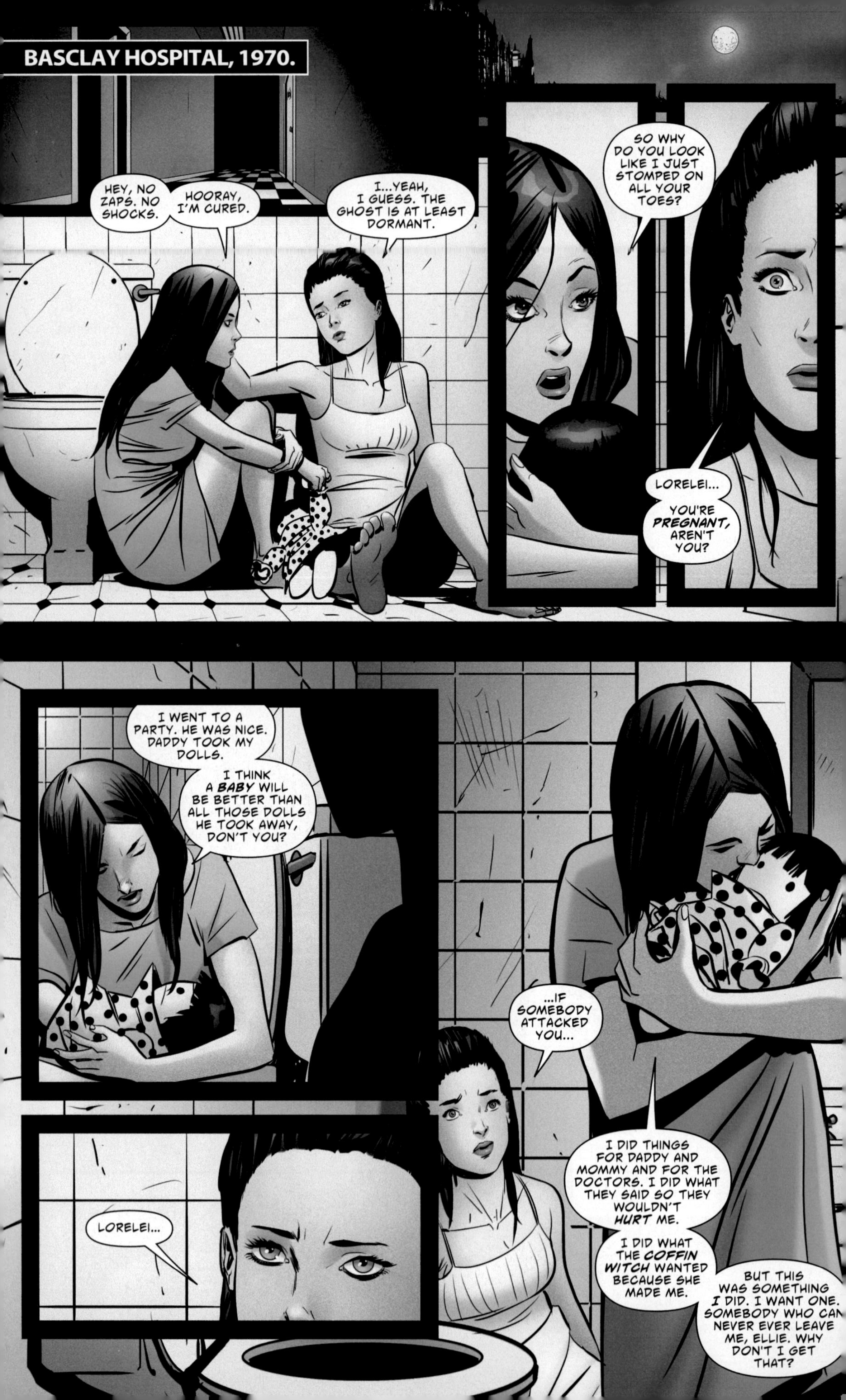
BASCLAY HOSPITAL, 1970.
HEY, NO ZAPS. NO SHOCKS.
HOORAY, I'M CURED.
I...YEAH, I GUESS. THE GHOST IS AT LEAST DORMANT.
SO WHY DO YOU LOOK LIKE I JUST STOMPED ON ALL YOUR TOES?
LORELEI...
YOU'RE PREGNANT, AREN'T YOU?
I WENT TO A PARTY. HE WAS NICE. DADDY TOOK MY DOLLS.
I THINK A BABY WILL BE BETTER THAN ALL THOSE DOLLS HE TOOK AWAY, DON'T YOU?
LORELEI...
...IF SOMEBODY ATTACKED YOU...
I DID THINGS FOR DADDY AND MOMMY AND FOR THE DOCTORS. I DID WHAT THEY SAID SO THEY WOULDN'T HURT ME.
I DID WHAT THE COFFIN WITCH WANTED BECAUSE SHE MADE ME.
BUT THIS WAS SOMETHING I DID. I WANT ONE. SOMEBODY WHO CAN NEVER EVER LEAVE ME, ELLIE. WHY DON'T I GET THAT?

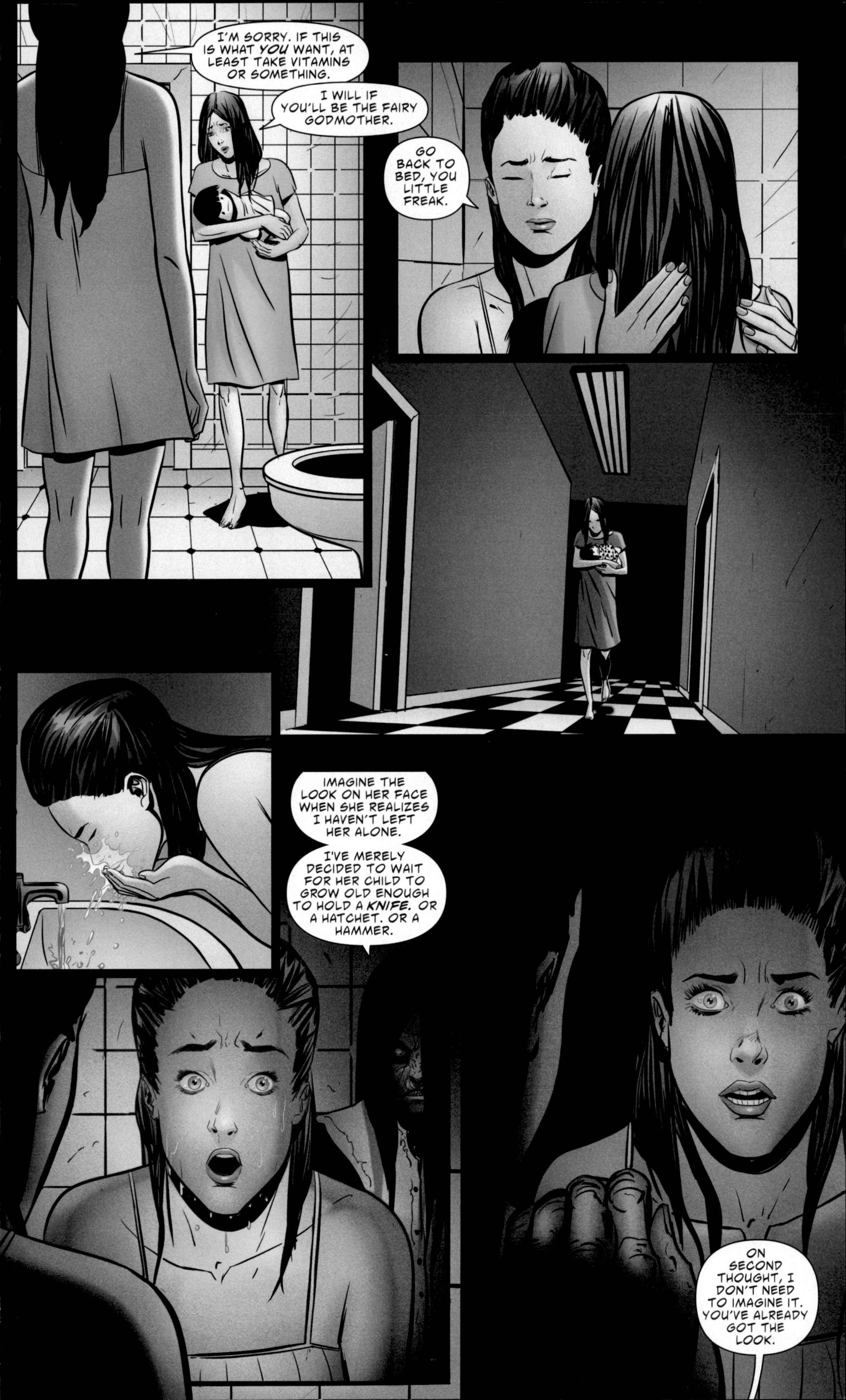
I'M SORRY. IF THIS IS WHAT YOU WANT, AT LEAST TAKE VITAMINS OR SOMETHING.
I WILL IF YOU'LL BE THE FAIRY GODMOTHER.
GO BACK TO BED, YOU LITTLE FREAK.
IMAGINE THE LOOK ON HER FACE WHEN SHE REALIZES I HAVEN'T LEFT HER ALONE.
I'VE MERELY DECIDED TO WAIT FOR HER CHILD TO GROW OLD ENOUGH TO HOLD A KNIFE. OR A HATCHET. OR A HAMMER.
ON SECOND THOUGHT, I DON'T NEED TO IMAGINE IT. YOU'VE ALREADY GOT THE LOOK.

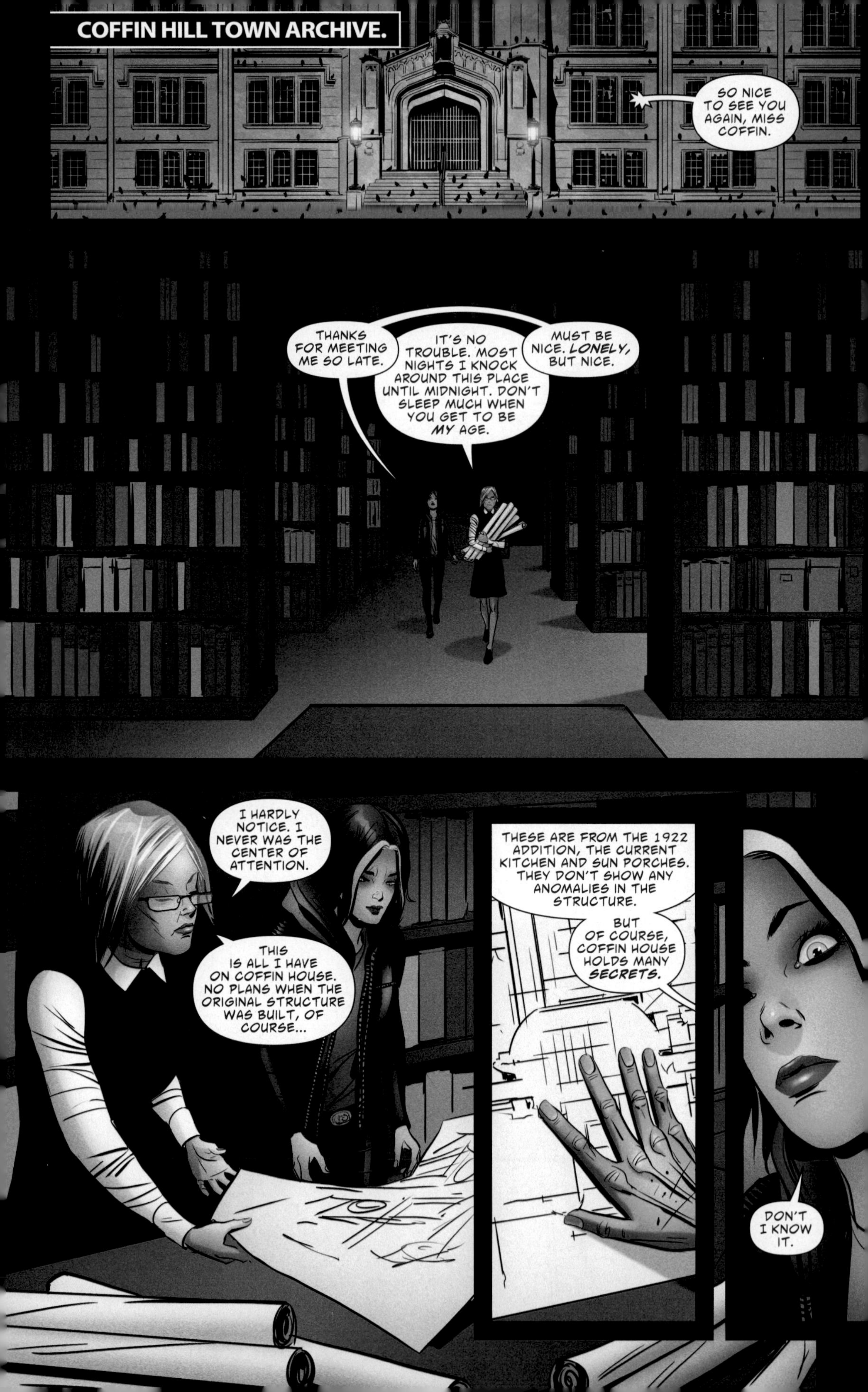
COFFIN HILL TOWN ARCHIVE.
SO NICE TO SEE YOU AGAIN, MISS COFFIN.
THANKS FOR MEETING ME SO LATE.
IT'S NO TROUBLE. MOST NIGHTS I KNOCK AROUND THIS PLACE UNTIL MIDNIGHT. DON'T SLEEP MUCH WHEN YOU GET TO BE MY AGE.
MUST BE NICE. LONELY, BUT NICE.
I HARDLY NOTICE. I NEVER WAS THE CENTER OF ATTENTION.
THIS IS ALL I HAVE ON COFFIN HOUSE. NO PLANS WHEN THE ORIGINAL STRUCTURE WAS BUILT, OF COURSE...
THESE ARE FROM THE 1922 ADDITION, THE CURRENT KITCHEN AND SUN PORCHES. THEY DON'T SHOW ANY ANOMALIES IN THE STRUCTURE.
BUT OF COURSE, COFFIN HOUSE HOLDS MANY SECRETS.
DON'T I KNOW IT.

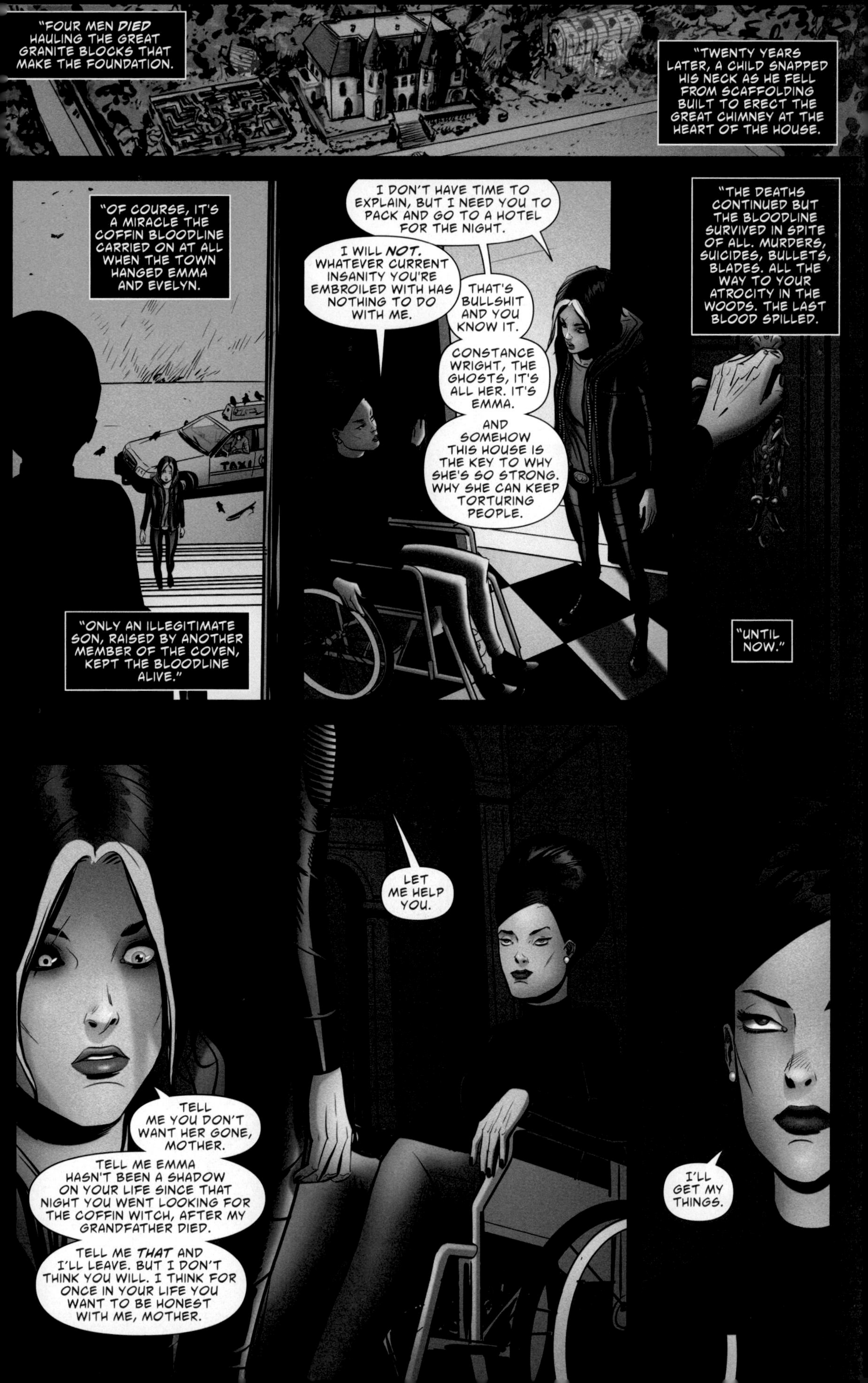
"FOUR MEN DIED HAULING THE GREAT GRANITE BLOCKS THAT MAKE THE FOUNDATION.
"TWENTY YEARS LATER, A CHILD SNAPPED HIS NECK AS HE FELL FROM SCAFFOLDING BUILT TO ERECT THE GREAT CHIMNEY AT THE HEART OF THE HOUSE.
"OF COURSE, IT'S A MIRACLE THE COFFIN BLOODLINE CARRIED ON AT ALL WHEN THE TOWN HANGED EMMA AND EVELYN.
TAXI
"ONLY AN ILLEGITIMATE SON, RAISED BY ANOTHER MEMBER OF THE COVEN, KEPT THE BLOODLINE ALIVE."
I DON'T HAVE TIME TO EXPLAIN, BUT I NEED YOU TO PACK AND GO TO A HOTEL FOR THE NIGHT.
I WILL NOT. WHATEVER CURRENT INSANITY YOU'RE EMBROILED WITH HAS NOTHING TO DO WITH ME.
THAT'S BULLSHIT AND YOU KNOW IT.
CONSTANCE WRIGHT, THE GHOSTS, IT'S ALL HER. IT'S EMMA.
AND SOMEHOW THIS HOUSE IS THE KEY TO WHY SHE'S SO STRONG. WHY SHE CAN KEEP TORTURING PEOPLE.
"THE DEATHS CONTINUED BUT THE BLOODLINE SURVIVED IN SPITE OF ALL. MURDERS, SUICIDES, BULLETS, BLADES. ALL THE WAY TO YOUR ATROCITY IN THE WOODS. THE LAST BLOOD SPILLED.
"UNTIL NOW."
TELL ME YOU DON'T WANT HER GONE, MOTHER.
TELL ME EMMA HASN'T BEEN A SHADOW ON YOUR LIFE SINCE THAT NIGHT YOU WENT LOOKING FOR THE COFFIN WITCH, AFTER MY GRANDFATHER DIED.
TELL ME THAT AND I'LL LEAVE. BUT I DON'T THINK YOU WILL. I THINK FOR ONCE IN YOUR LIFE YOU WANT TO BE HONEST WITH ME, MOTHER.
LET ME HELP YOU.
I'LL GET MY THINGS.

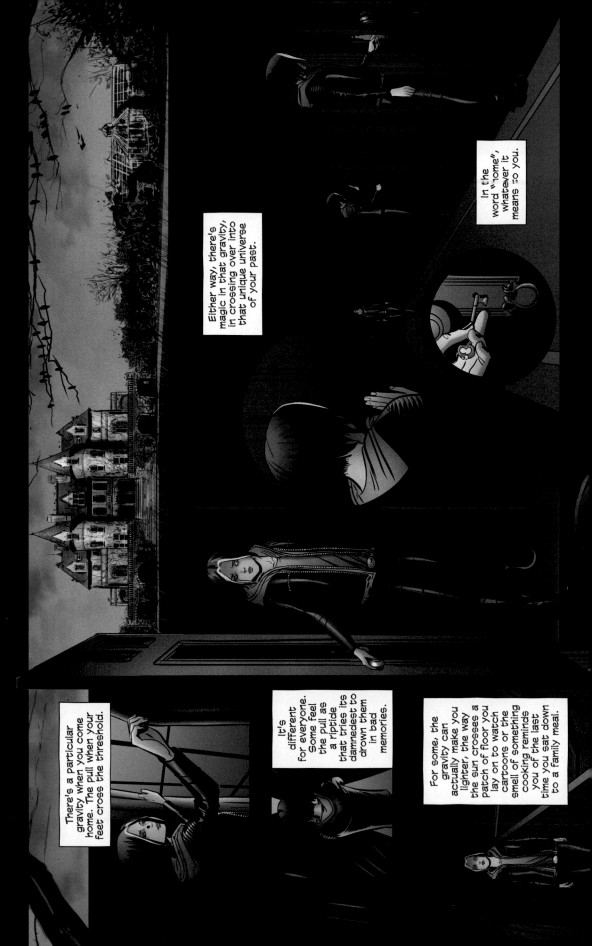

There's a particular gravity when you come home. The pull when your feet cross the threshold.

It's different for everyone. Some feel the pull as a riptide that tries its damnedest to drown them in bad memories.

For some, the gravity can actually make you lighter, the way the sun crosses a patch of floor you lay on to watch cartoons or the smell of something cooking reminds you of the last time you sat down to a family meal.

Either way, there's magic in that gravity, in crossing over into that unique universe of your past.

In the word "home", whatever it means to you.

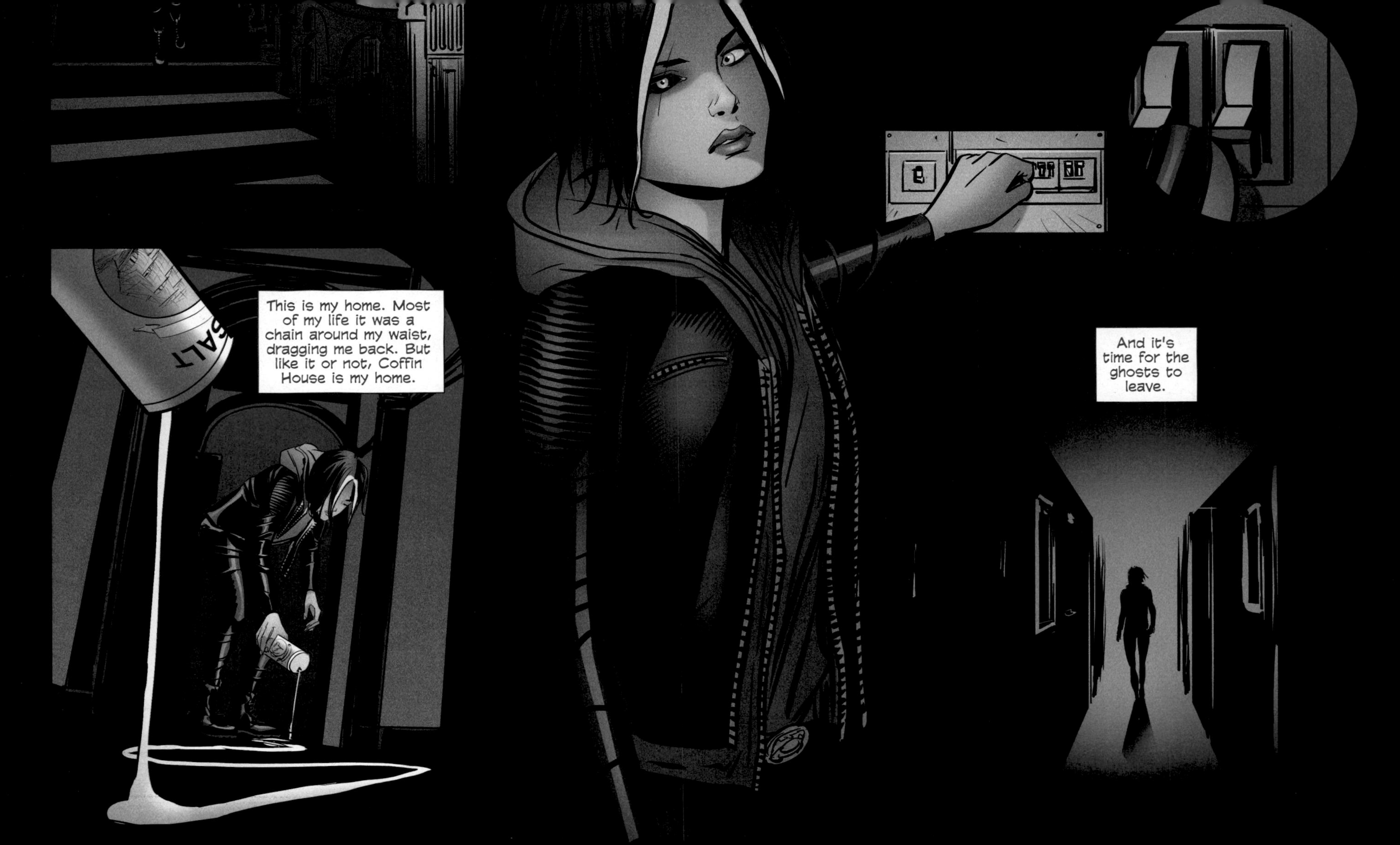
SALT
This is my home. Most of my life it was a chain around my waist, dragging me back. But like it or not, Coffin House is my home.
And it's time for the ghosts to leave.

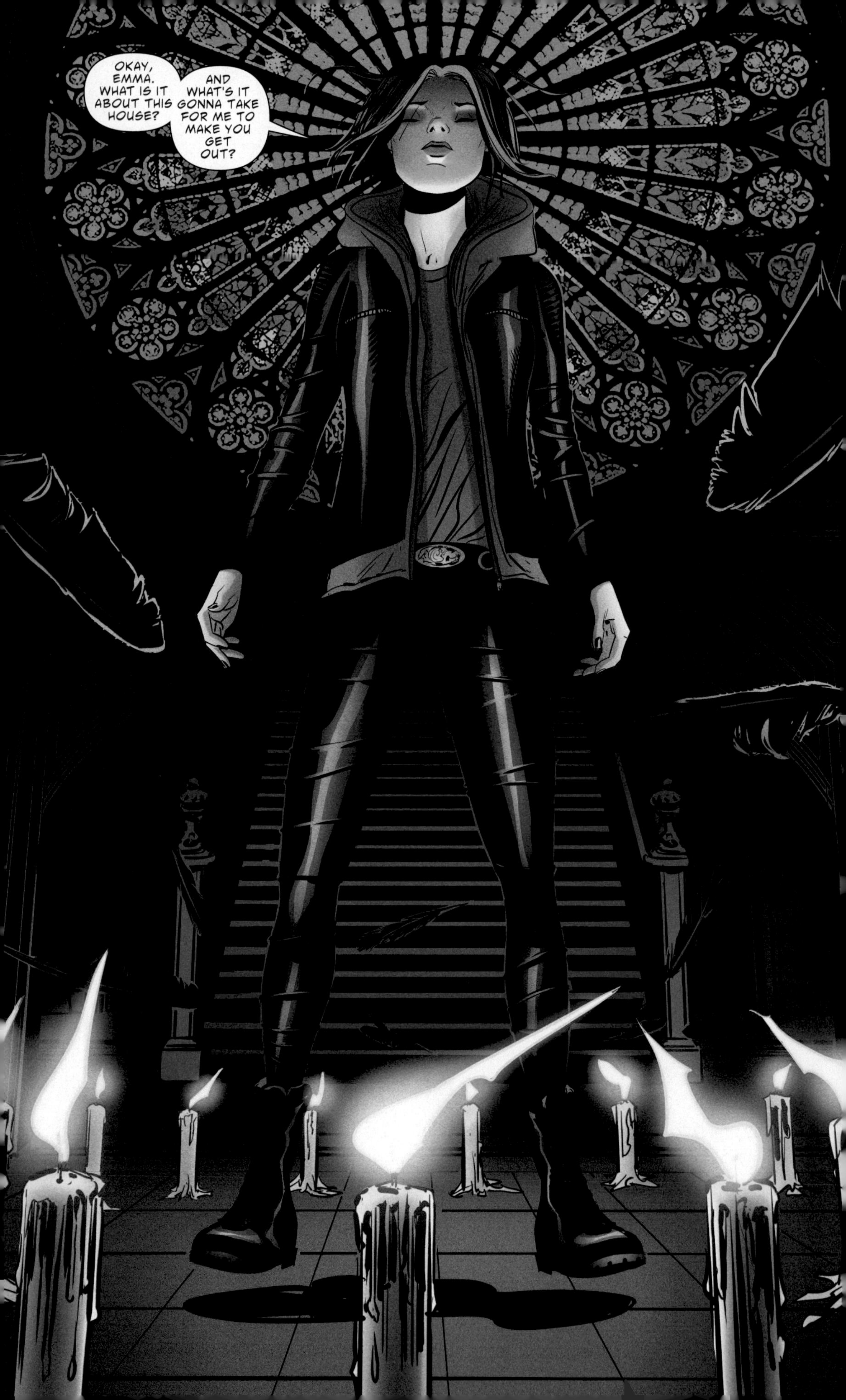
OKAY, EMMA. WHAT IS IT ABOUT THIS HOUSE?
AND WHAT'S IT GONNA TAKE FOR ME TO MAKE YOU GET OUT?

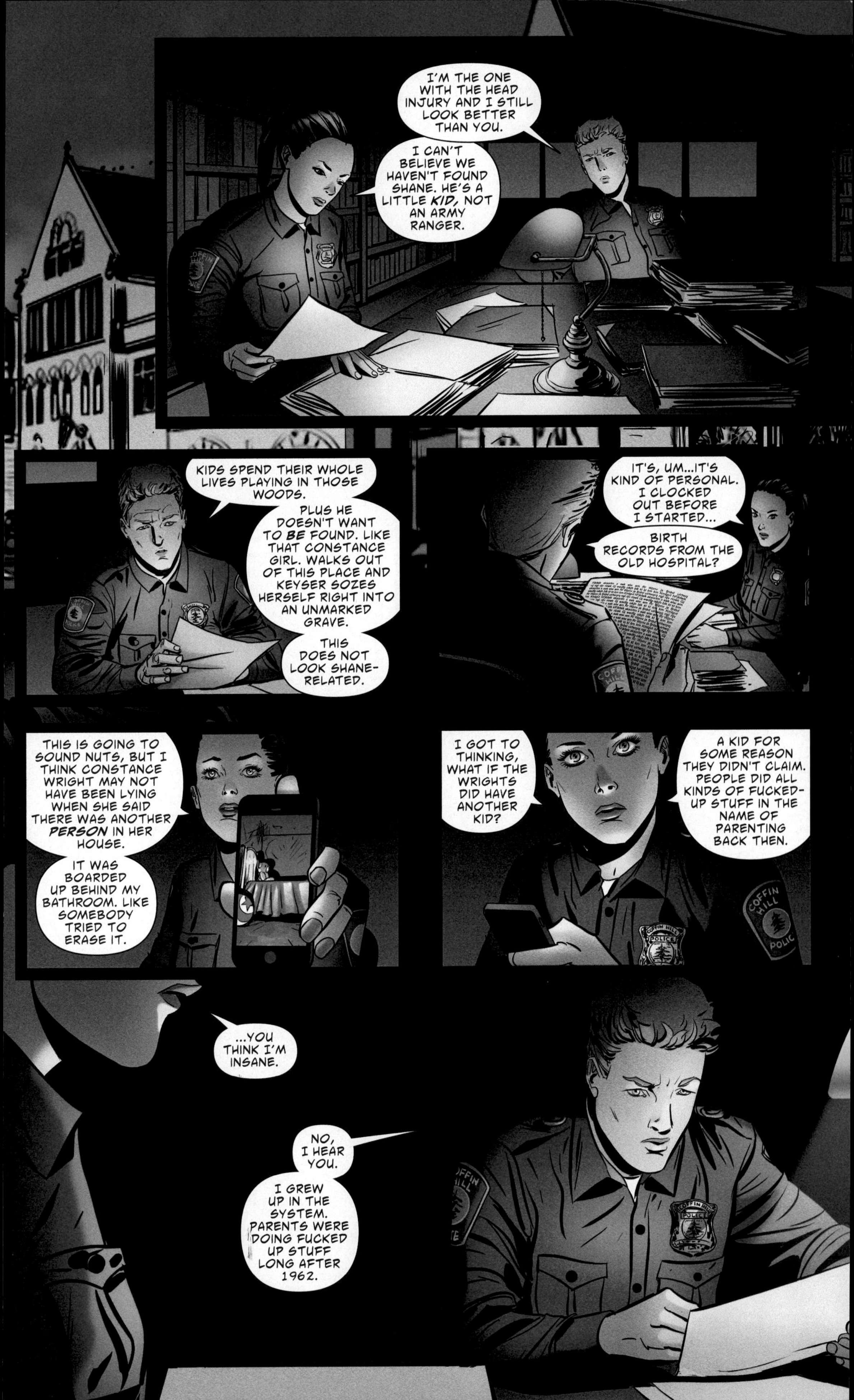
I'M THE ONE WITH THE HEAD INJURY AND I STILL LOOK BETTER THAN YOU.
I CAN'T BELIEVE WE HAVEN'T FOUND SHANE. HE'S A LITTLE KID, NOT AN ARMY RANGER.
KIDS SPEND THEIR WHOLE LIVES PLAYING IN THOSE WOODS.
PLUS HE DOESN'T WANT TO BE FOUND. LIKE THAT CONSTANCE GIRL. WALKS OUT OF THIS PLACE AND KEYSER SOZES HERSELF RIGHT INTO AN UNMARKED GRAVE.
THIS DOES NOT LOOK SHANE-RELATED.
IT'S, UM...IT'S KIND OF PERSONAL. I CLOCKED OUT BEFORE I STARTED...
BIRTH RECORDS FROM THE OLD HOSPITAL?
THIS IS GOING TO SOUND NUTS, BUT I THINK CONSTANCE WRIGHT MAY NOT HAVE BEEN LYING WHEN SHE SAID THERE WAS ANOTHER PERSON IN HER HOUSE.
IT WAS BOARDED UP BEHIND MY BATHROOM. LIKE SOMEBODY TRIED TO ERASE IT.
I GOT TO THINKING, WHAT IF THE WRIGHTS DID HAVE ANOTHER KID?
A KID FOR SOME REASON THEY DIDN'T CLAIM. PEOPLE DID ALL KINDS OF FUCKED-UP STUFF IN THE NAME OF PARENTING BACK THEN.
...YOU THINK I'M INSANE.
NO, I HEAR YOU.
I GREW UP IN THE SYSTEM. PARENTS WERE DOING FUCKED UP STUFF LONG AFTER 1962.

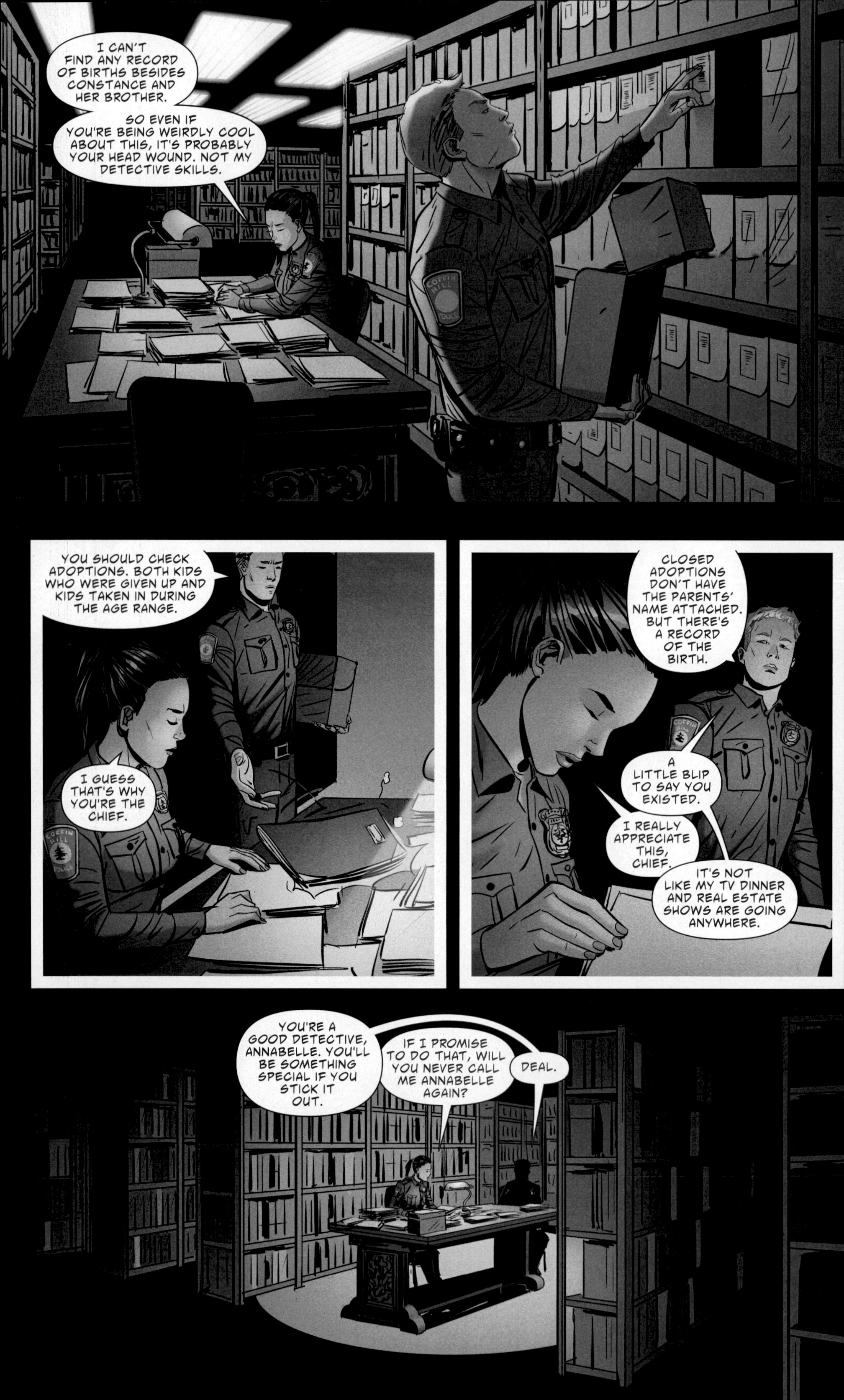
I CAN'T FIND ANY RECORD OF BIRTHS BESIDES CONSTANCE AND HER BROTHER.
SO EVEN IF YOU'RE BEING WEIRDLY COOL ABOUT THIS, IT'S PROBABLY YOUR HEAD WOUND. NOT MY DETECTIVE SKILLS.
YOU SHOULD CHECK ADOPTIONS. BOTH KIDS WHO WERE GIVEN UP AND KIDS TAKEN IN DURING THE AGE RANGE.
I GUESS THAT'S WHY YOU'RE THE CHIEF.
CLOSED ADOPTIONS DON'T HAVE THE PARENTS' NAME ATTACHED. BUT THERE'S A RECORD OF THE BIRTH.
A LITTLE BLIP TO SAY YOU EXISTED.
I REALLY APPRECIATE THIS, CHIEF.
IT'S NOT LIKE MY TV DINNER AND REAL ESTATE SHOWS ARE GOING ANYWHERE.
YOU'RE A GOOD DETECTIVE, ANNABELLE. YOU'LL BE SOMETHING SPECIAL IF YOU STICK IT OUT.
IF I PROMISE TO DO THAT, WILL YOU NEVER CALL ME ANNABELLE AGAIN?
DEAL.

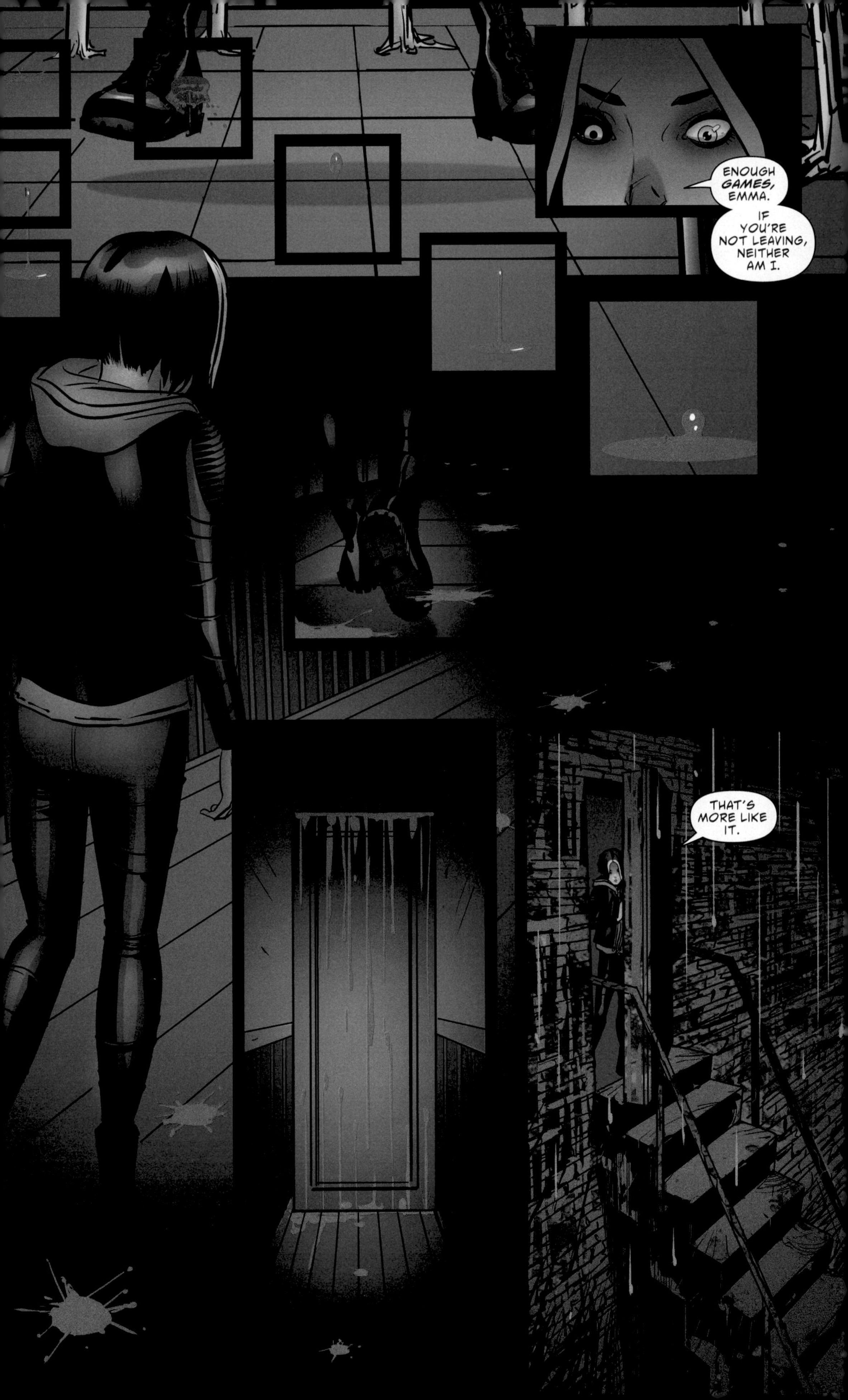

ENOUGH GAMES, EMMA.
IF YOU'RE NOT LEAVING, NEITHER AM I.
THAT'S MORE LIKE IT.

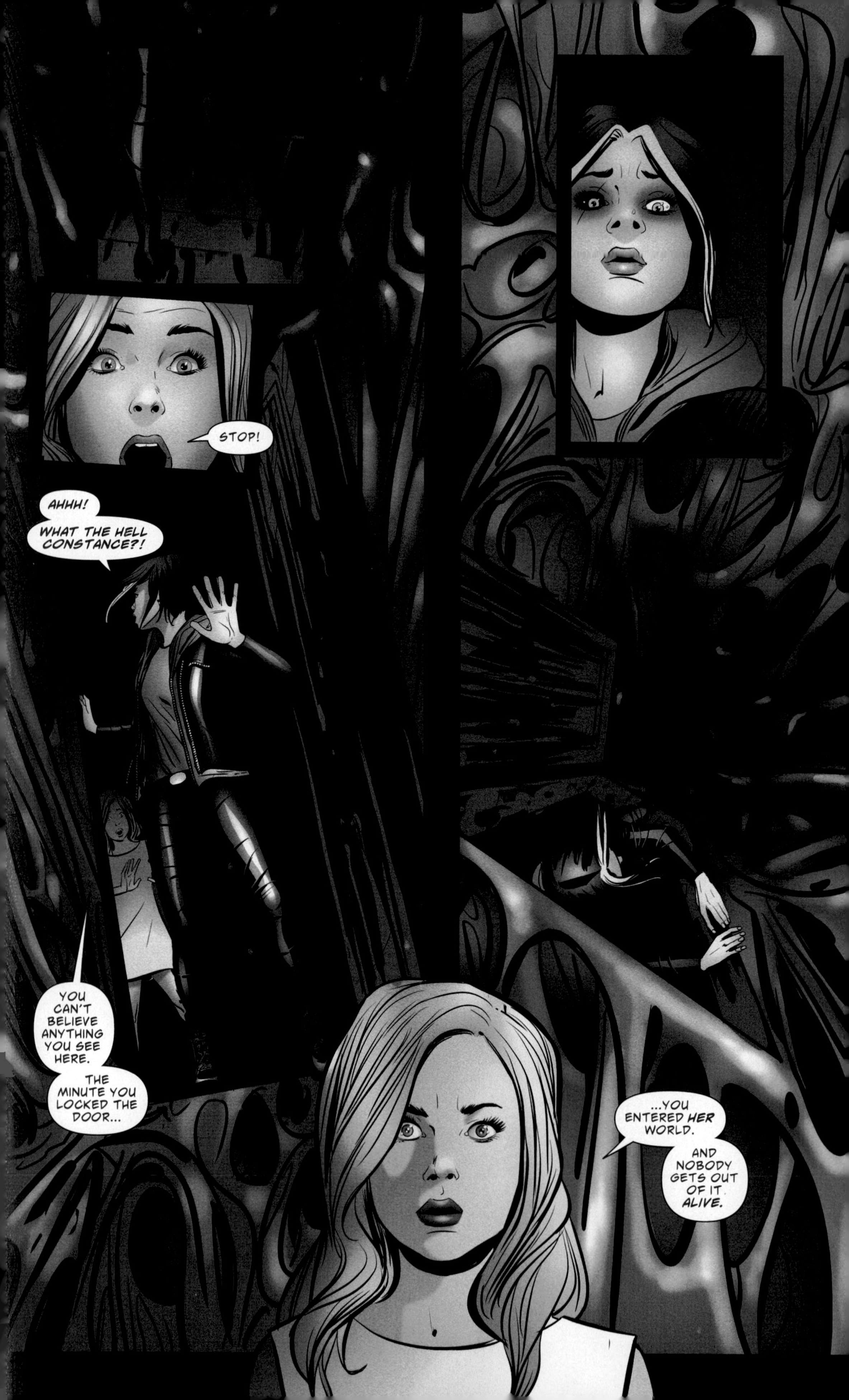
STOP!
AHHH!
WHAT THE HELL CONSTANCE?!
YOU CAN'T BELIEVE ANYTHING YOU SEE HERE.
THE MINUTE YOU LOCKED THE DOOR...
...YOU ENTERED HER WORLD.
AND NOBODY GETS OUT OF IT ALIVE.

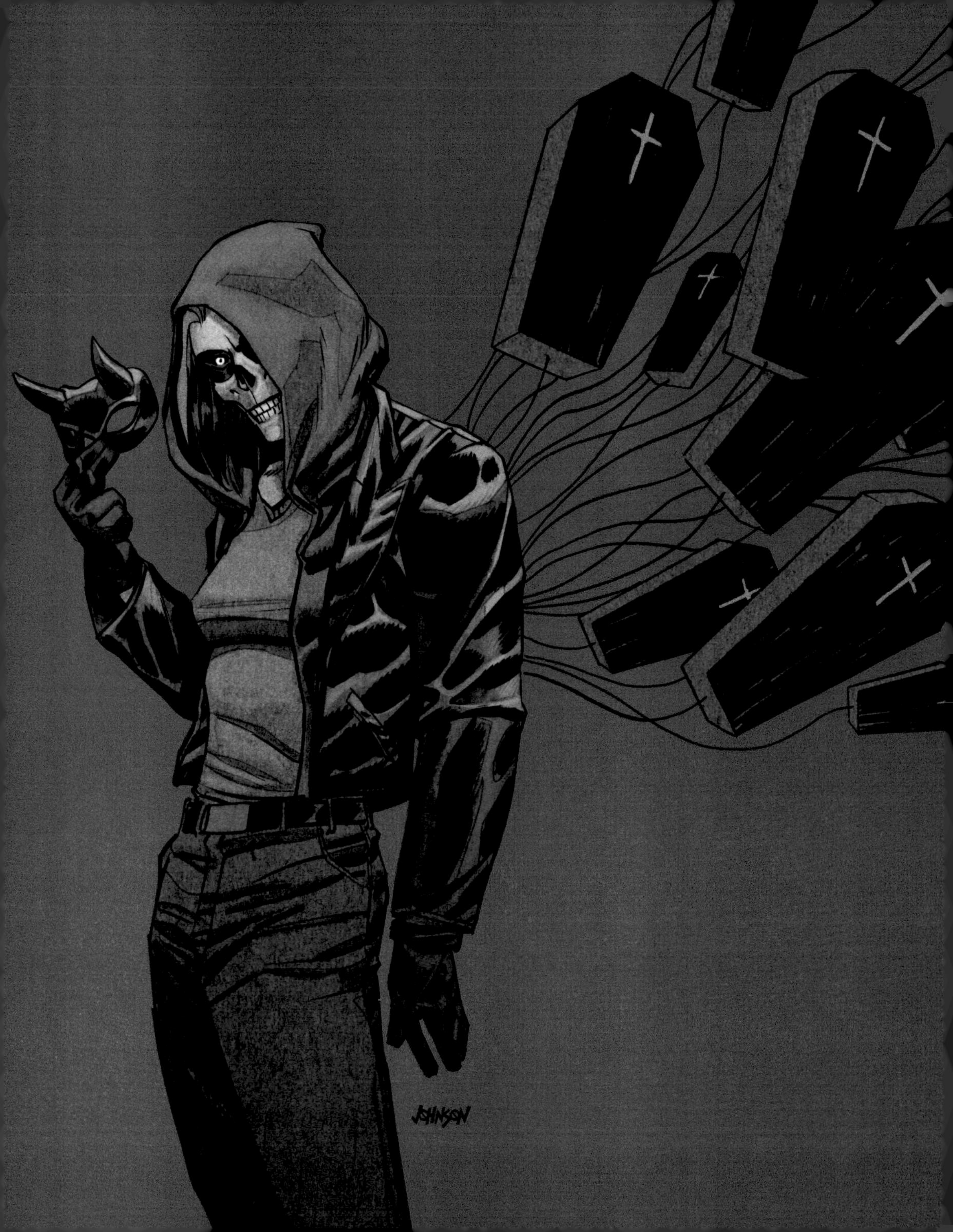
JOHNSON

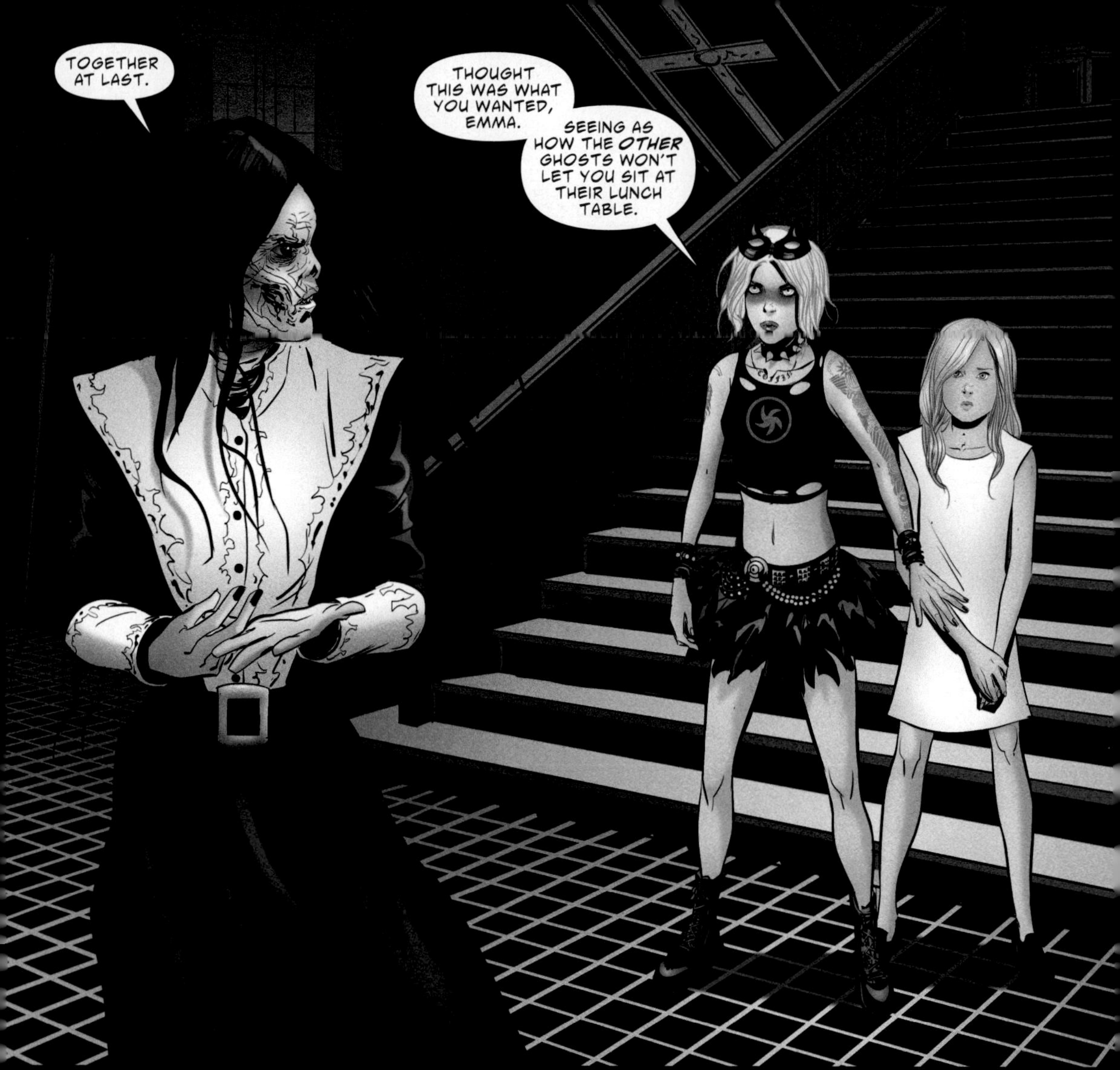
TOGETHER AT LAST.
THOUGHT THIS WAS WHAT YOU WANTED, EMMA.
SEEING AS HOW THE *OTHER* GHOSTS WON'T LET YOU SIT AT THEIR LUNCH TABLE.

COFFIN HOUSE...?

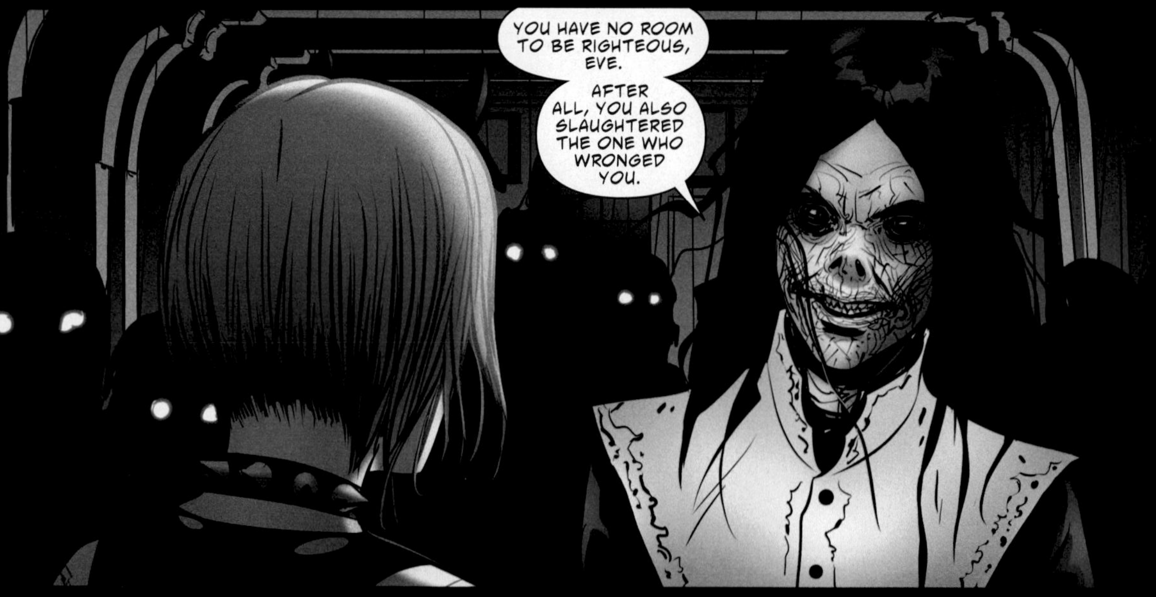
YOU HAVE NO ROOM TO BE RIGHTEOUS, EVE.
AFTER ALL, YOU ALSO SLAUGHTERED THE ONE WHO WRONGED YOU.

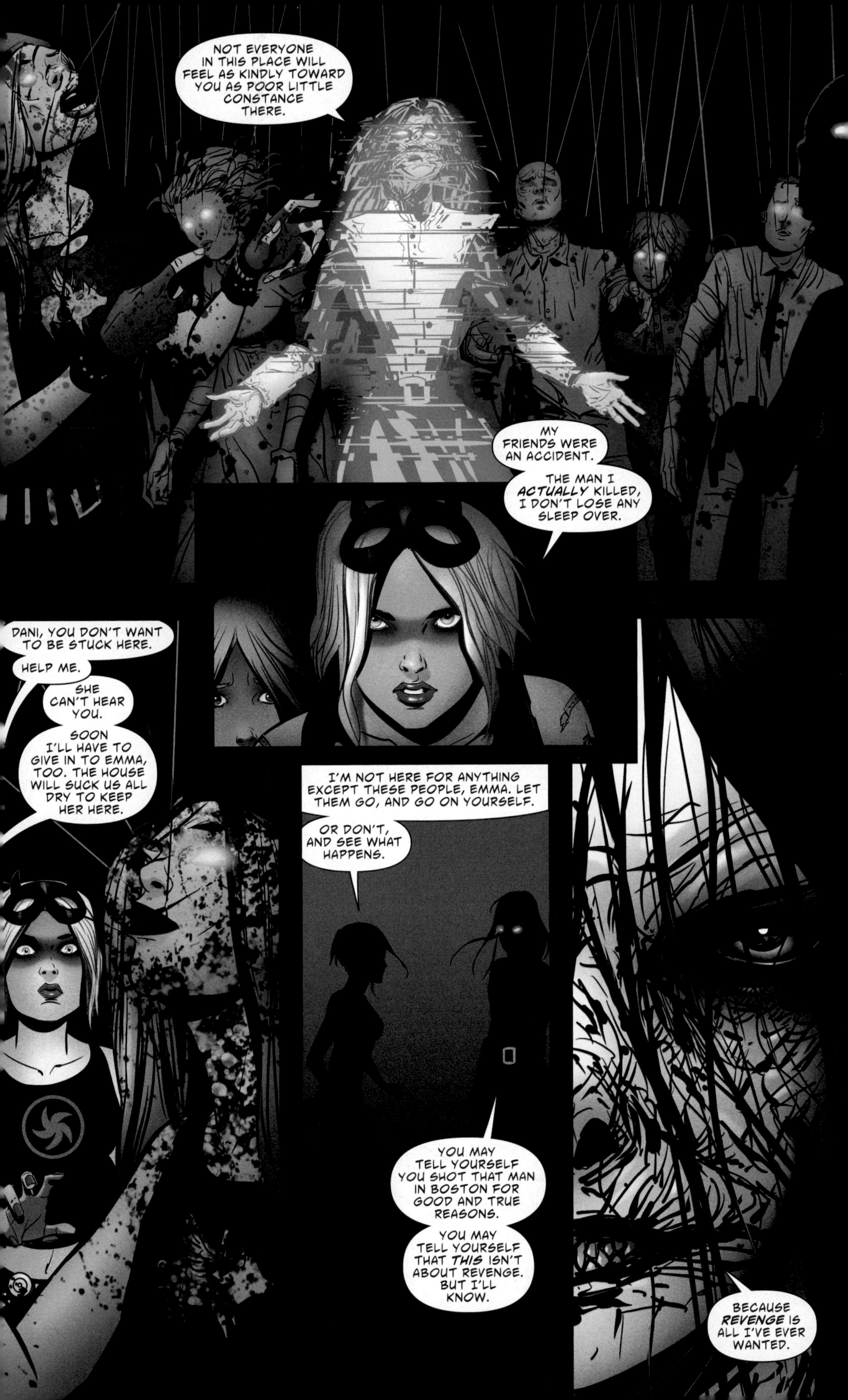
NOT EVERYONE IN THIS PLACE WILL FEEL AS KINDLY TOWARD YOU AS POOR LITTLE CONSTANCE THERE.
MY FRIENDS WERE AN ACCIDENT.
THE MAN I ACTUALLY KILLED, I DON'T LOSE ANY SLEEP OVER.
DANI, YOU DON'T WANT TO BE STUCK HERE.
HELP ME.
SHE CAN'T HEAR YOU.
SOON I'LL HAVE TO GIVE IN TO EMMA, TOO. THE HOUSE WILL SUCK US ALL DRY TO KEEP HER HERE.
I'M NOT HERE FOR ANYTHING EXCEPT THESE PEOPLE, EMMA. LET THEM GO, AND GO ON YOURSELF.
OR DON'T, AND SEE WHAT HAPPENS.
YOU MAY TELL YOURSELF YOU SHOT THAT MAN IN BOSTON FOR GOOD AND TRUE REASONS.
YOU MAY TELL YOURSELF THAT THIS ISN'T ABOUT REVENGE. BUT I'LL KNOW.
BECAUSE REVENGE IS ALL I'VE EVER WANTED.

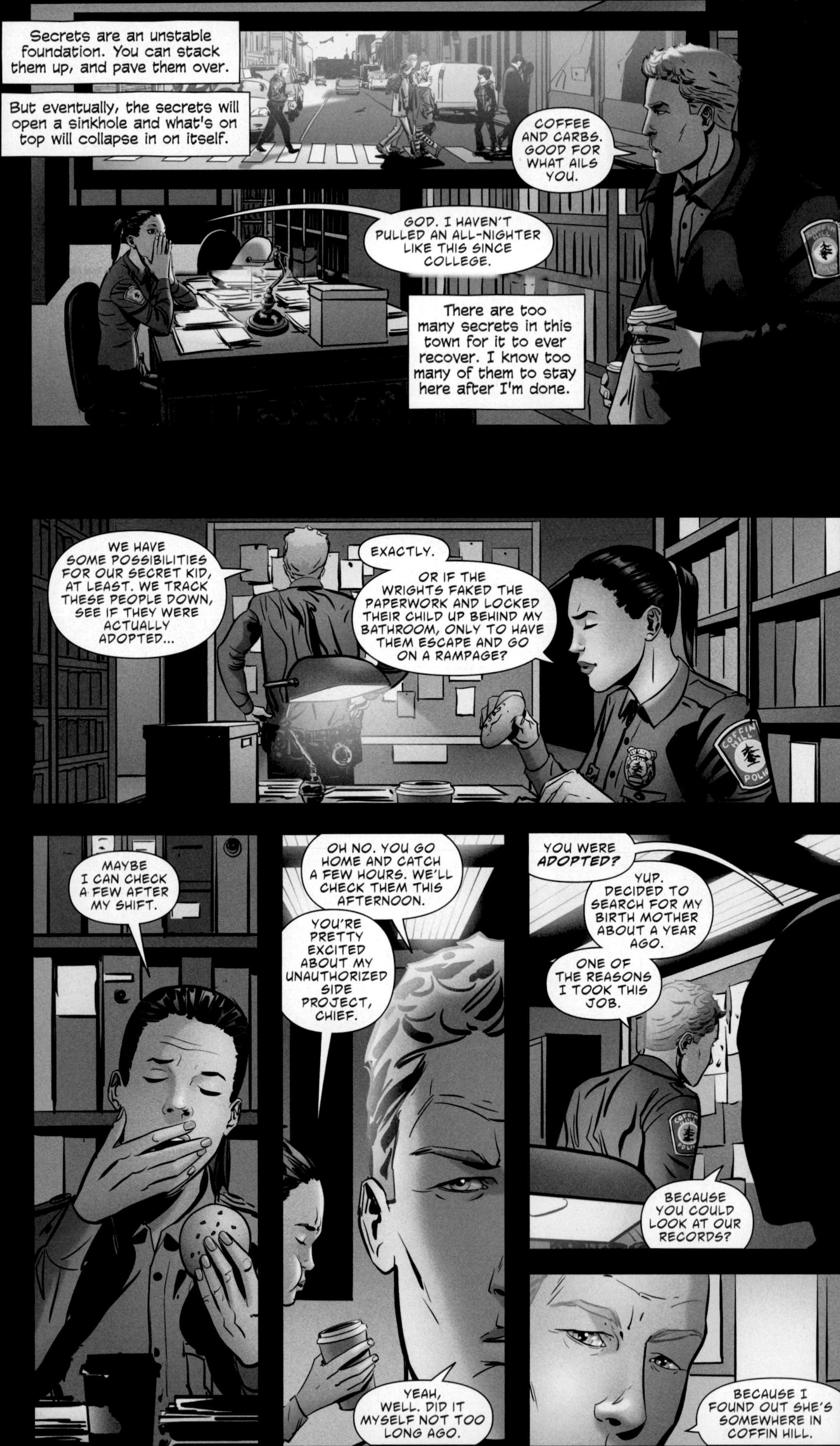
Secrets are an unstable foundation. You can stack them up, and pave them over.
But eventually, the secrets will open a sinkhole and what's on top will collapse in on itself.
COFFEE AND CARBS. GOOD FOR WHAT AILS YOU.
GOD. I HAVEN'T PULLED AN ALL-NIGHTER LIKE THIS SINCE COLLEGE.
There are too many secrets in this town for it to ever recover. I know too many of them to stay here after I'm done.
WE HAVE SOME POSSIBILITIES FOR OUR SECRET KID, AT LEAST. WE TRACK THESE PEOPLE DOWN, SEE IF THEY WERE ACTUALLY ADOPTED...
EXACTLY.
OR IF THE WRIGHTS FAKED THE PAPERWORK AND LOCKED THEIR CHILD UP BEHIND MY BATHROOM, ONLY TO HAVE THEM ESCAPE AND GO ON A RAMPAGE?
MAYBE I CAN CHECK A FEW AFTER MY SHIFT.
OH NO. YOU GO HOME AND CATCH A FEW HOURS. WE'LL CHECK THEM THIS AFTERNOON.
YOU'RE PRETTY EXCITED ABOUT MY UNAUTHORIZED SIDE PROJECT, CHIEF.
YEAH, WELL. DID IT MYSELF NOT TOO LONG AGO.
YOU WERE *ADOPTED?*
YUP. DECIDED TO SEARCH FOR MY BIRTH MOTHER ABOUT A YEAR AGO.
ONE OF THE REASONS I TOOK THIS JOB.
BECAUSE YOU COULD LOOK AT OUR RECORDS?
BECAUSE I FOUND OUT SHE'S SOMEWHERE IN COFFIN HILL.

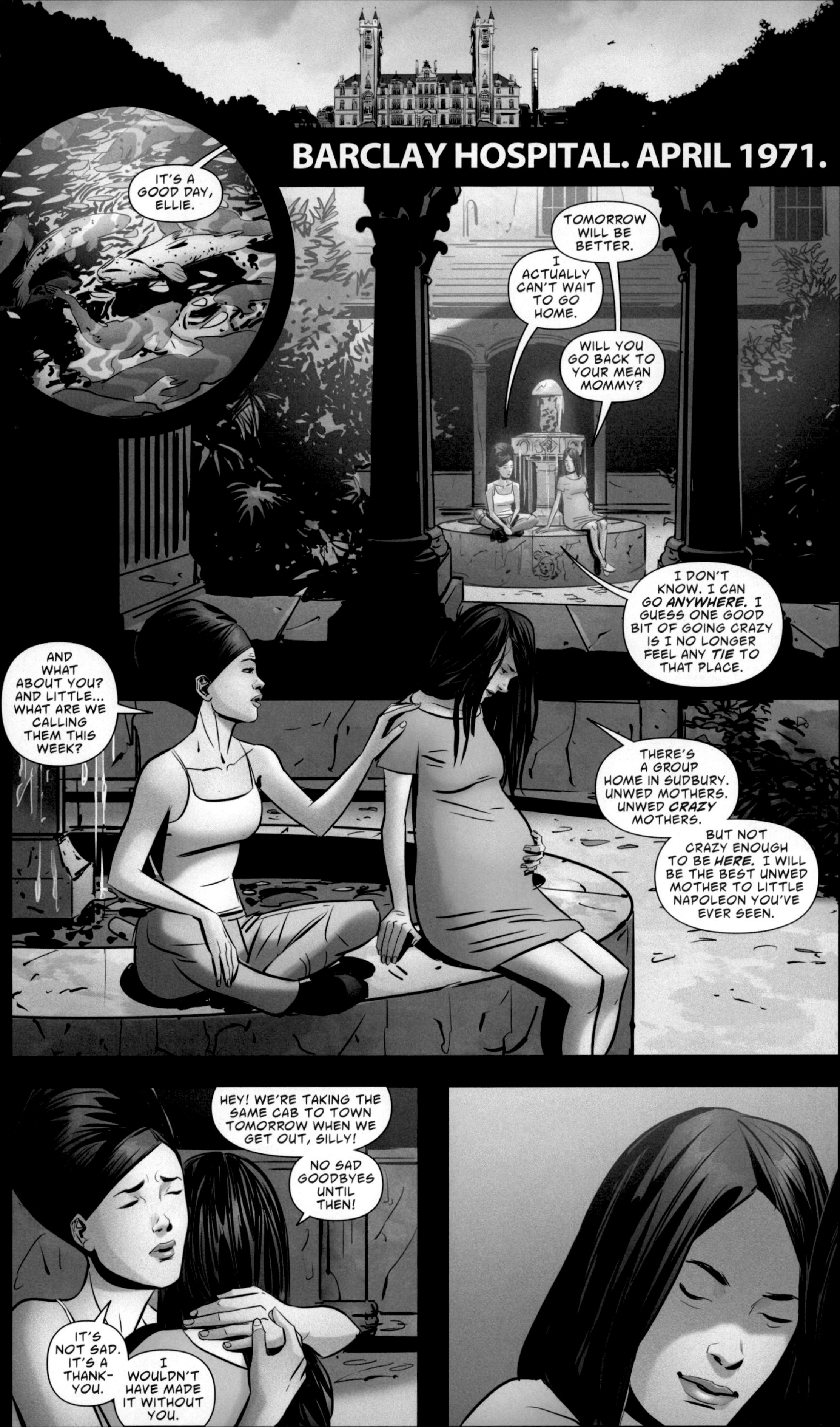
BARCLAY HOSPITAL. APRIL 1971.
IT'S A GOOD DAY, ELLIE.
TOMORROW WILL BE BETTER.
I ACTUALLY CAN'T WAIT TO GO HOME.
WILL YOU GO BACK TO YOUR MEAN MOMMY?
I DON'T KNOW. I CAN GO ANYWHERE. I GUESS ONE GOOD BIT OF GOING CRAZY IS I NO LONGER FEEL ANY TIE TO THAT PLACE.
AND WHAT ABOUT YOU? AND LITTLE... WHAT ARE WE CALLING THEM THIS WEEK?
THERE'S A GROUP HOME IN SUDBURY. UNWED MOTHERS. UNWED CRAZY MOTHERS.
BUT NOT CRAZY ENOUGH TO BE HERE. I WILL BE THE BEST UNWED MOTHER TO LITTLE NAPOLEON YOU'VE EVER SEEN.
HEY! WE'RE TAKING THE SAME CAB TO TOWN TOMORROW WHEN WE GET OUT, SILLY!
NO SAD GOODBYES UNTIL THEN!
IT'S NOT SAD. IT'S A THANK-YOU.
I WOULDN'T HAVE MADE IT WITHOUT YOU.

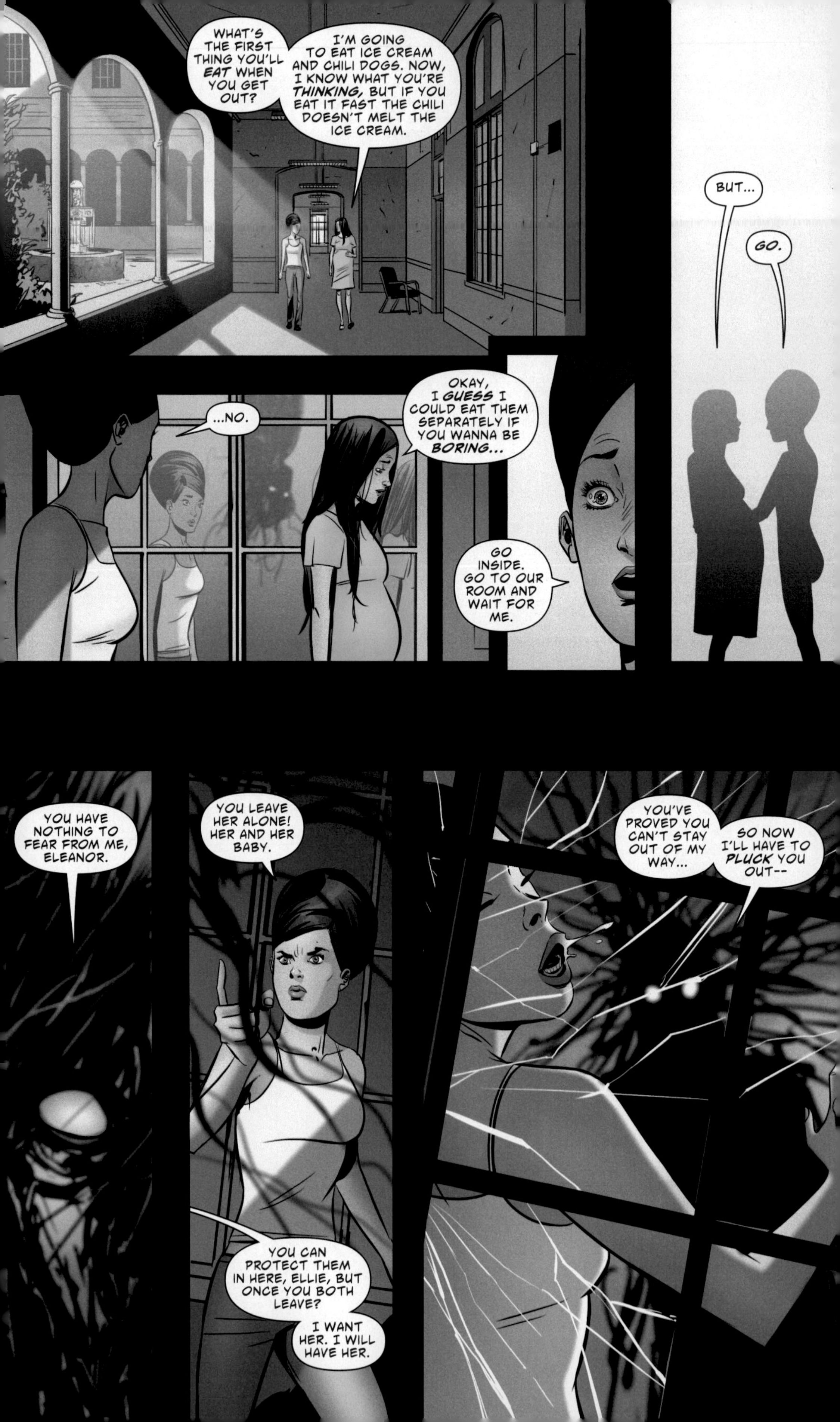
WHAT'S THE FIRST THING YOU'LL *EAT* WHEN YOU GET OUT?
I'M GOING TO EAT ICE CREAM AND CHILI DOGS. NOW, I KNOW WHAT YOU'RE *THINKING,* BUT IF YOU EAT IT FAST THE CHILI DOESN'T MELT THE ICE CREAM.
...NO.
OKAY, I *GUESS* I COULD EAT THEM SEPARATELY IF YOU WANNA BE *BORING...*
GO INSIDE. GO TO OUR ROOM AND WAIT FOR ME.
BUT...
GO.
YOU HAVE NOTHING TO FEAR FROM ME, ELEANOR.
YOU LEAVE HER ALONE! HER AND HER BABY.
YOU CAN PROTECT THEM IN HERE, ELLIE, BUT ONCE YOU BOTH LEAVE?
I WANT HER. I WILL HAVE HER.
YOU'VE PROVED YOU CAN'T STAY OUT OF MY WAY...
SO NOW I'LL HAVE TO *PLUCK* YOU OUT--

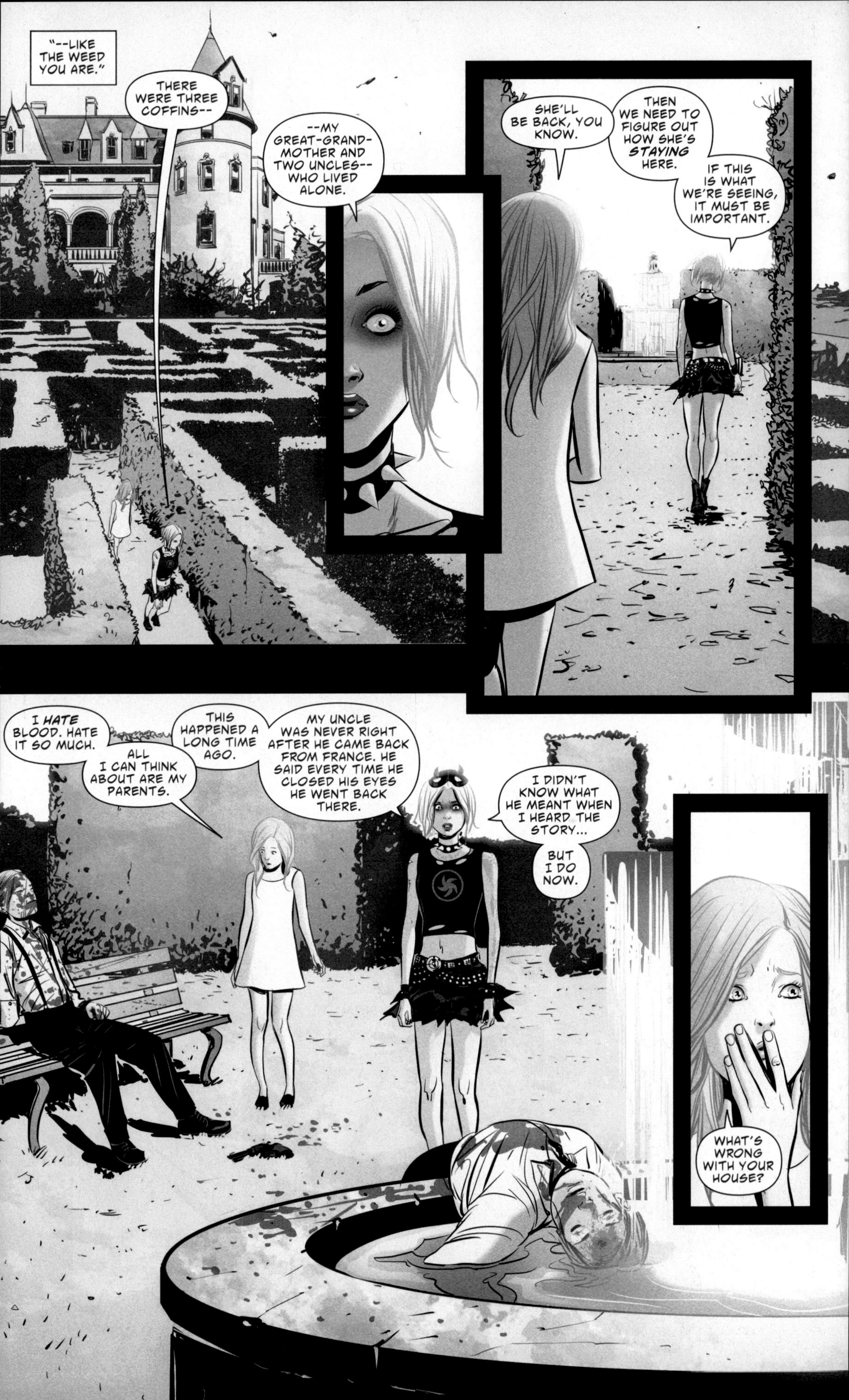
"--LIKE THE WEED YOU ARE."
THERE WERE THREE COFFINS--
--MY GREAT-GRAND-MOTHER AND TWO UNCLES--WHO LIVED ALONE.
SHE'LL BE BACK, YOU KNOW.
THEN WE NEED TO FIGURE OUT HOW SHE'S *STAYING* HERE.
IF THIS IS WHAT WE'RE SEEING, IT MUST BE IMPORTANT.
I *HATE* BLOOD. HATE IT SO MUCH.
ALL I CAN THINK ABOUT ARE MY PARENTS.
THIS HAPPENED A LONG TIME AGO.
MY UNCLE WAS NEVER RIGHT AFTER HE CAME BACK FROM FRANCE. HE SAID EVERY TIME HE CLOSED HIS EYES HE WENT BACK THERE.
I DIDN'T KNOW WHAT HE MEANT WHEN I HEARD THE STORY...
BUT I DO NOW.
WHAT'S WRONG WITH YOUR HOUSE?

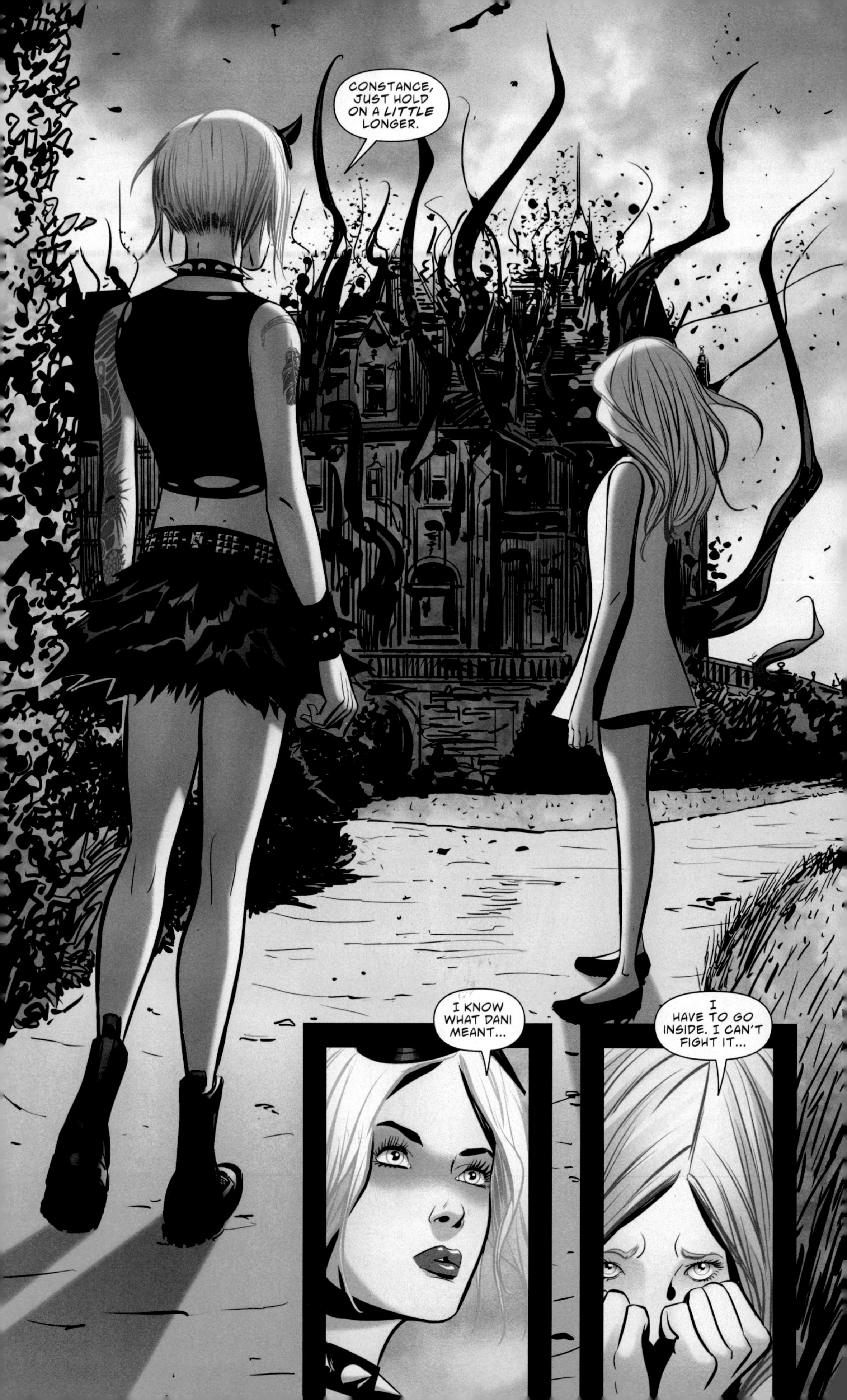
CONSTANCE, JUST HOLD ON A *LITTLE* LONGER.
I KNOW WHAT DANI MEANT...
I HAVE TO GO INSIDE. I CAN'T FIGHT IT...

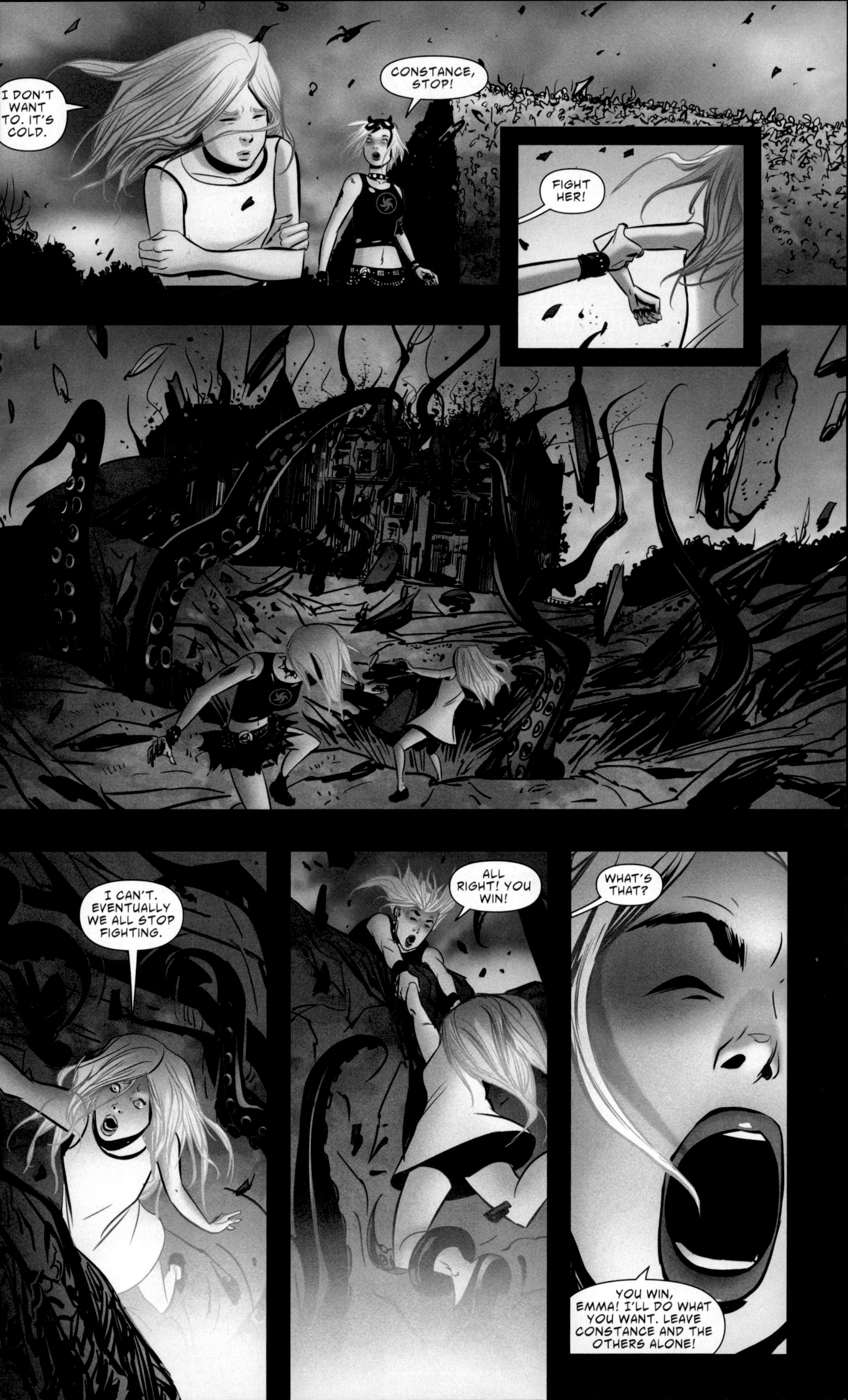
I DON'T WANT TO. IT'S COLD.
CONSTANCE, STOP!
FIGHT HER!
I CAN'T. EVENTUALLY WE ALL STOP FIGHTING.
ALL RIGHT! YOU WIN!
WHAT'S THAT?
YOU WIN, EMMA! I'LL DO WHAT YOU WANT. LEAVE CONSTANCE AND THE OTHERS ALONE!

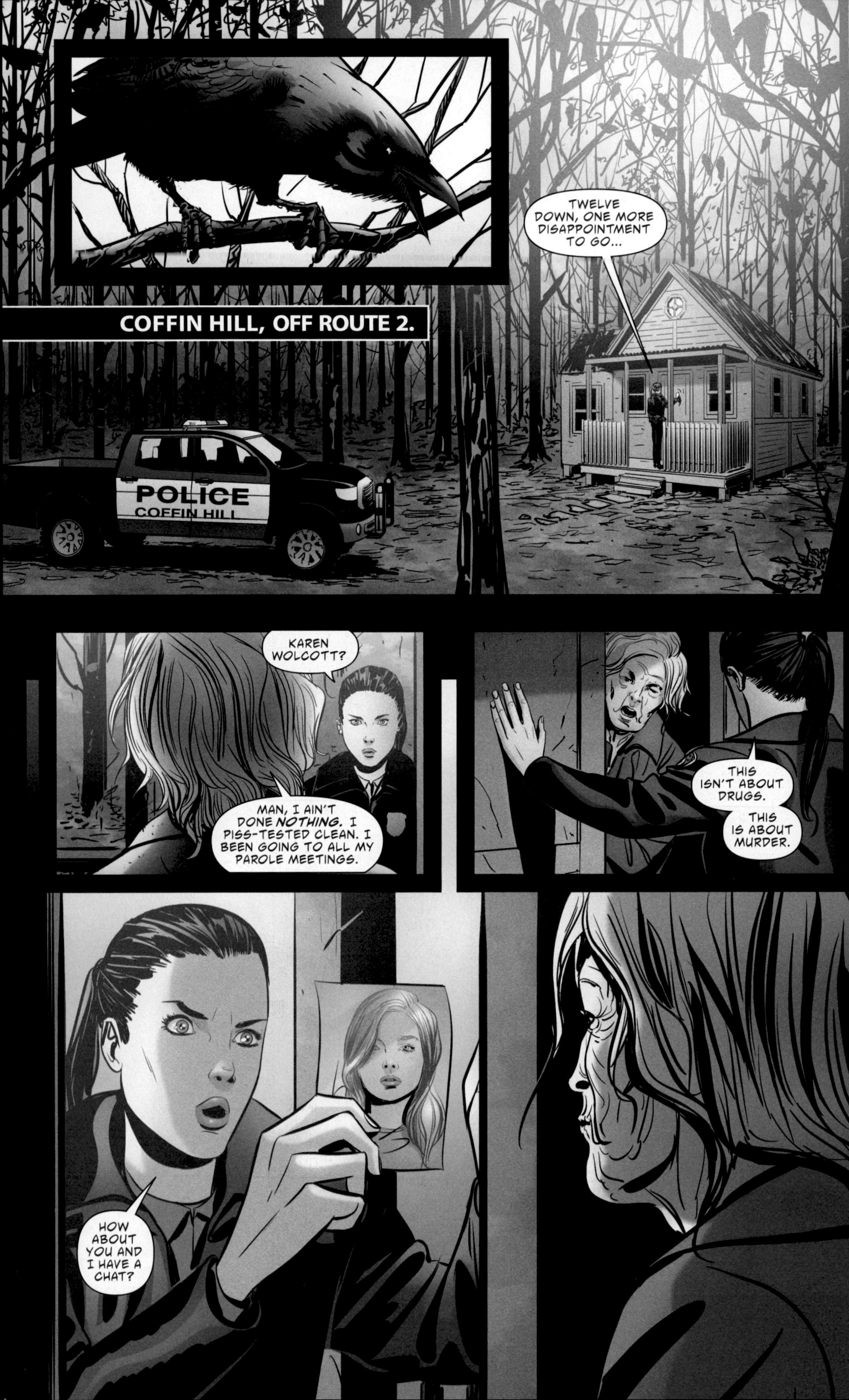
COFFIN HILL, OFF ROUTE 2.
TWELVE DOWN, ONE MORE DISAPPOINTMENT TO GO...
POLICE
COFFIN HILL
KAREN WOLCOTT?
MAN, I AIN'T DONE *NOTHING*. I PISS-TESTED CLEAN. I BEEN GOING TO ALL MY PAROLE MEETINGS.
THIS ISN'T ABOUT DRUGS.
THIS IS ABOUT MURDER.
HOW ABOUT YOU AND I HAVE A CHAT?

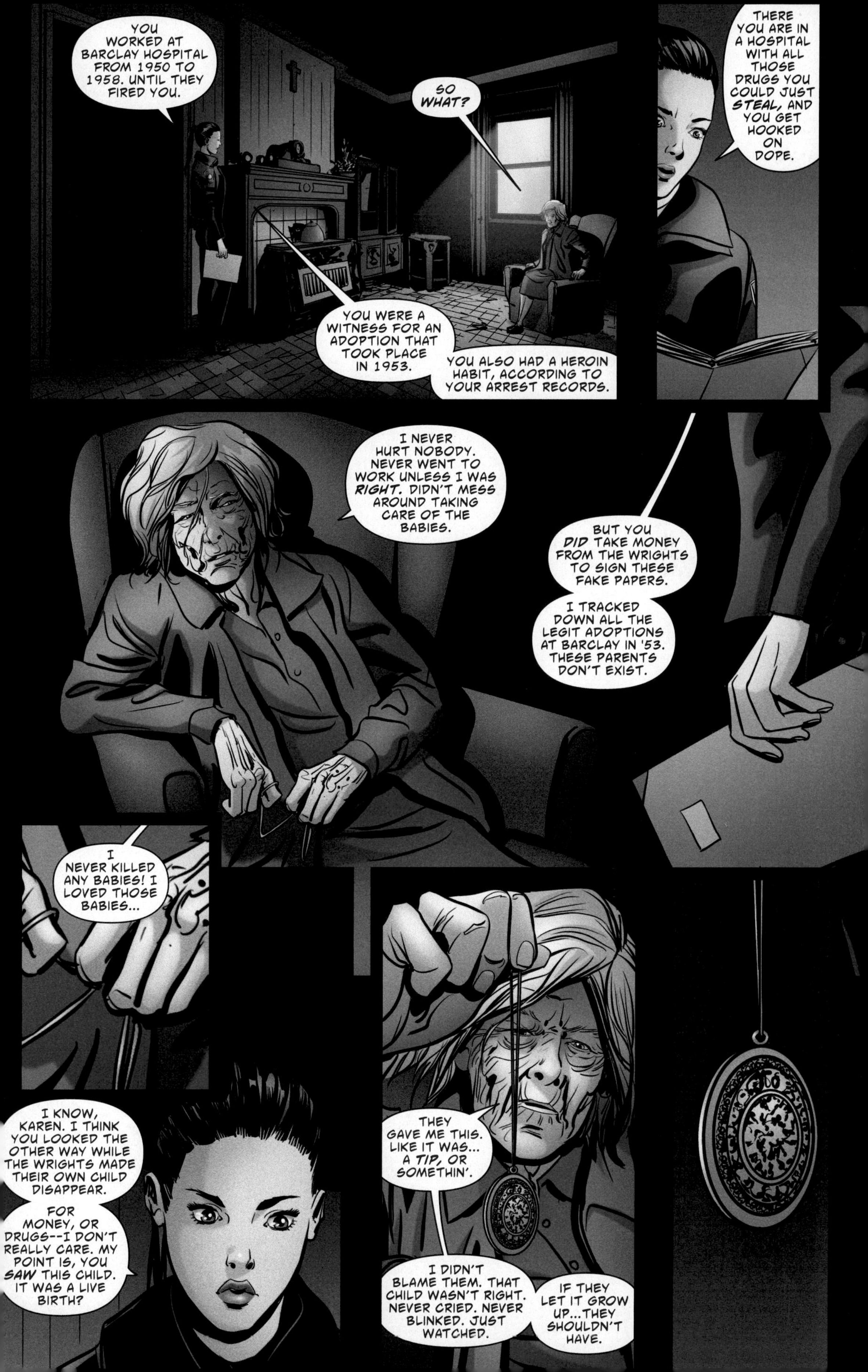
YOU WORKED AT BARCLAY HOSPITAL FROM 1950 TO 1958. UNTIL THEY FIRED YOU.
SO WHAT?
YOU WERE A WITNESS FOR AN ADOPTION THAT TOOK PLACE IN 1953.
YOU ALSO HAD A HEROIN HABIT, ACCORDING TO YOUR ARREST RECORDS.
THERE YOU ARE IN A HOSPITAL WITH ALL THOSE DRUGS YOU COULD JUST STEAL, AND YOU GET HOOKED ON DOPE.
I NEVER HURT NOBODY. NEVER WENT TO WORK UNLESS I WAS RIGHT. DIDN'T MESS AROUND TAKING CARE OF THE BABIES.
BUT YOU DID TAKE MONEY FROM THE WRIGHTS TO SIGN THESE FAKE PAPERS.
I TRACKED DOWN ALL THE LEGIT ADOPTIONS AT BARCLAY IN '53. THESE PARENTS DON'T EXIST.
I NEVER KILLED ANY BABIES! I LOVED THOSE BABIES...
I KNOW, KAREN. I THINK YOU LOOKED THE OTHER WAY WHILE THE WRIGHTS MADE THEIR OWN CHILD DISAPPEAR.
FOR MONEY, OR DRUGS--I DON'T REALLY CARE. MY POINT IS, YOU SAW THIS CHILD. IT WAS A LIVE BIRTH?
THEY GAVE ME THIS. LIKE IT WAS... A TIP, OR SOMETHIN'.
I DIDN'T BLAME THEM. THAT CHILD WASN'T RIGHT. NEVER CRIED. NEVER BLINKED. JUST WATCHED.
IF THEY LET IT GROW UP...THEY SHOULDN'T HAVE.

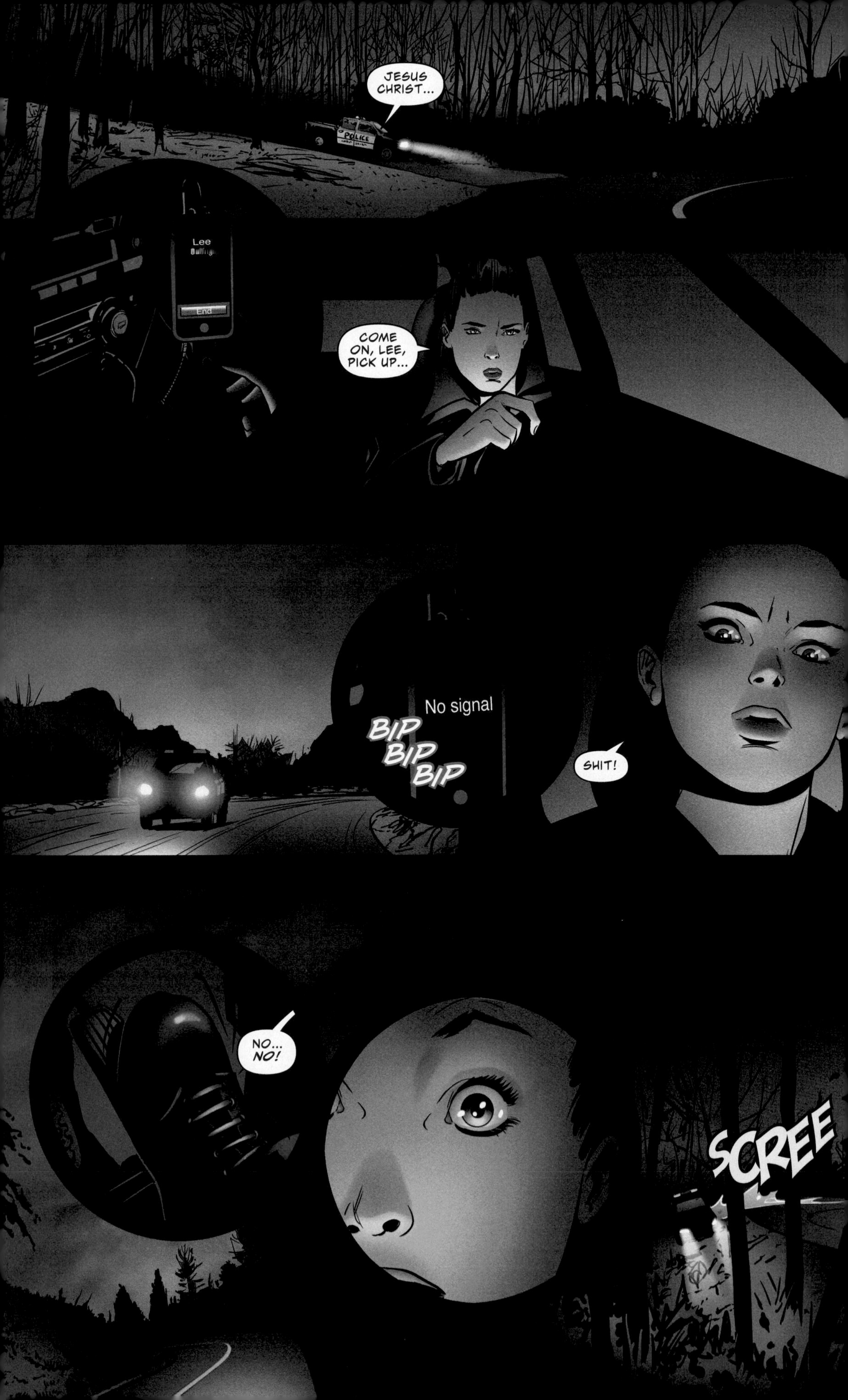
JESUS CHRIST...
POLICE
Lee
End
COME ON, LEE, PICK UP...
No signal
BIP BIP BIP
SHIT!
NO... NO!
SCREE

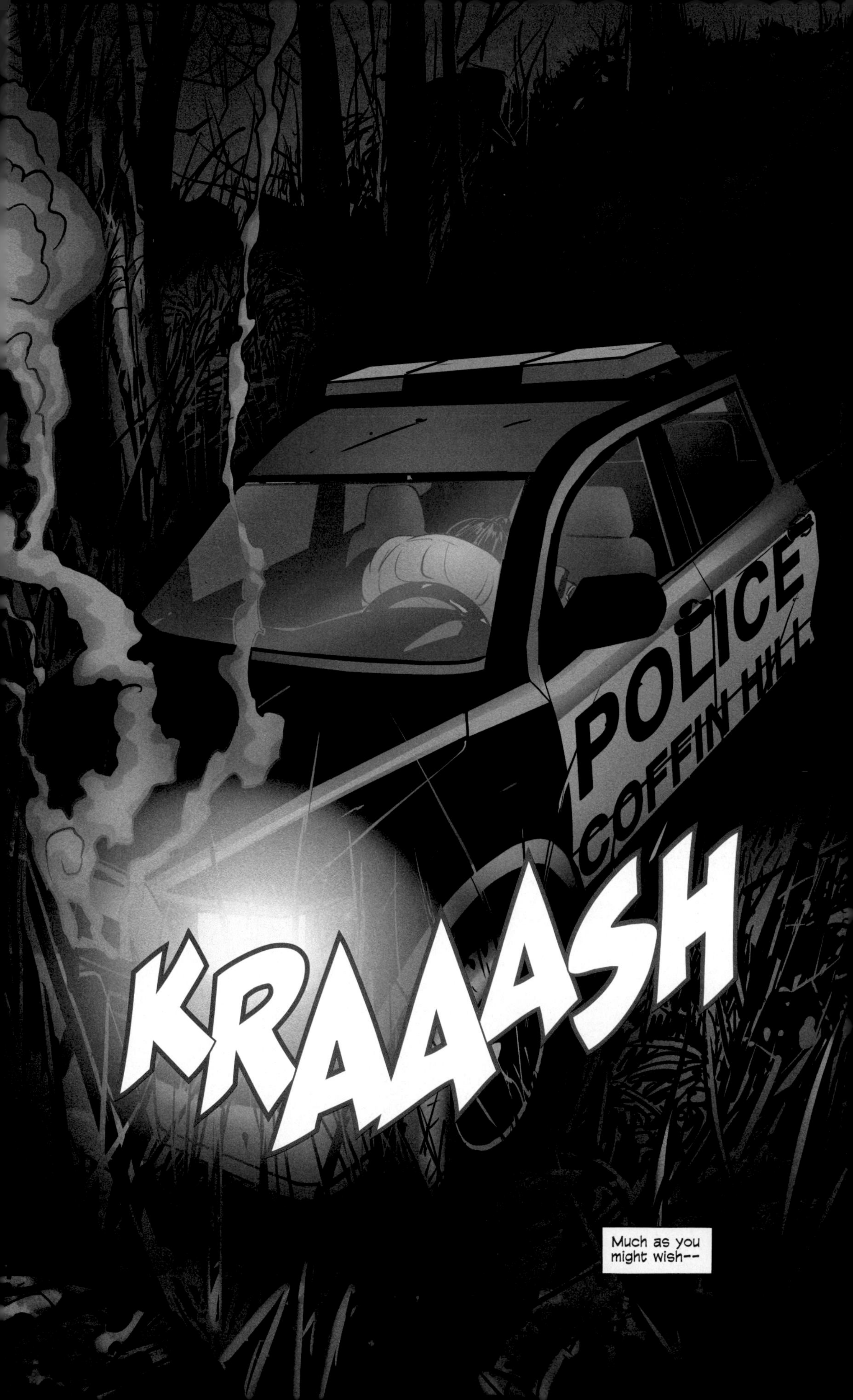
POLICE
COFFIN HILL
KRAAASH
Much as you might wish--

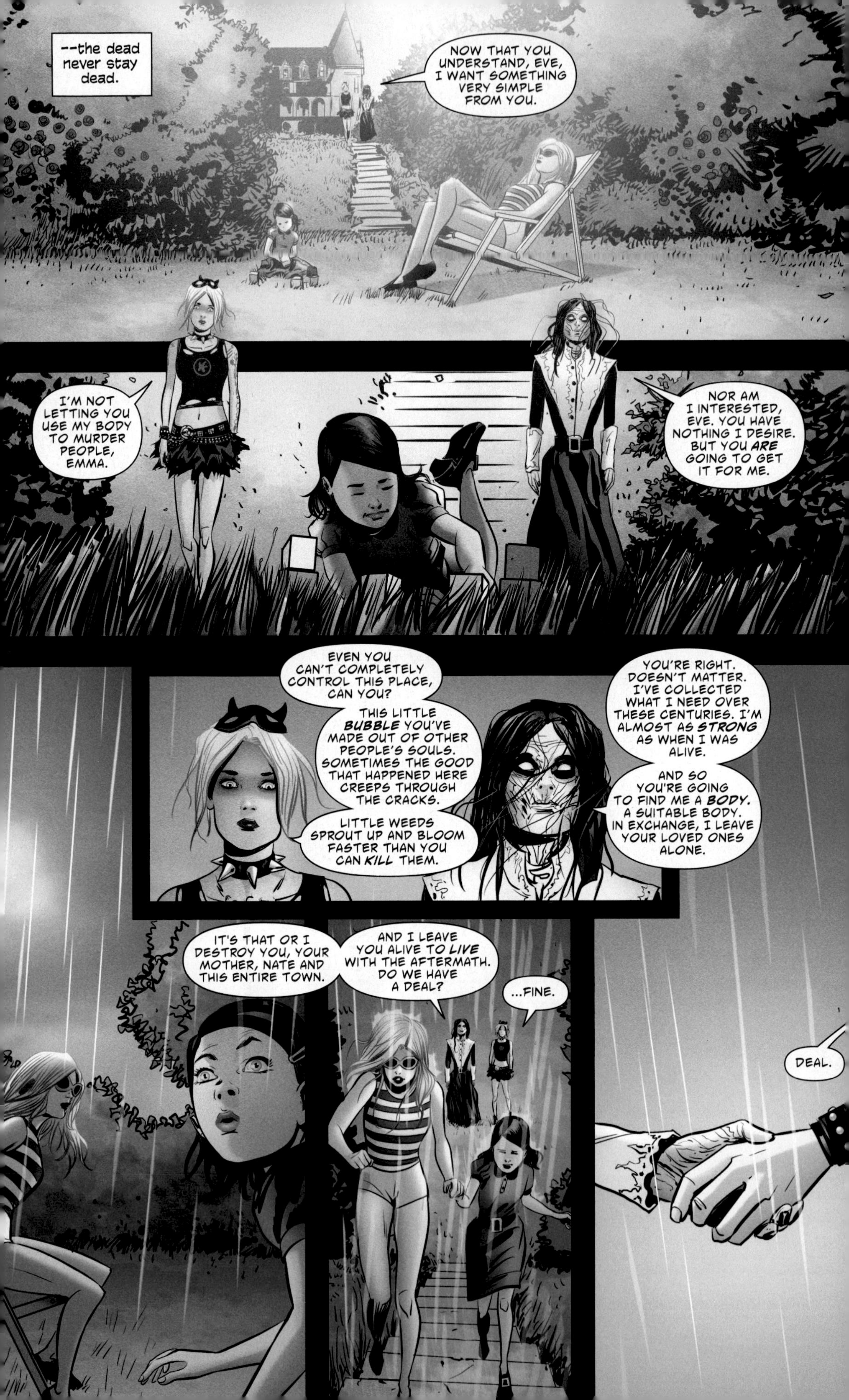
--the dead never stay dead.
NOW THAT YOU UNDERSTAND, EVE, I WANT SOMETHING VERY SIMPLE FROM YOU.
I'M NOT LETTING YOU USE MY BODY TO MURDER PEOPLE, EMMA.
NOR AM I INTERESTED, EVE. YOU HAVE NOTHING I DESIRE. BUT YOU ARE GOING TO GET IT FOR ME.
EVEN YOU CAN'T COMPLETELY CONTROL THIS PLACE, CAN YOU?
THIS LITTLE BUBBLE YOU'VE MADE OUT OF OTHER PEOPLE'S SOULS. SOMETIMES THE GOOD THAT HAPPENED HERE CREEPS THROUGH THE CRACKS.
LITTLE WEEDS SPROUT UP AND BLOOM FASTER THAN YOU CAN KILL THEM.
YOU'RE RIGHT. DOESN'T MATTER. I'VE COLLECTED WHAT I NEED OVER THESE CENTURIES. I'M ALMOST AS STRONG AS WHEN I WAS ALIVE.
AND SO YOU'RE GOING TO FIND ME A BODY. A SUITABLE BODY. IN EXCHANGE, I LEAVE YOUR LOVED ONES ALONE.
IT'S THAT OR I DESTROY YOU, YOUR MOTHER, NATE AND THIS ENTIRE TOWN.
AND I LEAVE YOU ALIVE TO LIVE WITH THE AFTERMATH. DO WE HAVE A DEAL?
...FINE.
DEAL.

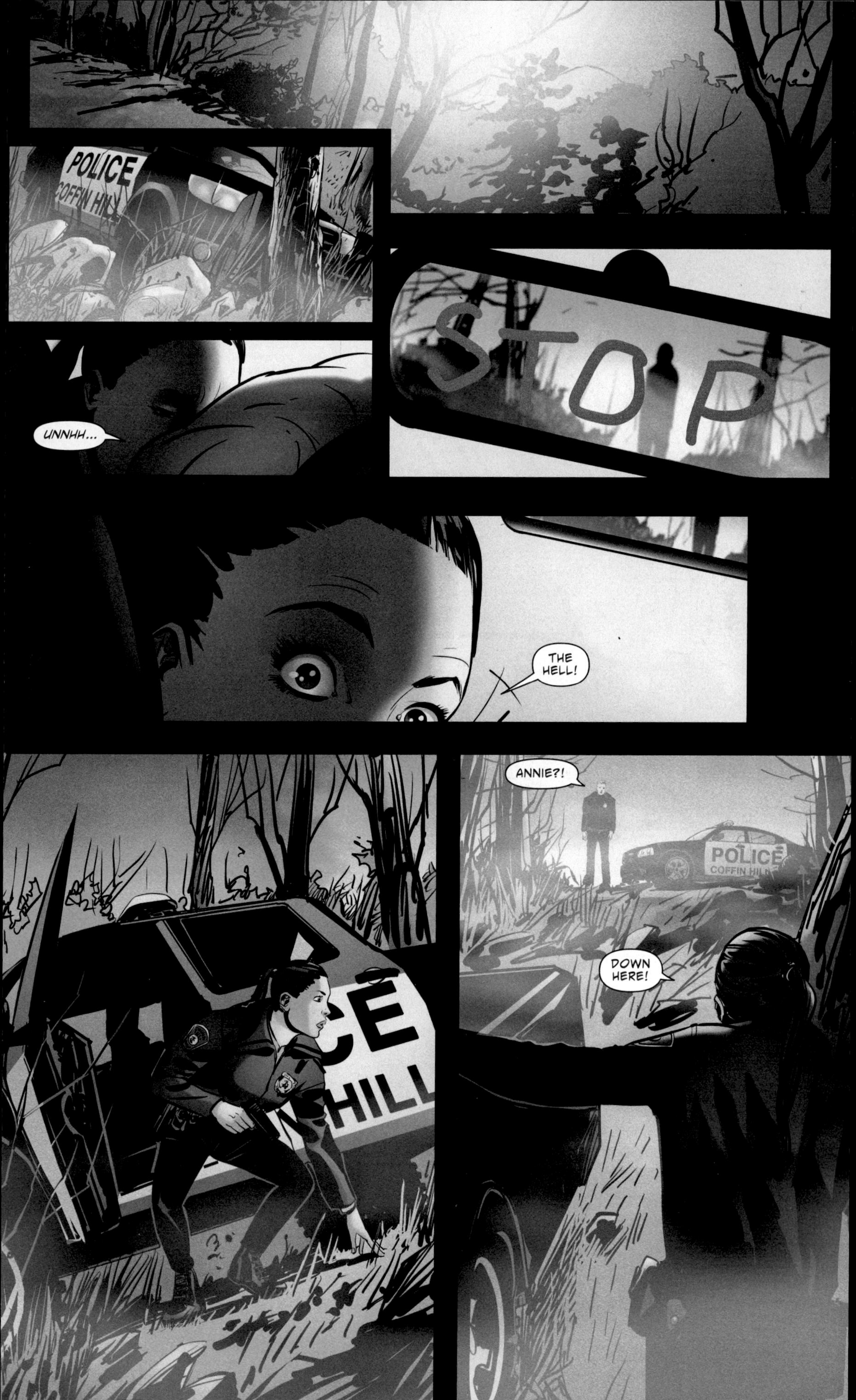
POLICE
COFFIN HILL
UNNHH...
STOP
THE HELL!
ANNIE?!
POLICE
COFFIN HILL
DOWN HERE!
CE
HILL

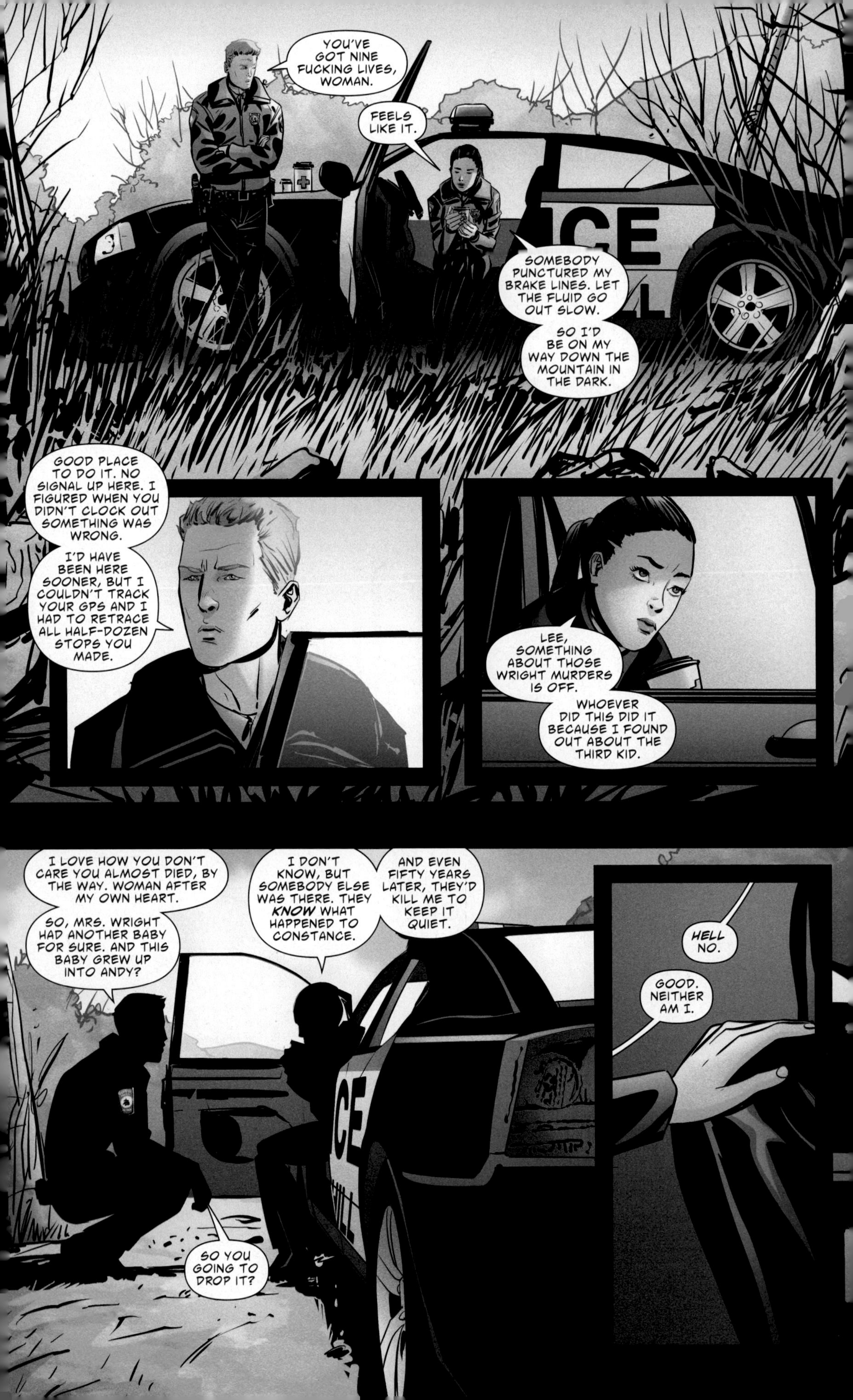
YOU'VE GOT NINE FUCKING LIVES, WOMAN.
FEELS LIKE IT.
SOMEBODY PUNCTURED MY BRAKE LINES. LET THE FLUID GO OUT SLOW.
SO I'D BE ON MY WAY DOWN THE MOUNTAIN IN THE DARK.
GOOD PLACE TO DO IT. NO SIGNAL UP HERE. I FIGURED WHEN YOU DIDN'T CLOCK OUT SOMETHING WAS WRONG.
I'D HAVE BEEN HERE SOONER, BUT I COULDN'T TRACK YOUR GPS AND I HAD TO RETRACE ALL HALF-DOZEN STOPS YOU MADE.
LEE, SOMETHING ABOUT THOSE WRIGHT MURDERS IS OFF.
WHOEVER DID THIS DID IT BECAUSE I FOUND OUT ABOUT THE THIRD KID.
I LOVE HOW YOU DON'T CARE YOU ALMOST DIED, BY THE WAY. WOMAN AFTER MY OWN HEART.
SO, MRS. WRIGHT HAD ANOTHER BABY FOR SURE. AND THIS BABY GREW UP INTO ANDY?
I DON'T KNOW, BUT SOMEBODY ELSE WAS THERE. THEY ***KNOW*** WHAT HAPPENED TO CONSTANCE.
AND EVEN FIFTY YEARS LATER, THEY'D KILL ME TO KEEP IT QUIET.
SO YOU GOING TO DROP IT?
HELL NO.
GOOD. NEITHER AM I.

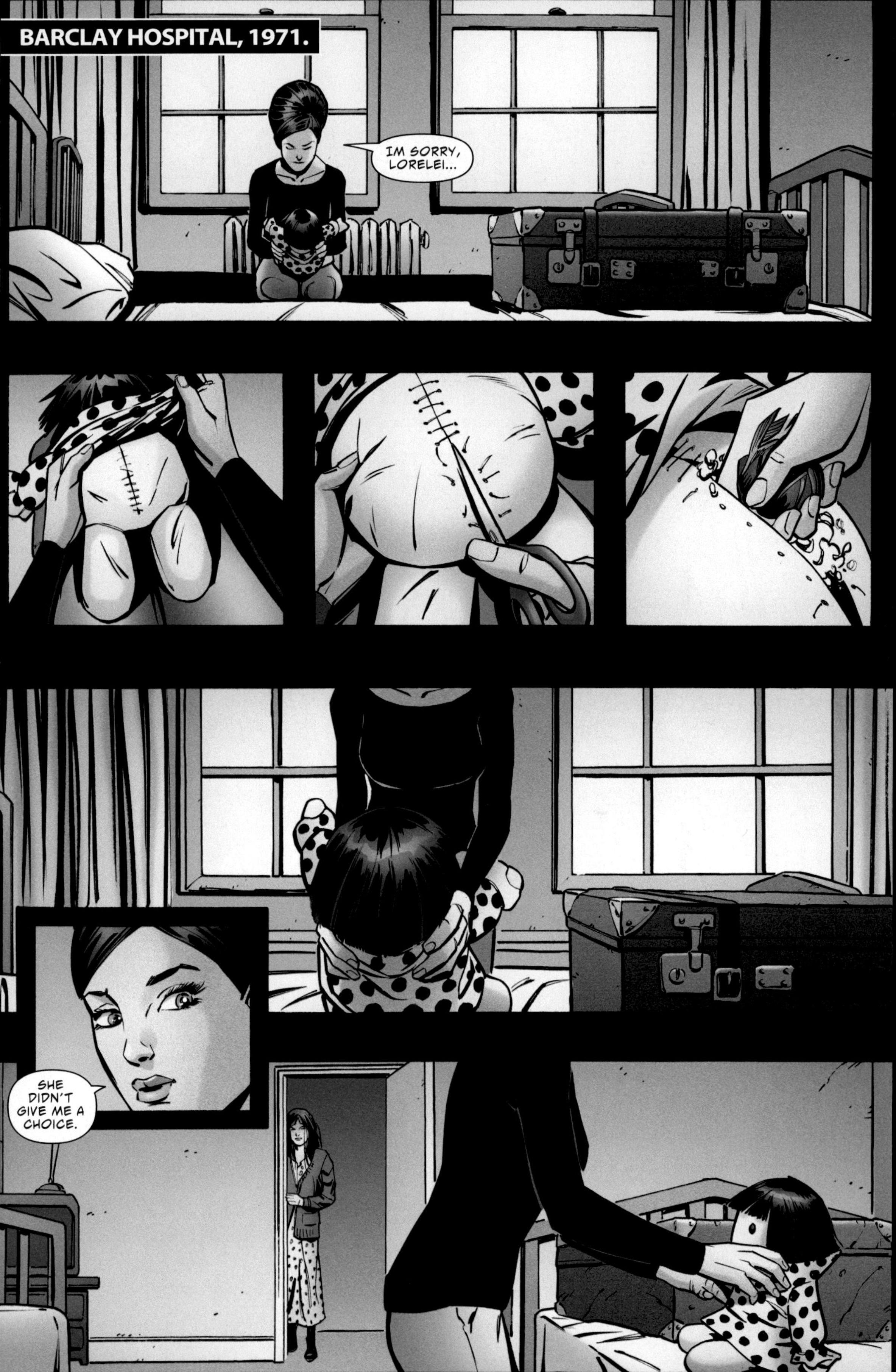
BARCLAY HOSPITAL, 1971.
IM SORRY, LORELEI...
SHE DIDN'T GIVE ME A CHOICE.

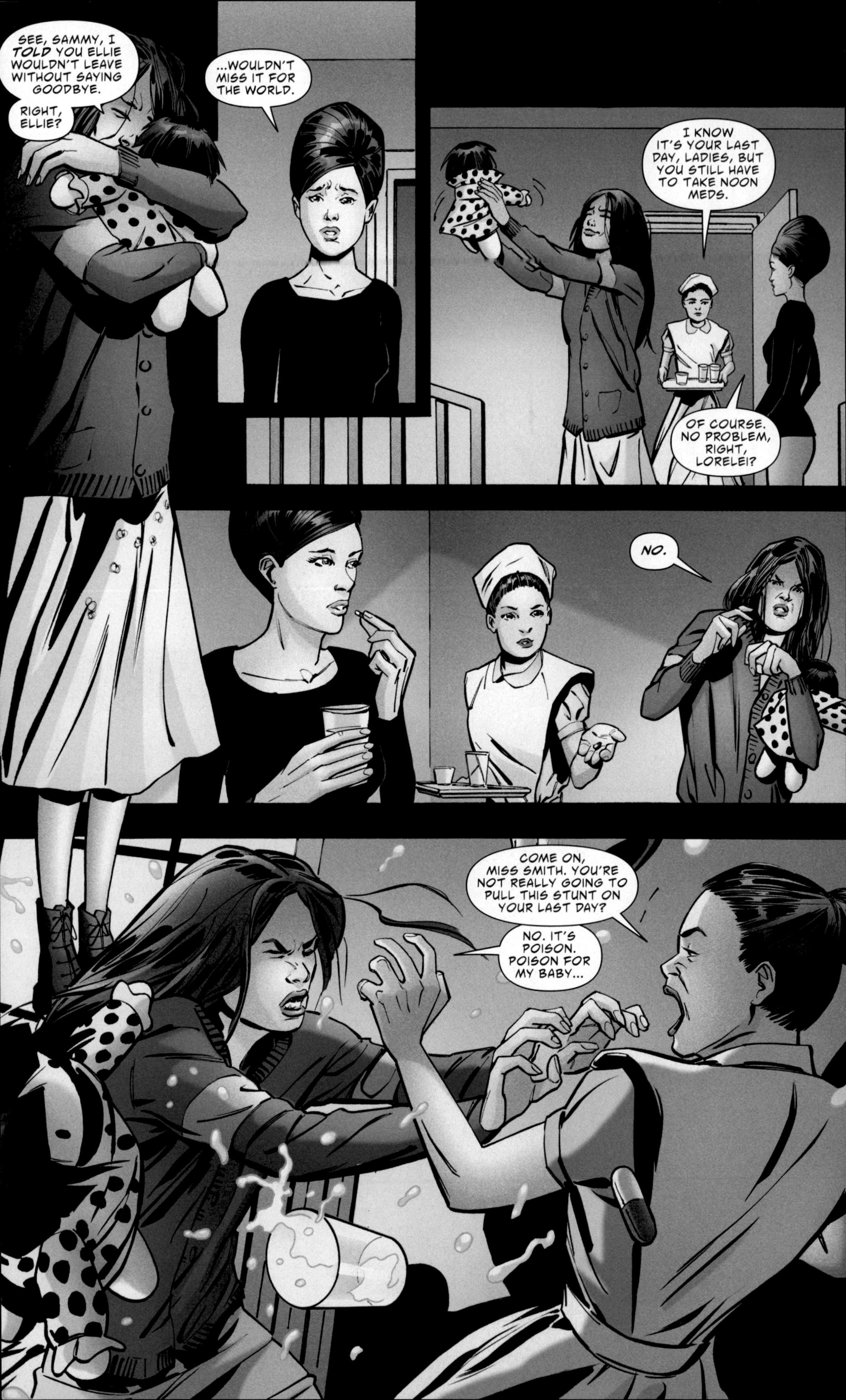
SEE, SAMMY, I TOLD YOU ELLIE WOULDN'T LEAVE WITHOUT SAYING GOODBYE.
RIGHT, ELLIE?
...WOULDN'T MISS IT FOR THE WORLD.
I KNOW IT'S YOUR LAST DAY, LADIES, BUT YOU STILL HAVE TO TAKE NOON MEDS.
OF COURSE. NO PROBLEM, RIGHT, LORELEI?
NO.
COME ON, MISS SMITH. YOU'RE NOT REALLY GOING TO PULL THIS STUNT ON YOUR LAST DAY?
NO. IT'S POISON. POISON FOR MY BABY...

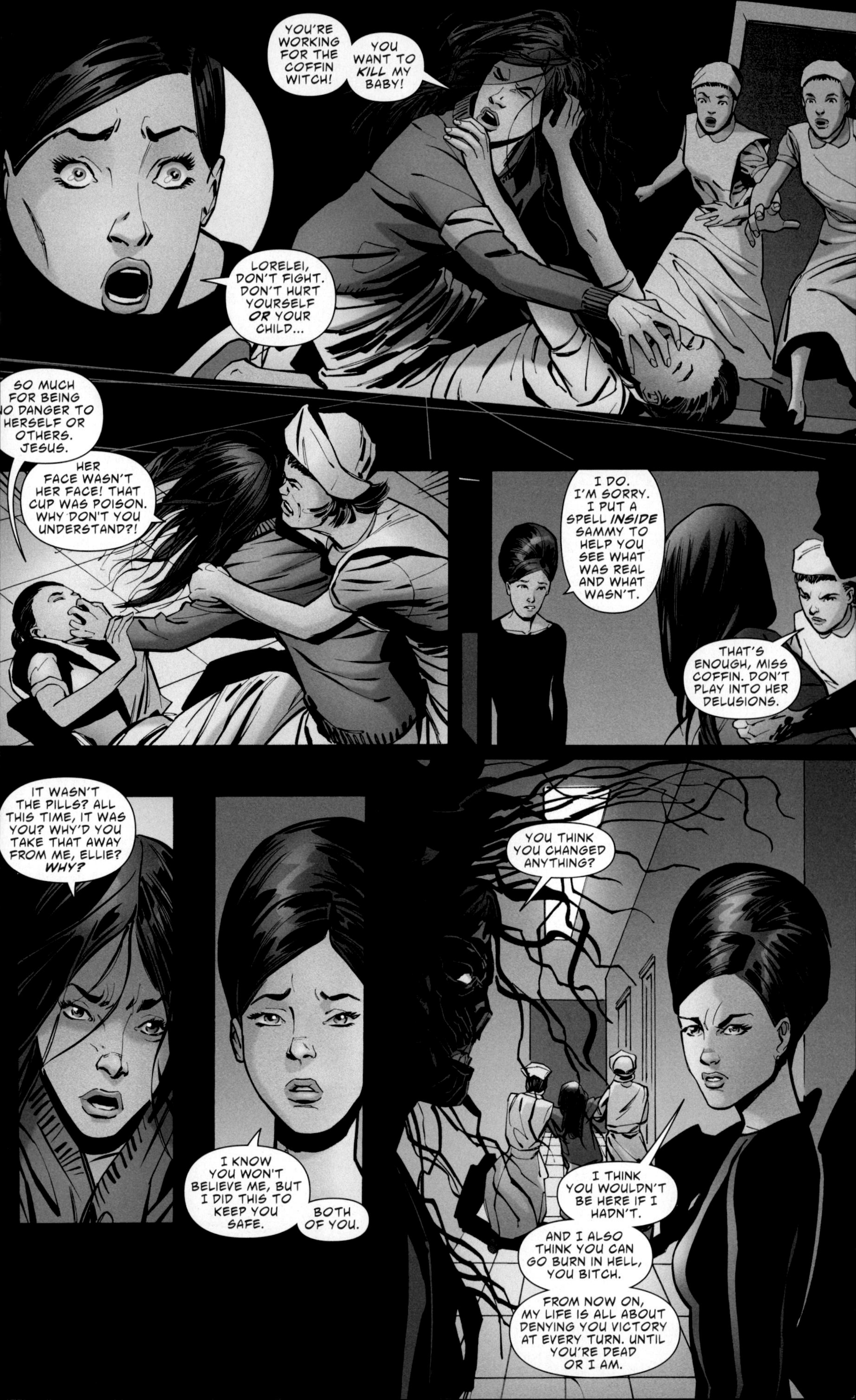
YOU'RE WORKING FOR THE COFFIN WITCH!
YOU WANT TO KILL MY BABY!
LORELEI, DON'T FIGHT. DON'T HURT YOURSELF OR YOUR CHILD...
SO MUCH FOR BEING NO DANGER TO HERSELF OR OTHERS. JESUS.
HER FACE WASN'T HER FACE! THAT CUP WAS POISON. WHY DON'T YOU UNDERSTAND?!
I DO. I'M SORRY. I PUT A SPELL INSIDE SAMMY TO HELP YOU SEE WHAT WAS REAL AND WHAT WASN'T.
THAT'S ENOUGH, MISS COFFIN. DON'T PLAY INTO HER DELUSIONS.
IT WASN'T THE PILLS? ALL THIS TIME, IT WAS YOU? WHY'D YOU TAKE THAT AWAY FROM ME, ELLIE? WHY?
I KNOW YOU WON'T BELIEVE ME, BUT I DID THIS TO KEEP YOU SAFE.
BOTH OF YOU.
YOU THINK YOU CHANGED ANYTHING?
I THINK YOU WOULDN'T BE HERE IF I HADN'T.
AND I ALSO THINK YOU CAN GO BURN IN HELL, YOU BITCH.
FROM NOW ON, MY LIFE IS ALL ABOUT DENYING YOU VICTORY AT EVERY TURN. UNTIL YOU'RE DEAD OR I AM.

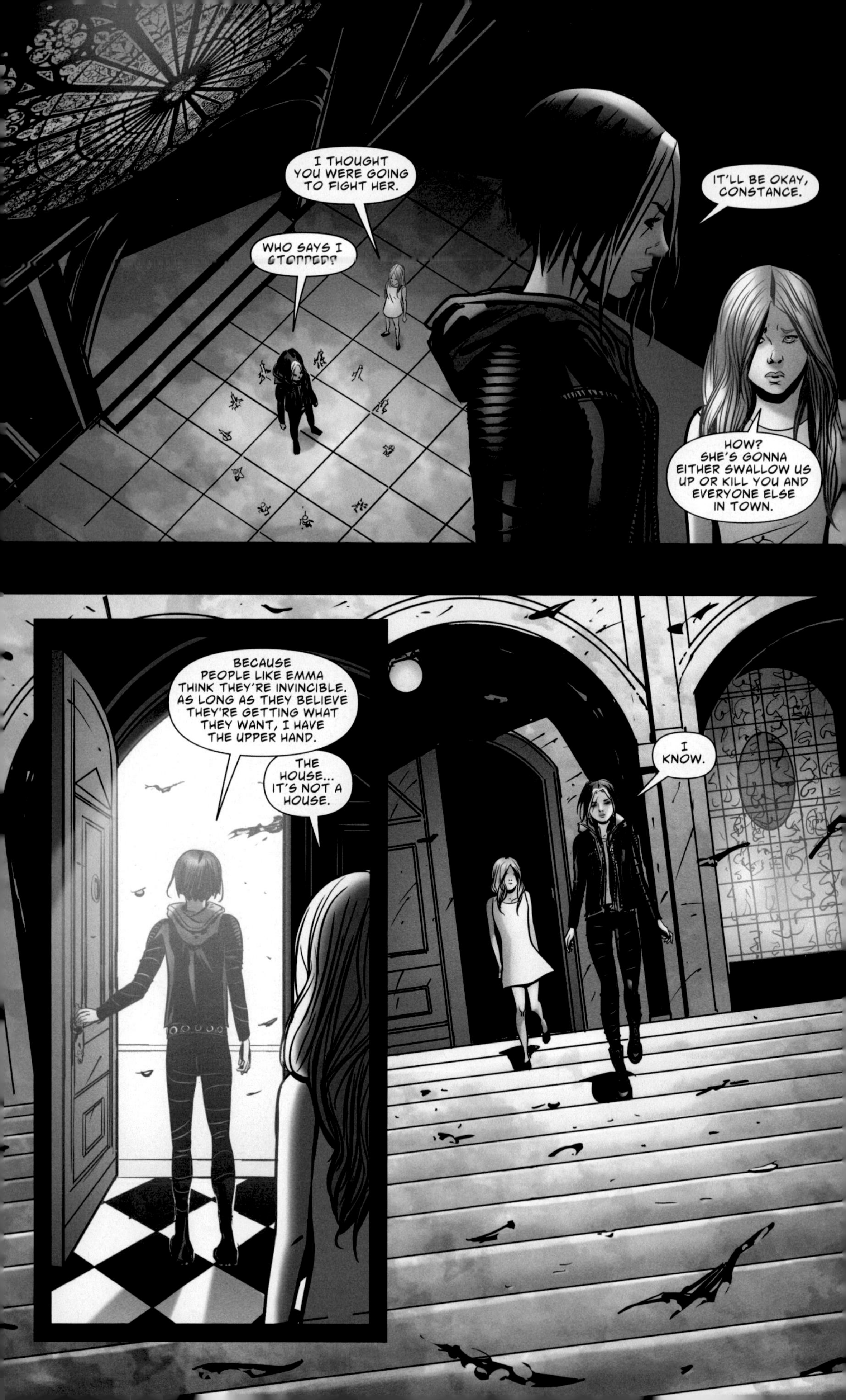
I THOUGHT YOU WERE GOING TO FIGHT HER.
WHO SAYS I STOPPED?
IT'LL BE OKAY, CONSTANCE.
HOW? SHE'S GONNA EITHER SWALLOW US UP OR KILL YOU AND EVERYONE ELSE IN TOWN.
BECAUSE PEOPLE LIKE EMMA THINK THEY'RE INVINCIBLE. AS LONG AS THEY BELIEVE THEY'RE GETTING WHAT THEY WANT, I HAVE THE UPPER HAND.
THE HOUSE... IT'S NOT A HOUSE.
I KNOW.

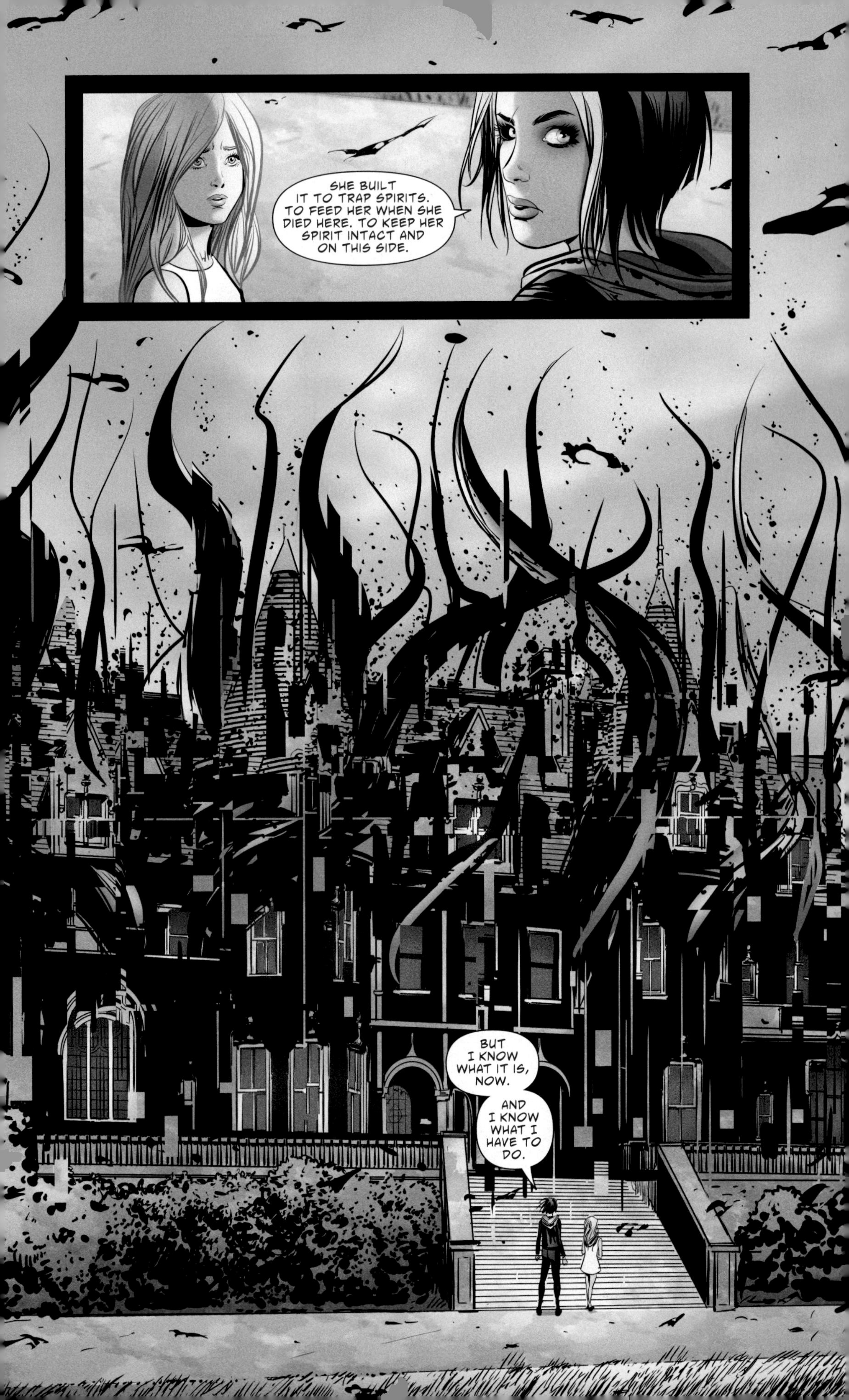
SHE BUILT IT TO TRAP SPIRITS. TO FEED HER WHEN SHE DIED HERE. TO KEEP HER SPIRIT INTACT AND ON THIS SIDE.
BUT I KNOW WHAT IT IS, NOW.
AND I KNOW WHAT I HAVE TO DO.

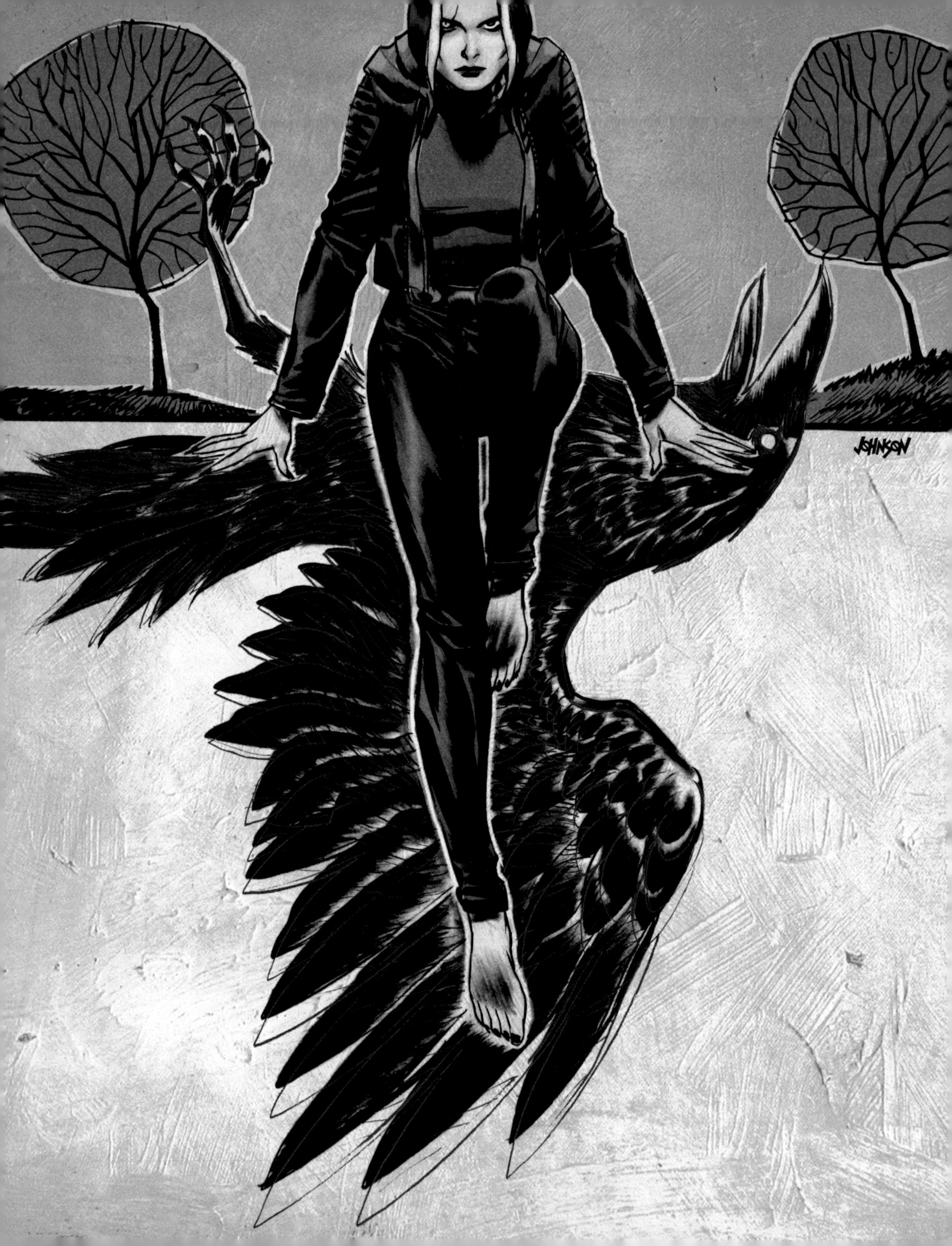
JOHNSON

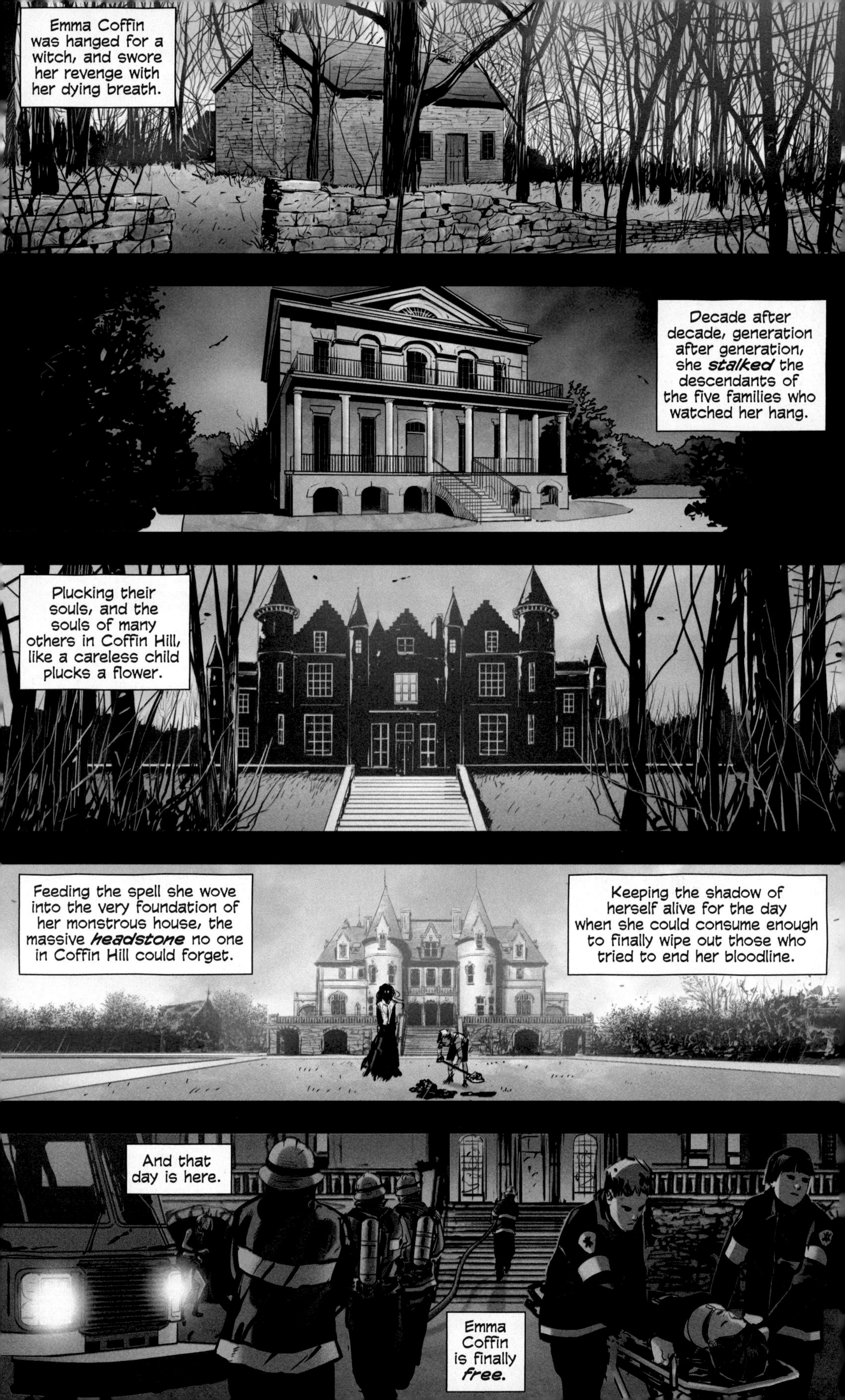
Emma Coffin was hanged for a witch, and swore her revenge with her dying breath.
Decade after decade, generation after generation, she *stalked* the descendants of the five families who watched her hang.
Plucking their souls, and the souls of many others in Coffin Hill, like a careless child plucks a flower.
Feeding the spell she wove into the very foundation of her monstrous house, the massive *headstone* no one in Coffin Hill could forget.
Keeping the shadow of herself alive for the day when she could consume enough to finally wipe out those who tried to end her bloodline.
And that day is here.
Emma Coffin is finally *free*.

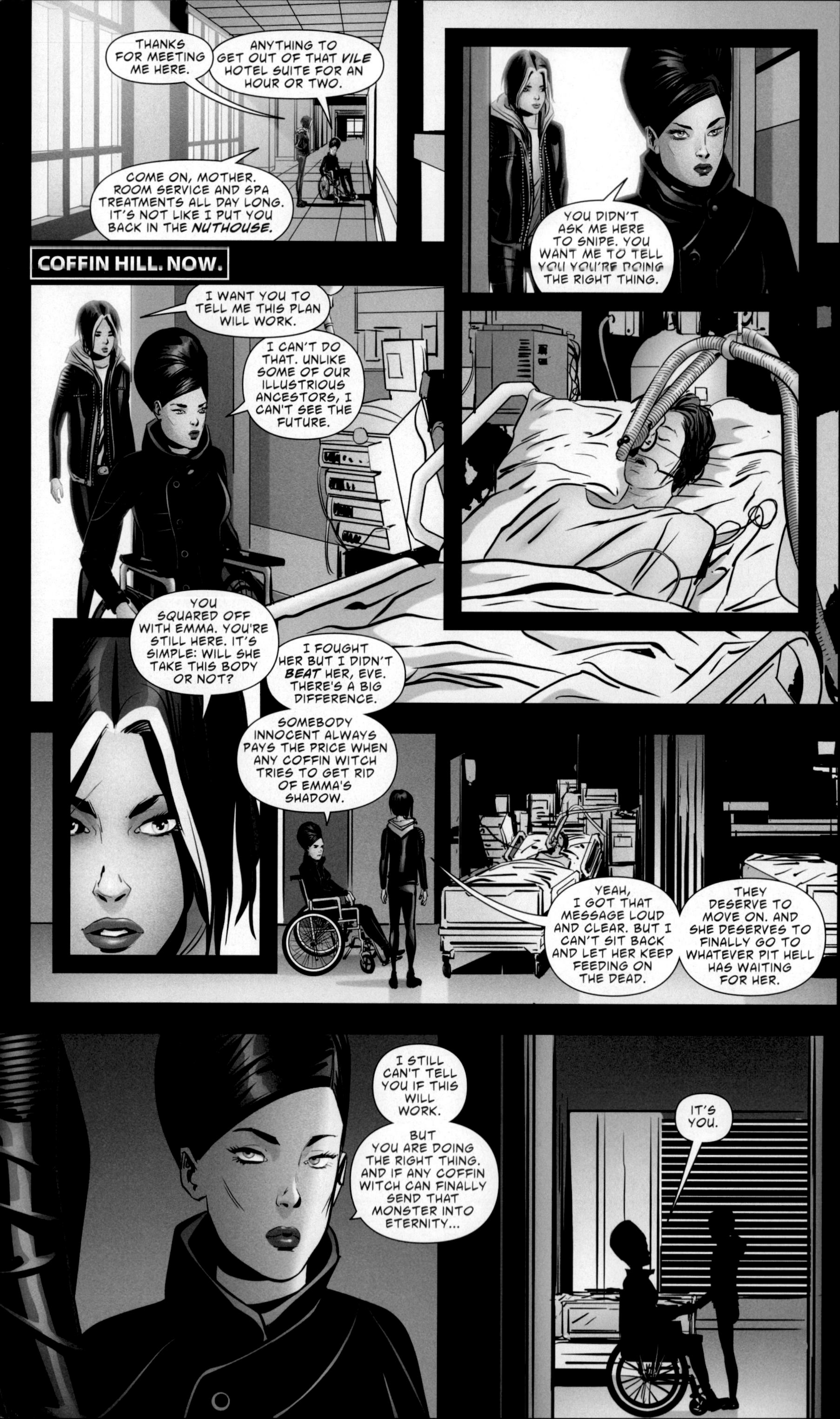
THANKS FOR MEETING ME HERE.
ANYTHING TO GET OUT OF THAT *VILE* HOTEL SUITE FOR AN HOUR OR TWO.
COME ON, MOTHER. ROOM SERVICE AND SPA TREATMENTS ALL DAY LONG. IT'S NOT LIKE I PUT YOU BACK IN THE ***NUTHOUSE.***
YOU DIDN'T ASK ME HERE TO SNIPE. YOU WANT ME TO TELL YOU YOU'RE DOING THE RIGHT THING.
COFFIN HILL. NOW.
I WANT YOU TO TELL ME THIS PLAN WILL WORK.
I CAN'T DO THAT. UNLIKE SOME OF OUR ILLUSTRIOUS ANCESTORS, I CAN'T SEE THE FUTURE.
YOU SQUARED OFF WITH EMMA. YOU'RE STILL HERE. IT'S SIMPLE: WILL SHE TAKE THIS BODY OR NOT?
I FOUGHT HER BUT I DIDN'T ***BEAT*** HER, EVE. THERE'S A BIG DIFFERENCE.
SOMEBODY INNOCENT ALWAYS PAYS THE PRICE WHEN ANY COFFIN WITCH TRIES TO GET RID OF EMMA'S SHADOW.
YEAH, I GOT THAT MESSAGE LOUD AND CLEAR. BUT I CAN'T SIT BACK AND LET HER KEEP FEEDING ON THE DEAD.
THEY DESERVE TO MOVE ON. AND SHE DESERVES TO FINALLY GO TO WHATEVER PIT HELL HAS WAITING FOR HER.
I STILL CAN'T TELL YOU IF THIS WILL WORK.
BUT YOU ARE DOING THE RIGHT THING. AND IF ANY COFFIN WITCH CAN FINALLY SEND THAT MONSTER INTO ETERNITY...
IT'S YOU.

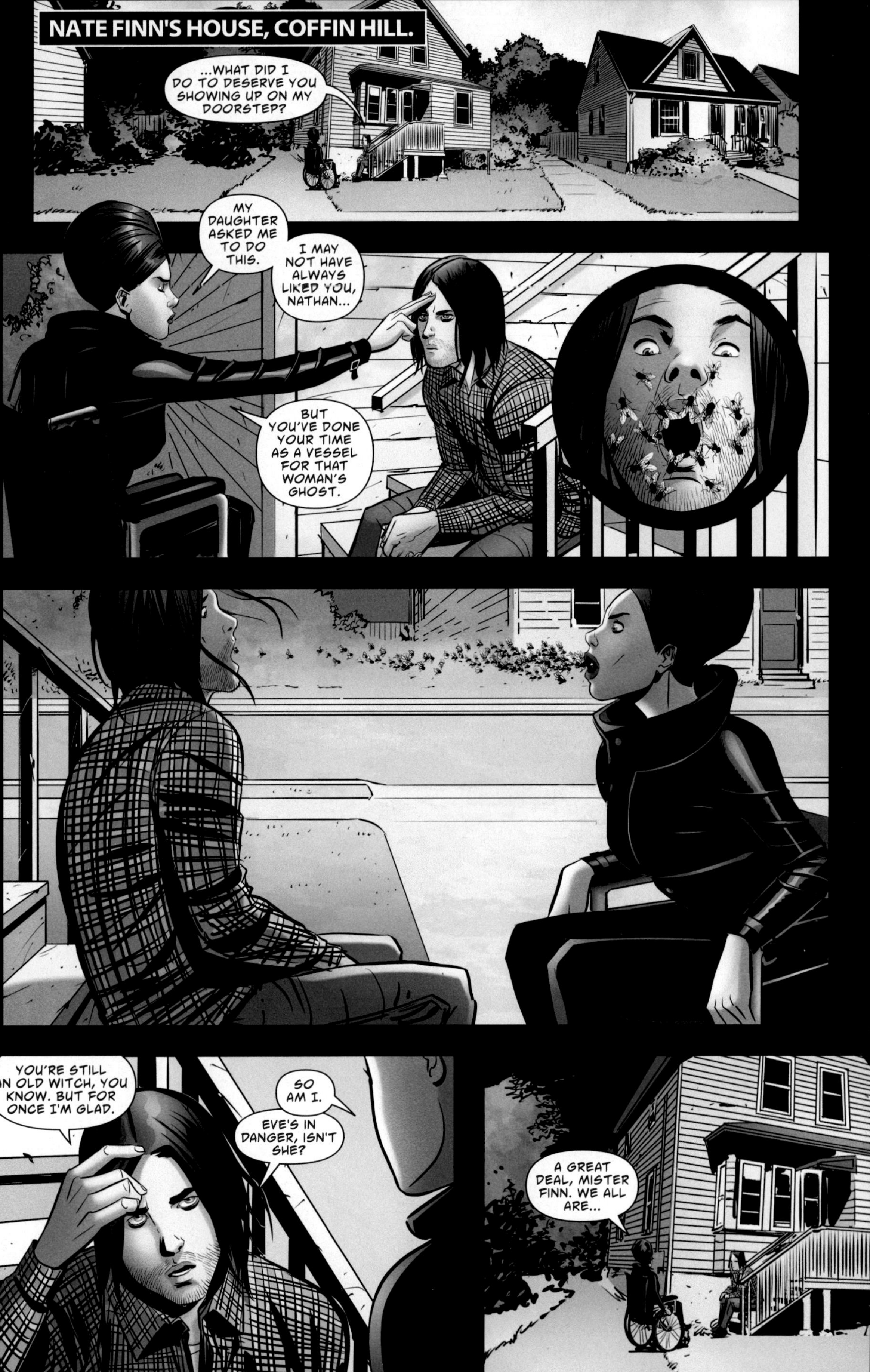
NATE FINN'S HOUSE, COFFIN HILL.
...WHAT DID I DO TO DESERVE YOU SHOWING UP ON MY DOORSTEP?
MY DAUGHTER ASKED ME TO DO THIS.
I MAY NOT HAVE ALWAYS LIKED YOU, NATHAN...
BUT YOU'VE DONE YOUR TIME AS A VESSEL FOR THAT WOMAN'S GHOST.
YOU'RE STILL AN OLD WITCH, YOU KNOW. BUT FOR ONCE I'M GLAD.
SO AM I.
EVE'S IN DANGER, ISN'T SHE?
A GREAT DEAL, MISTER FINN. WE ALL ARE...

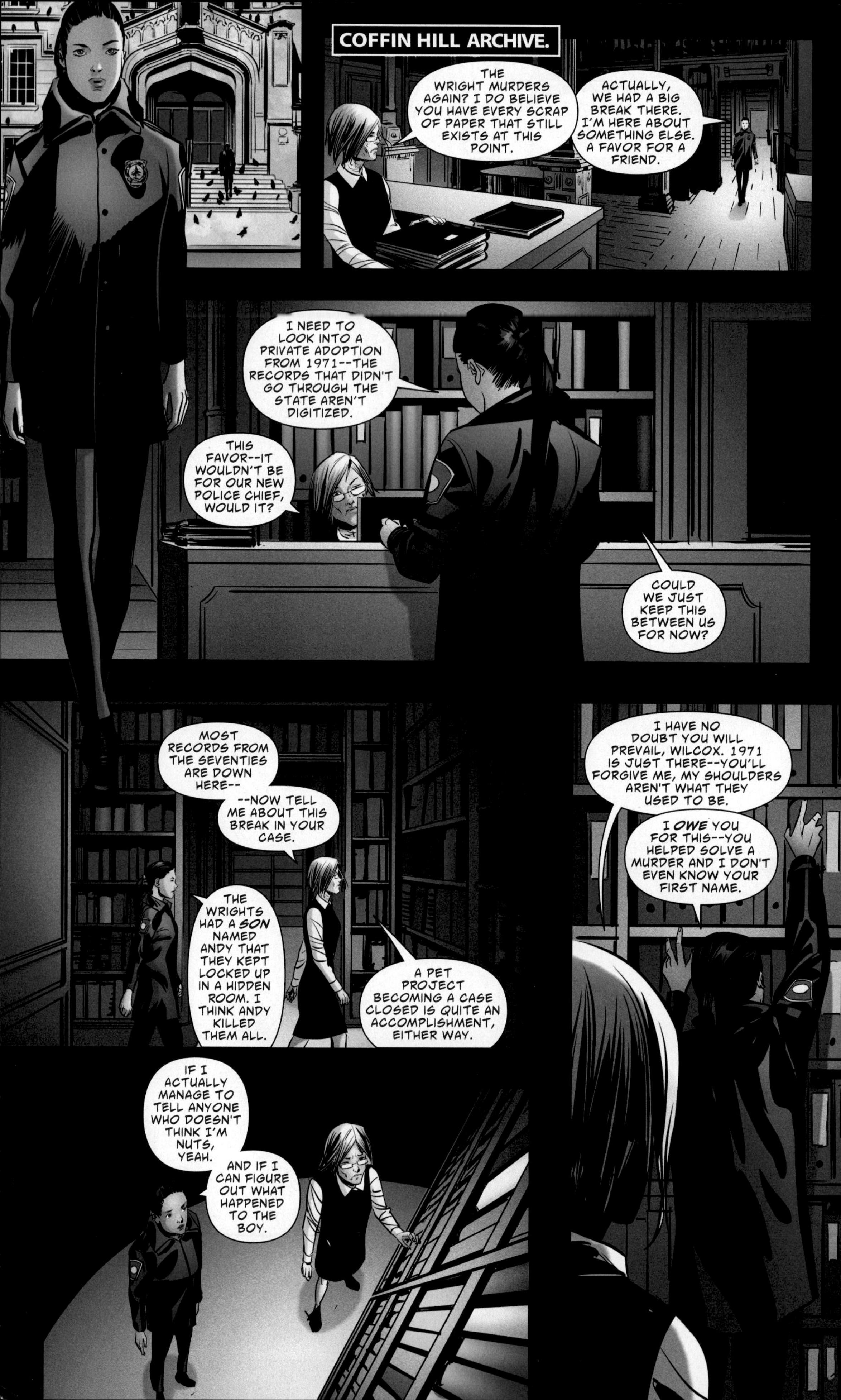
COFFIN HILL ARCHIVE.
THE WRIGHT MURDERS AGAIN? I DO BELIEVE YOU HAVE EVERY SCRAP OF PAPER THAT STILL EXISTS AT THIS POINT.
ACTUALLY, WE HAD A BIG BREAK THERE. I'M HERE ABOUT SOMETHING ELSE. A FAVOR FOR A FRIEND.
I NEED TO LOOK INTO A PRIVATE ADOPTION FROM 1971--THE RECORDS THAT DIDN'T GO THROUGH THE STATE AREN'T DIGITIZED.
THIS FAVOR--IT WOULDN'T BE FOR OUR NEW POLICE CHIEF, WOULD IT?
COULD WE JUST KEEP THIS BETWEEN US FOR NOW?
MOST RECORDS FROM THE SEVENTIES ARE DOWN HERE--
--NOW TELL ME ABOUT THIS BREAK IN YOUR CASE.
THE WRIGHTS HAD A SON NAMED ANDY THAT THEY KEPT LOCKED UP IN A HIDDEN ROOM. I THINK ANDY KILLED THEM ALL.
A PET PROJECT BECOMING A CASE CLOSED IS QUITE AN ACCOMPLISHMENT, EITHER WAY.
I HAVE NO DOUBT YOU WILL PREVAIL, WILCOX. 1971 IS JUST THERE--YOU'LL FORGIVE ME, MY SHOULDERS AREN'T WHAT THEY USED TO BE.
I OWE YOU FOR THIS--YOU HELPED SOLVE A MURDER AND I DON'T EVEN KNOW YOUR FIRST NAME.
IF I ACTUALLY MANAGE TO TELL ANYONE WHO DOESN'T THINK I'M NUTS, YEAH.
AND IF I CAN FIGURE OUT WHAT HAPPENED TO THE BOY.

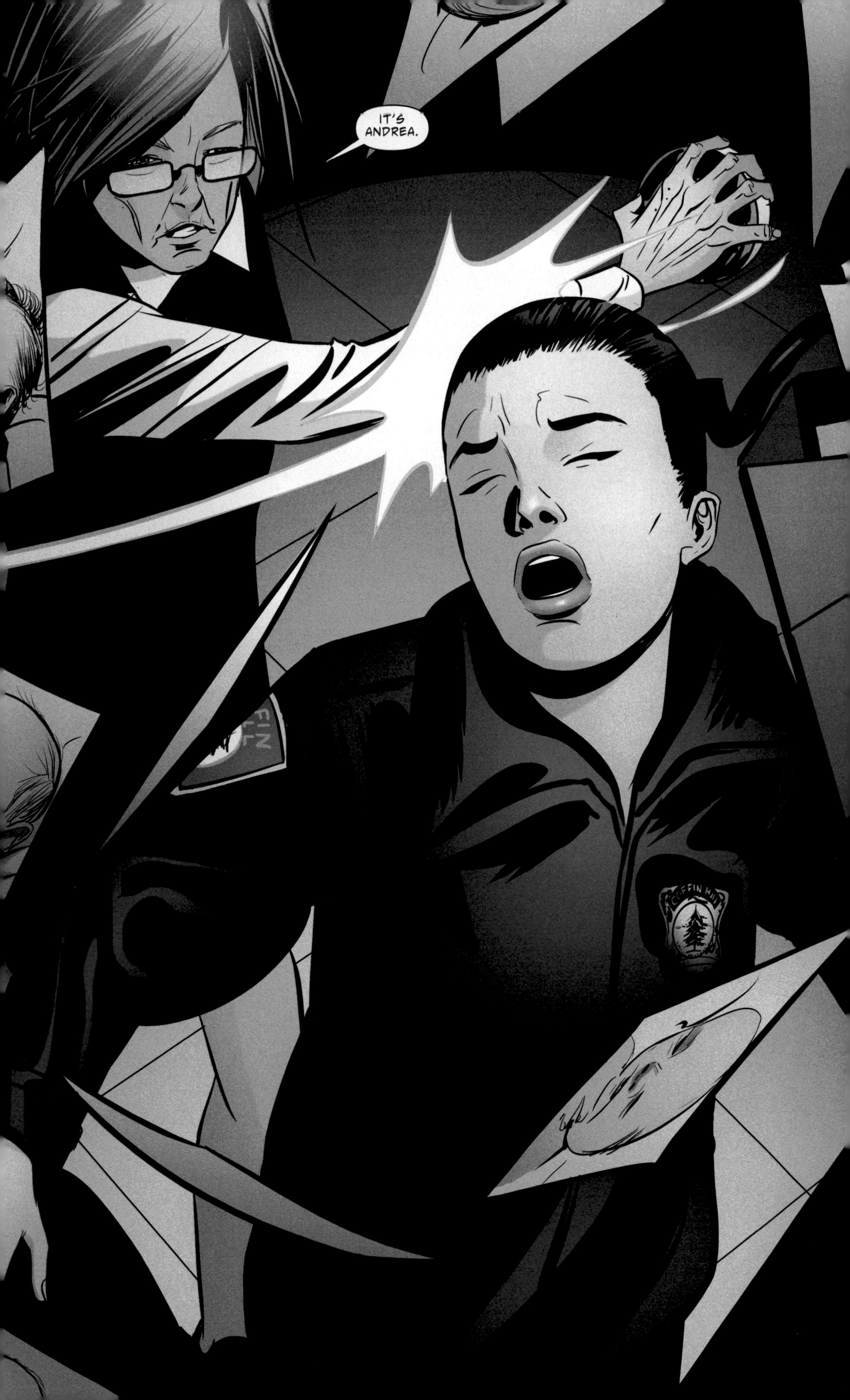
IT'S ANDREA.

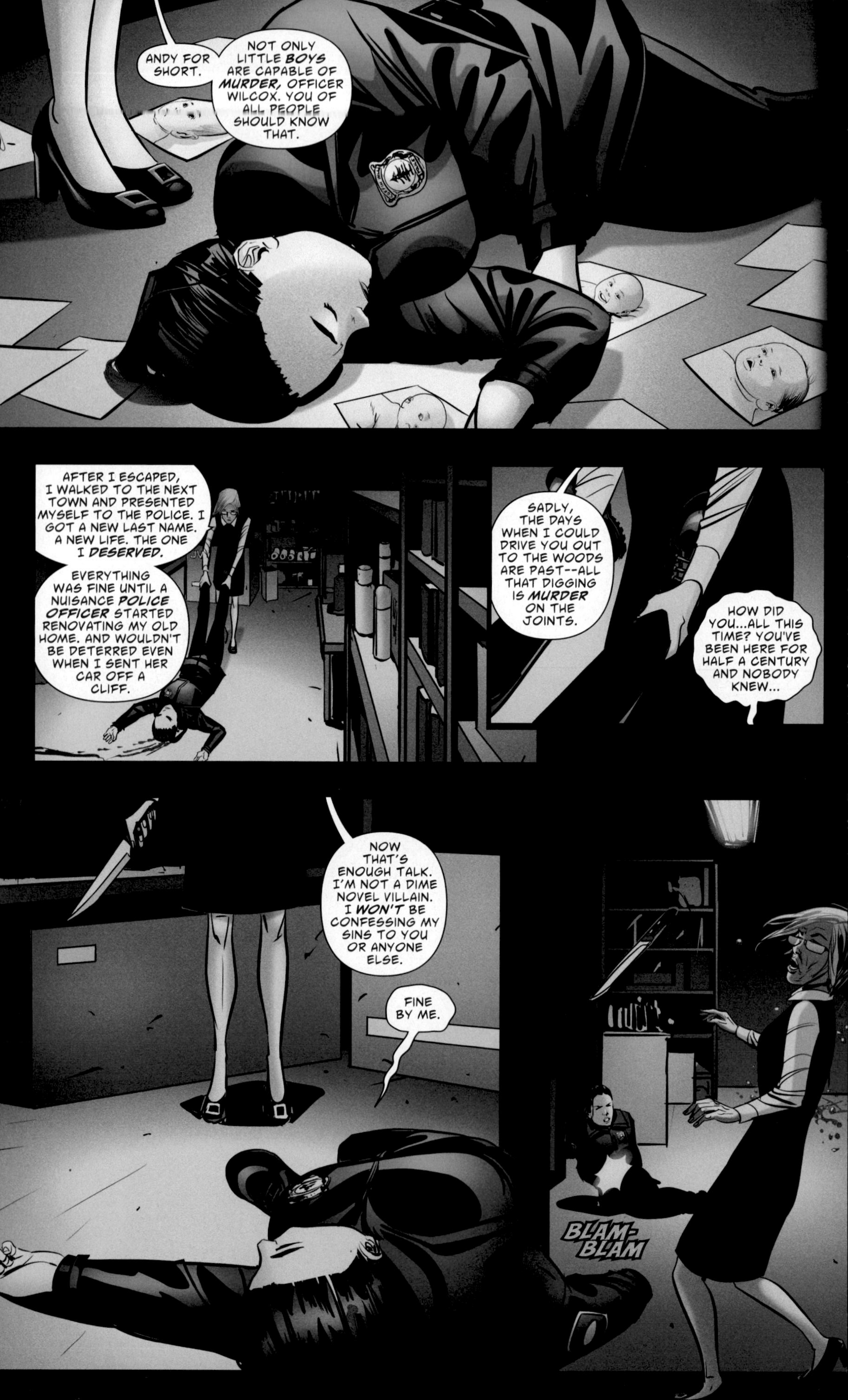
ANDY FOR SHORT.
NOT ONLY LITTLE BOYS ARE CAPABLE OF MURDER, OFFICER WILCOX. YOU OF ALL PEOPLE SHOULD KNOW THAT.
AFTER I ESCAPED, I WALKED TO THE NEXT TOWN AND PRESENTED MYSELF TO THE POLICE. I GOT A NEW LAST NAME. A NEW LIFE. THE ONE I DESERVED.
EVERYTHING WAS FINE UNTIL A NUISANCE POLICE OFFICER STARTED RENOVATING MY OLD HOME. AND WOULDN'T BE DETERRED EVEN WHEN I SENT HER CAR OFF A CLIFF.
SADLY, THE DAYS WHEN I COULD DRIVE YOU OUT TO THE WOODS ARE PAST--ALL THAT DIGGING IS MURDER ON THE JOINTS.
HOW DID YOU...ALL THIS TIME? YOU'VE BEEN HERE FOR HALF A CENTURY AND NOBODY KNEW...
NOW THAT'S ENOUGH TALK. I'M NOT A DIME NOVEL VILLAIN. I WON'T BE CONFESSING MY SINS TO YOU OR ANYONE ELSE.
FINE BY ME.
BLAM-BLAM

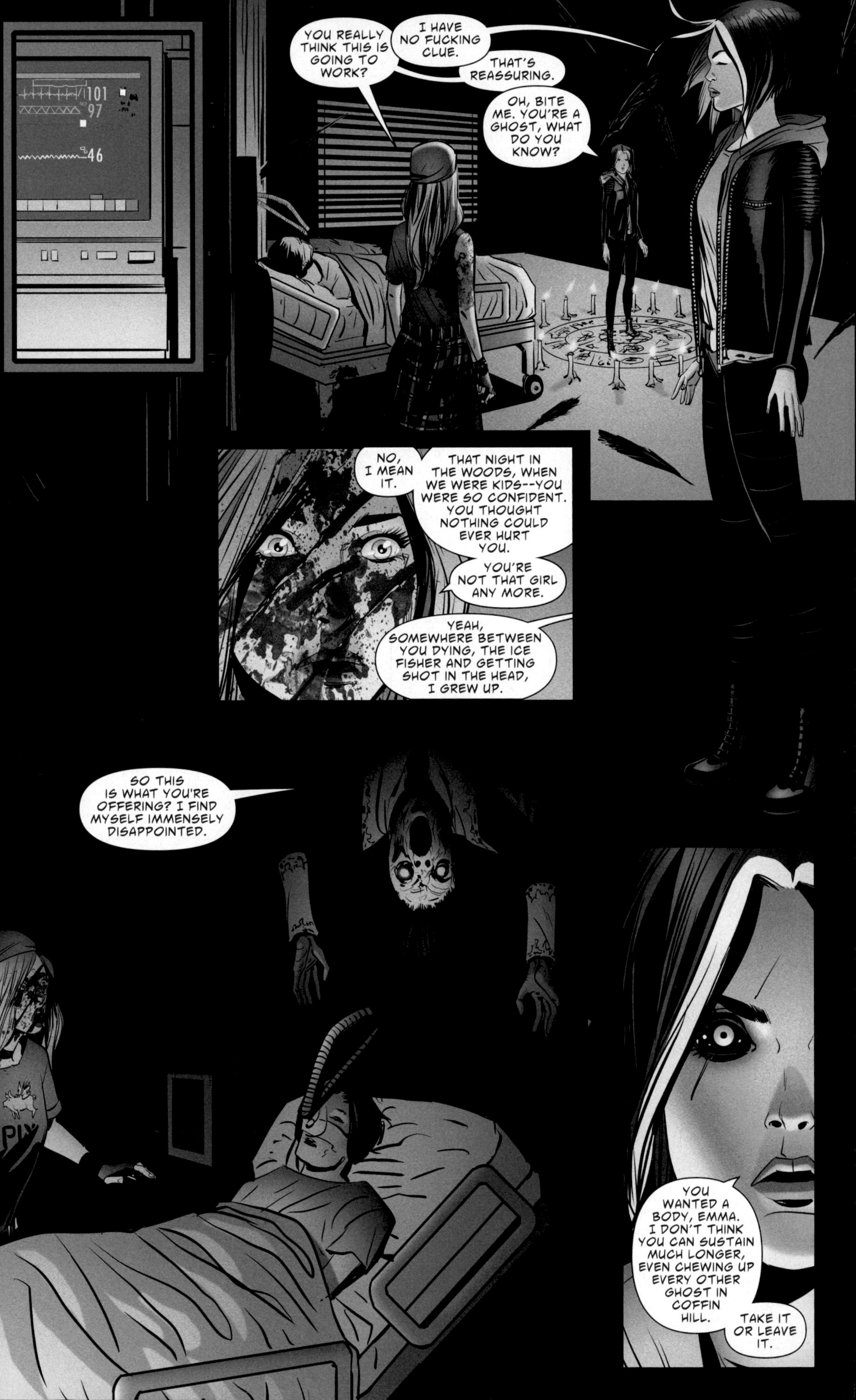
YOU REALLY THINK THIS IS GOING TO WORK?
I HAVE NO FUCKING CLUE.
THAT'S REASSURING.
OH, BITE ME. YOU'RE A GHOST, WHAT DO YOU KNOW?
NO, I MEAN IT.
THAT NIGHT IN THE WOODS, WHEN WE WERE KIDS--YOU WERE SO CONFIDENT. YOU THOUGHT NOTHING COULD EVER HURT YOU.
YOU'RE NOT THAT GIRL ANY MORE.
YEAH, SOMEWHERE BETWEEN YOU DYING, THE ICE FISHER AND GETTING SHOT IN THE HEAD, I GREW UP.
SO THIS IS WHAT YOU'RE OFFERING? I FIND MYSELF IMMENSELY DISAPPOINTED.
YOU WANTED A BODY, EMMA. I DON'T THINK YOU CAN SUSTAIN MUCH LONGER, EVEN CHEWING UP EVERY OTHER GHOST IN COFFIN HILL.
TAKE IT OR LEAVE IT.

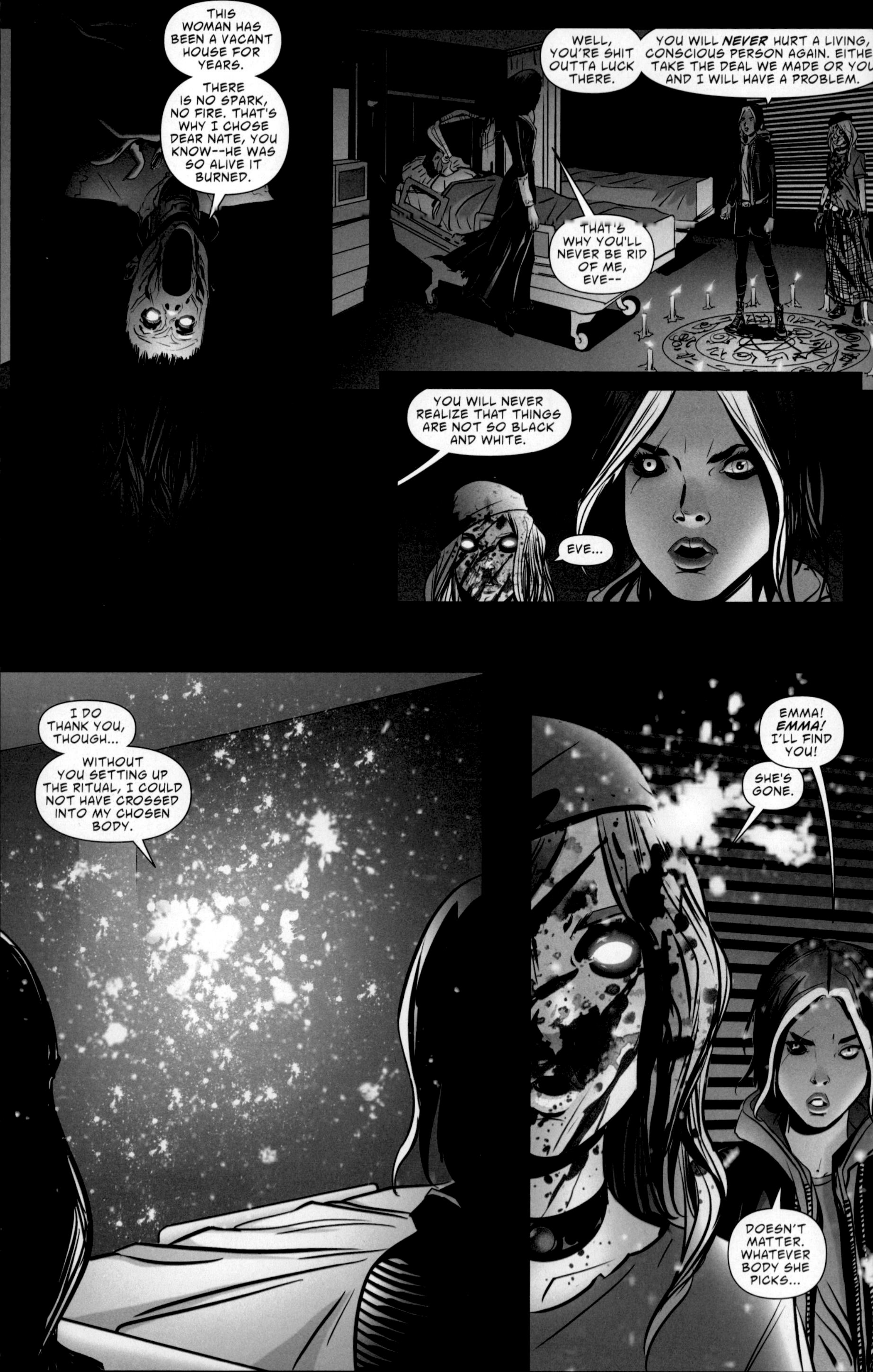
THIS WOMAN HAS BEEN A VACANT HOUSE FOR YEARS.
THERE IS NO SPARK, NO FIRE. THAT'S WHY I CHOSE DEAR NATE, YOU KNOW--HE WAS SO ALIVE IT BURNED.
WELL, YOU'RE SHIT OUTTA LUCK THERE.
YOU WILL NEVER HURT A LIVING, CONSCIOUS PERSON AGAIN. EITHER TAKE THE DEAL WE MADE OR YOU AND I WILL HAVE A PROBLEM.
THAT'S WHY YOU'LL NEVER BE RID OF ME, EVE--
YOU WILL NEVER REALIZE THAT THINGS ARE NOT SO BLACK AND WHITE.
EVE...
I DO THANK YOU, THOUGH...
WITHOUT YOU SETTING UP THE RITUAL, I COULD NOT HAVE CROSSED INTO MY CHOSEN BODY.
EMMA! EMMA! I'LL FIND YOU!
SHE'S GONE.
DOESN'T MATTER. WHATEVER BODY SHE PICKS...

"I KNOW WHERE SHE'S GOING."

LEE, I NEED BACKUP AT THE TOWN ARCHIVE.

I'LL EXPLAIN WHEN YOU GET HERE. JUST COME!

YOU'RE TOO LATE.

I HAVE INFLICTED ENOUGH FATAL BLOWS IN MY TIME.

I'LL BE DEAD BEFORE THE MINUTE RUNS OUT.

MY SISTER CONSTANCE--SHE MADE A WISH TO THE COFFIN WITCH. BUT IT DIDN'T COME TRUE.

SHE WISHED FOR OUR PARENTS TO LOVE ME. FOR ME TO BE FREE OF THE PRISON THEY KEPT ME IN.

SHE WAS SO TRUSTING...

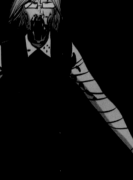

AH. THAT'S BETTER.

THE MOMENT OF DEATH IS IDEAL FOR THIS SORT OF THING. OLDER THAN I WOULD HAVE PREFERRED, BUT OH, SO ALIVE.

H-HOLD IT! YOU STOP RIGHT THERE!

YOU WON'T NEED THAT GUN. IF YOU SEE MY DEAR DESCENDANT EVE...YOU TELL HER I'M WAITING.

SHIT!!!

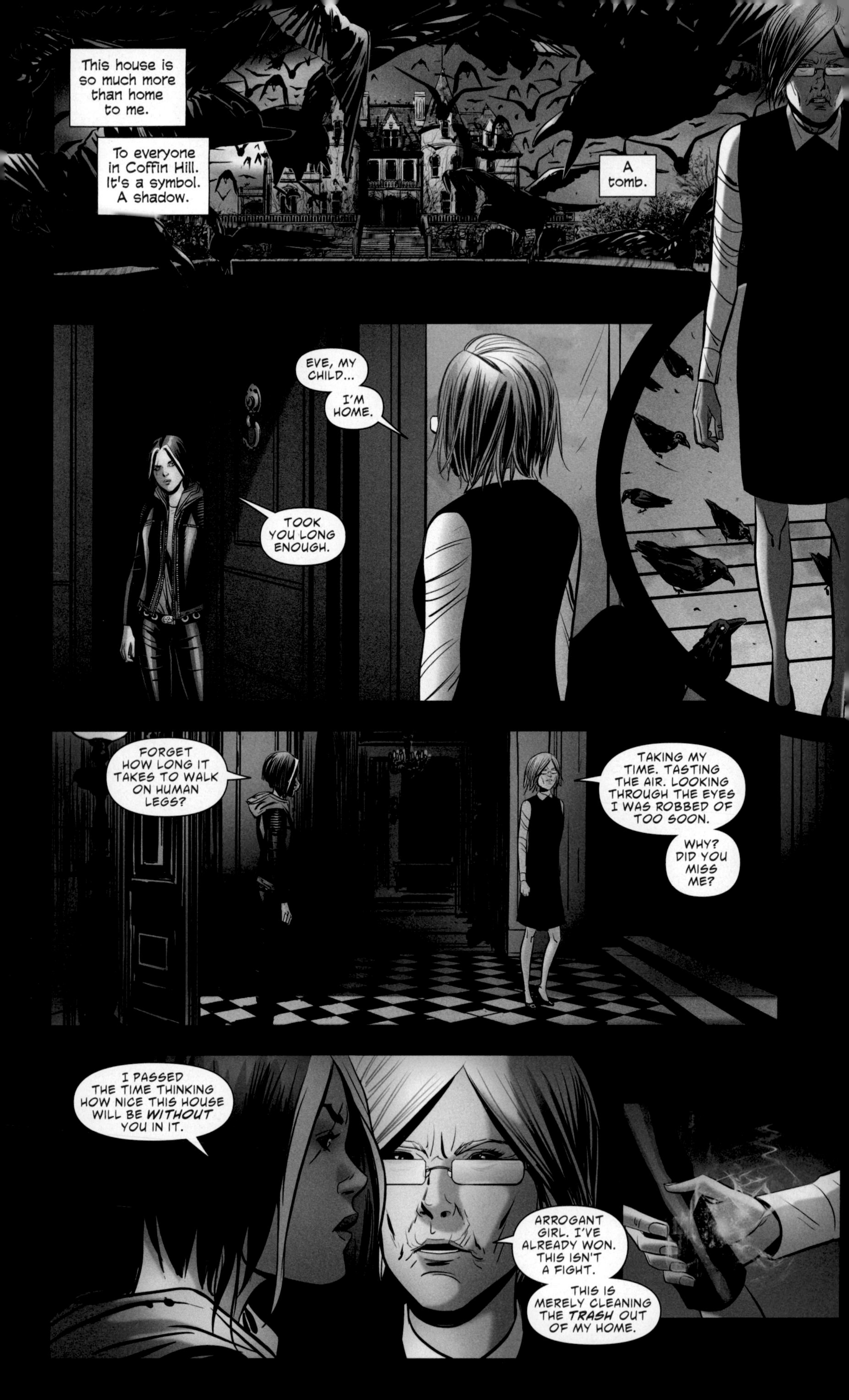
This house is so much more than home to me.
To everyone in Coffin Hill. It's a symbol. A shadow.
A tomb.
EVE, MY CHILD... I'M HOME.
TOOK YOU LONG ENOUGH.
FORGET HOW LONG IT TAKES TO WALK ON HUMAN LEGS?
TAKING MY TIME. TASTING THE AIR. LOOKING THROUGH THE EYES I WAS ROBBED OF TOO SOON.
WHY? DID YOU MISS ME?
I PASSED THE TIME THINKING HOW NICE THIS HOUSE WILL BE WITHOUT YOU IN IT.
ARROGANT GIRL. I'VE ALREADY WON. THIS ISN'T A FIGHT.
THIS IS MERELY CLEANING THE TRASH OUT OF MY HOME.

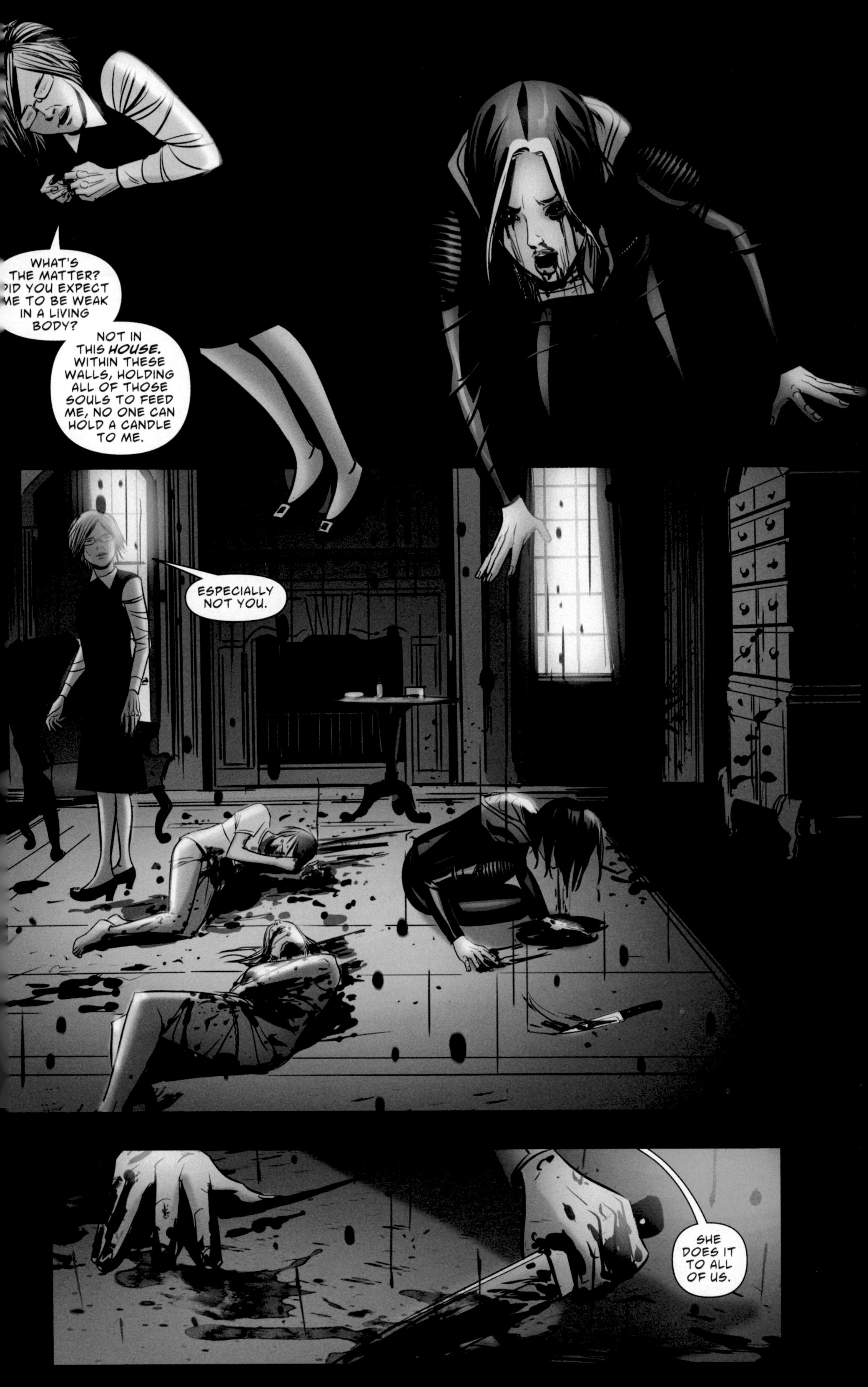

WHAT'S THE MATTER? DID YOU EXPECT ME TO BE WEAK IN A LIVING BODY?
NOT IN THIS *HOUSE.* WITHIN THESE WALLS, HOLDING ALL OF THOSE SOULS TO FEED ME, NO ONE CAN HOLD A CANDLE TO ME.
ESPECIALLY NOT YOU.
SHE DOES IT TO ALL OF US.

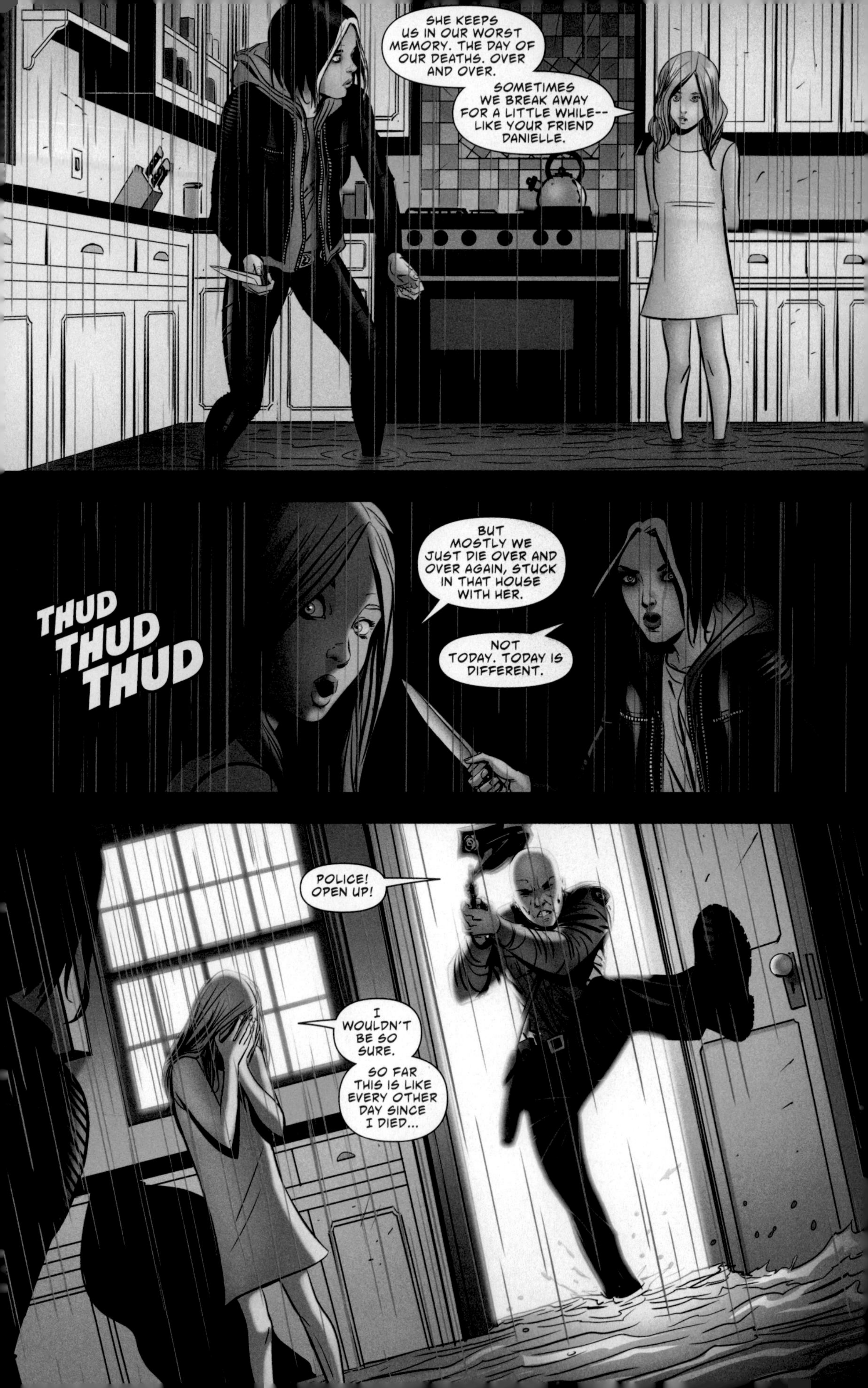
SHE KEEPS US IN OUR WORST MEMORY. THE DAY OF OUR DEATHS. OVER AND OVER.
SOMETIMES WE BREAK AWAY FOR A LITTLE WHILE--LIKE YOUR FRIEND DANIELLE.
THUD THUD THUD
BUT MOSTLY WE JUST DIE OVER AND OVER AGAIN, STUCK IN THAT HOUSE WITH HER.
NOT TODAY. TODAY IS DIFFERENT.
POLICE! OPEN UP!
I WOULDN'T BE SO SURE.
SO FAR THIS IS LIKE EVERY OTHER DAY SINCE I DIED...

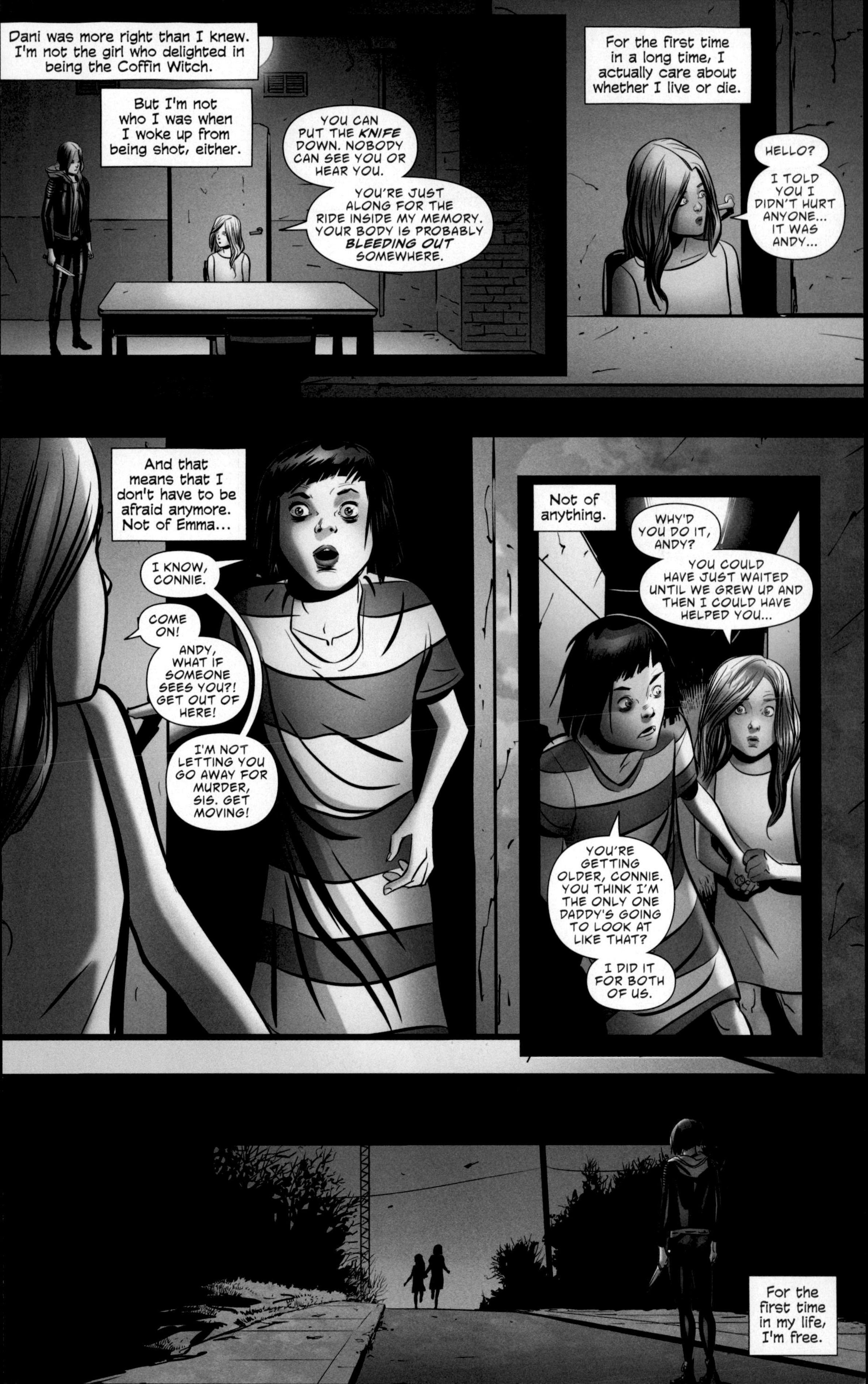

Dani was more right than I knew. I'm not the girl who delighted in being the Coffin Witch.
But I'm not who I was when I woke up from being shot, either.
YOU CAN PUT THE KNIFE DOWN. NOBODY CAN SEE YOU OR HEAR YOU.
YOU'RE JUST ALONG FOR THE RIDE INSIDE MY MEMORY. YOUR BODY IS PROBABLY BLEEDING OUT SOMEWHERE.
For the first time in a long time, I actually care about whether I live or die.
HELLO?
I TOLD YOU I DIDN'T HURT ANYONE... IT WAS ANDY...
And that means that I don't have to be afraid anymore. Not of Emma...
I KNOW, CONNIE.
COME ON!
ANDY, WHAT IF SOMEONE SEES YOU?! GET OUT OF HERE!
I'M NOT LETTING YOU GO AWAY FOR MURDER, SIS. GET MOVING!
Not of anything.
WHY'D YOU DO IT, ANDY?
YOU COULD HAVE JUST WAITED UNTIL WE GREW UP AND THEN I COULD HAVE HELPED YOU...
YOU'RE GETTING OLDER, CONNIE. YOU THINK I'M THE ONLY ONE DADDY'S GOING TO LOOK AT LIKE THAT?
I DID IT FOR BOTH OF US.
For the first time in my life, I'm free.

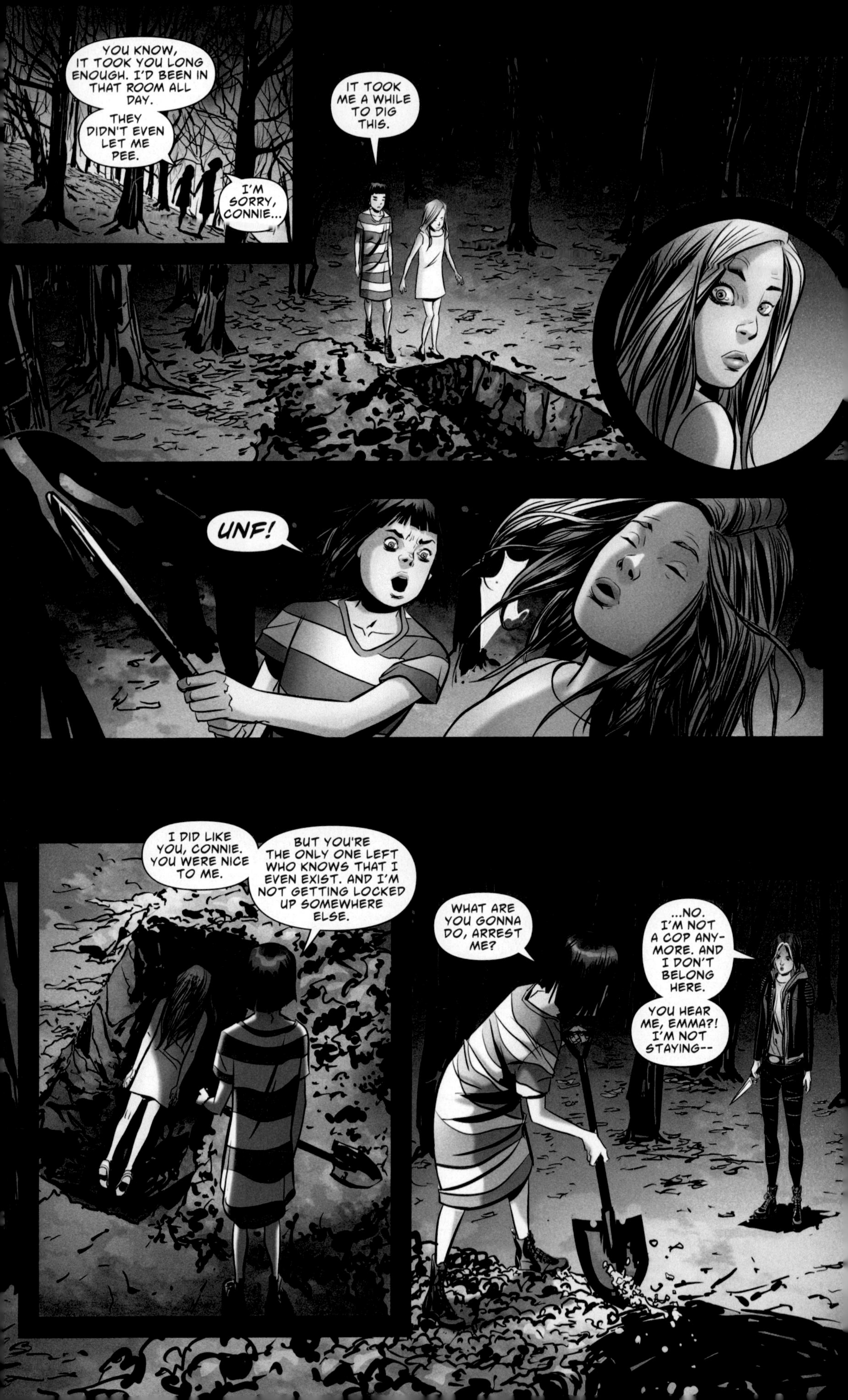
YOU KNOW, IT TOOK YOU LONG ENOUGH. I'D BEEN IN THAT ROOM ALL DAY.
THEY DIDN'T EVEN LET ME PEE.
I'M SORRY, CONNIE...
IT TOOK ME A WHILE TO DIG THIS.
UNF!
I DID LIKE YOU, CONNIE. YOU WERE NICE TO ME.
BUT YOU'RE THE ONLY ONE LEFT WHO KNOWS THAT I EVEN EXIST. AND I'M NOT GETTING LOCKED UP SOMEWHERE ELSE.
WHAT ARE YOU GONNA DO, ARREST ME?
...NO. I'M NOT A COP ANY-MORE. AND I DON'T BELONG HERE.
YOU HEAR ME, EMMA?! I'M NOT STAYING--

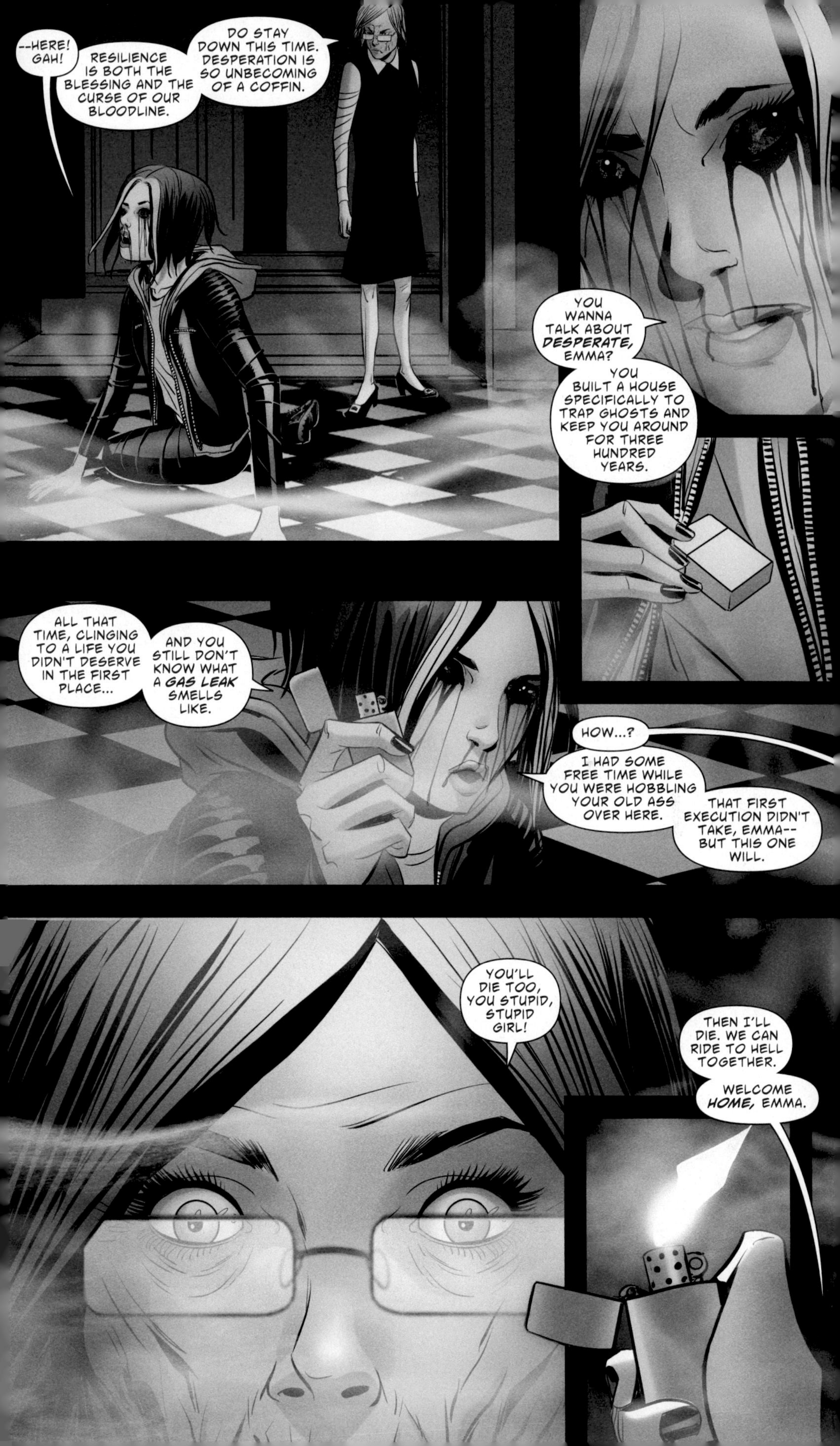

--HERE! GAH!
RESILIENCE IS BOTH THE BLESSING AND THE CURSE OF OUR BLOODLINE.
DO STAY DOWN THIS TIME. DESPERATION IS SO UNBECOMING OF A COFFIN.
YOU WANNA TALK ABOUT DESPERATE, EMMA?
YOU BUILT A HOUSE SPECIFICALLY TO TRAP GHOSTS AND KEEP YOU AROUND FOR THREE HUNDRED YEARS.
ALL THAT TIME, CLINGING TO A LIFE YOU DIDN'T DESERVE IN THE FIRST PLACE...
AND YOU STILL DON'T KNOW WHAT A GAS LEAK SMELLS LIKE.
HOW...?
I HAD SOME FREE TIME WHILE YOU WERE HOBBLING YOUR OLD ASS OVER HERE.
THAT FIRST EXECUTION DIDN'T TAKE, EMMA--BUT THIS ONE WILL.
YOU'LL DIE TOO, YOU STUPID, STUPID GIRL!
THEN I'LL DIE. WE CAN RIDE TO HELL TOGETHER.
WELCOME HOME, EMMA.

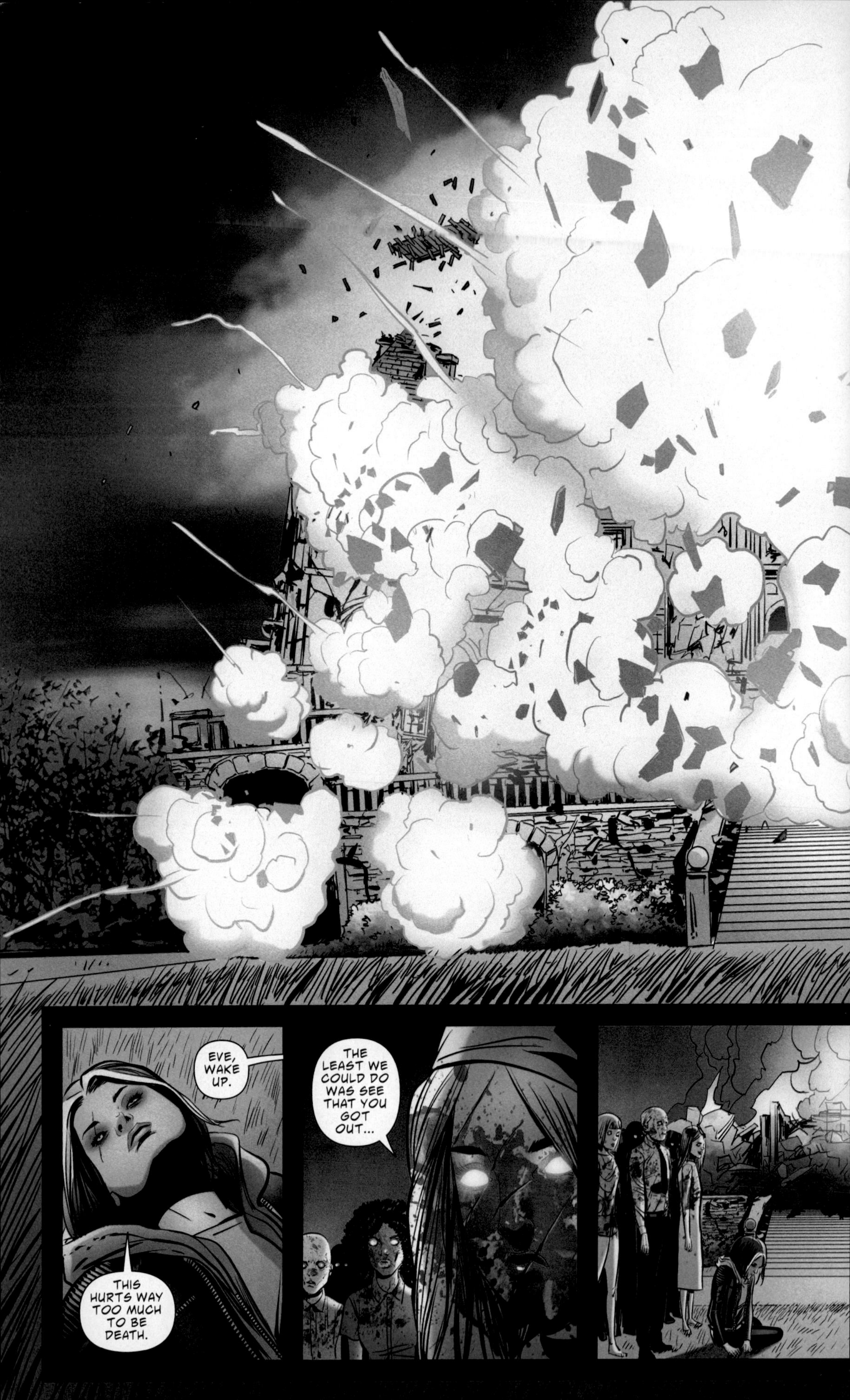
EVE, WAKE UP.
THIS HURTS WAY TOO MUCH TO BE DEATH.
THE LEAST WE COULD DO WAS SEE THAT YOU GOT OUT...

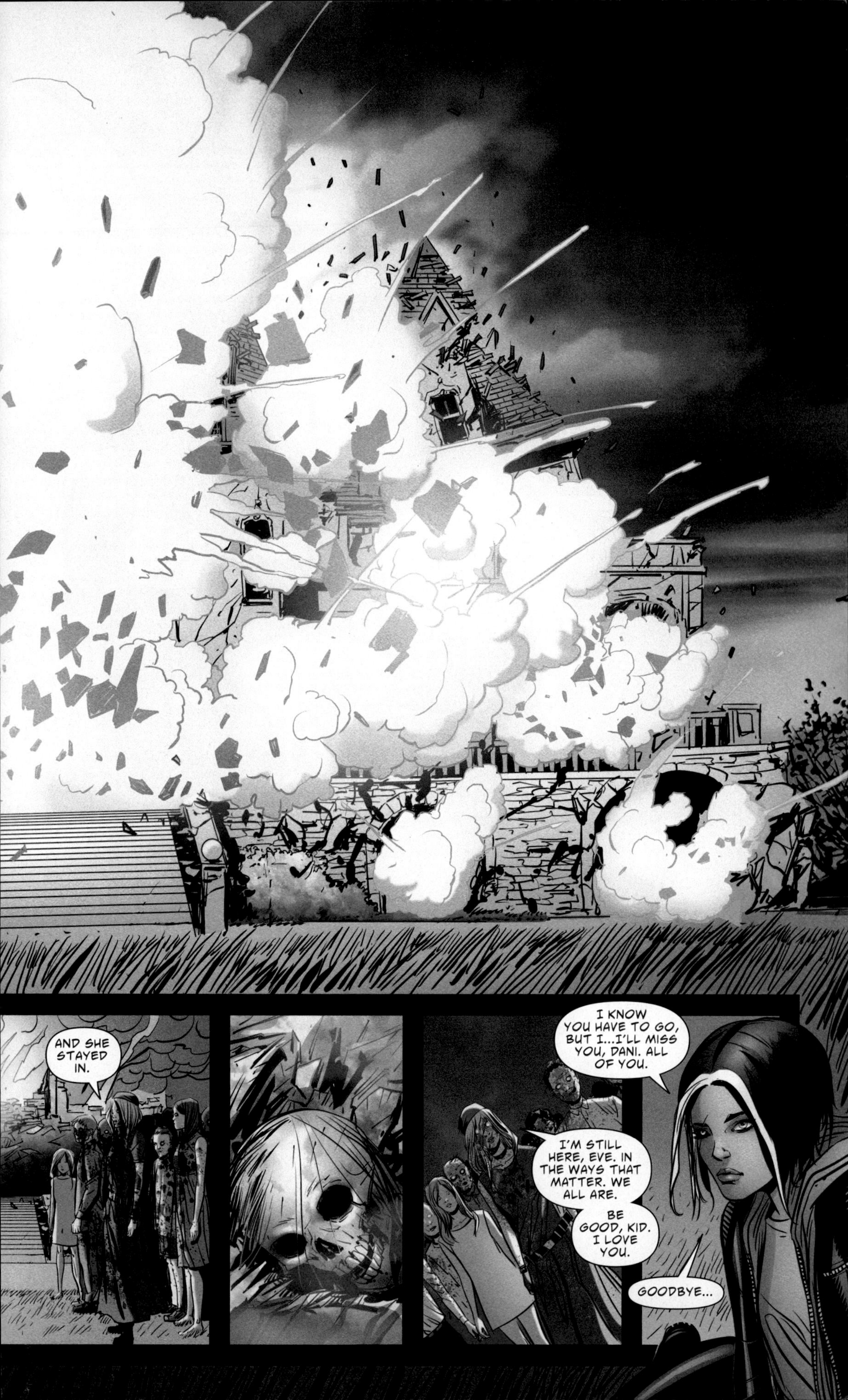
AND SHE STAYED IN.
I KNOW YOU HAVE TO GO, BUT I...I'LL MISS YOU, DANI. ALL OF YOU.
I'M STILL HERE, EVE. IN THE WAYS THAT MATTER. WE ALL ARE.
BE GOOD, KID. I LOVE YOU.
GOODBYE...

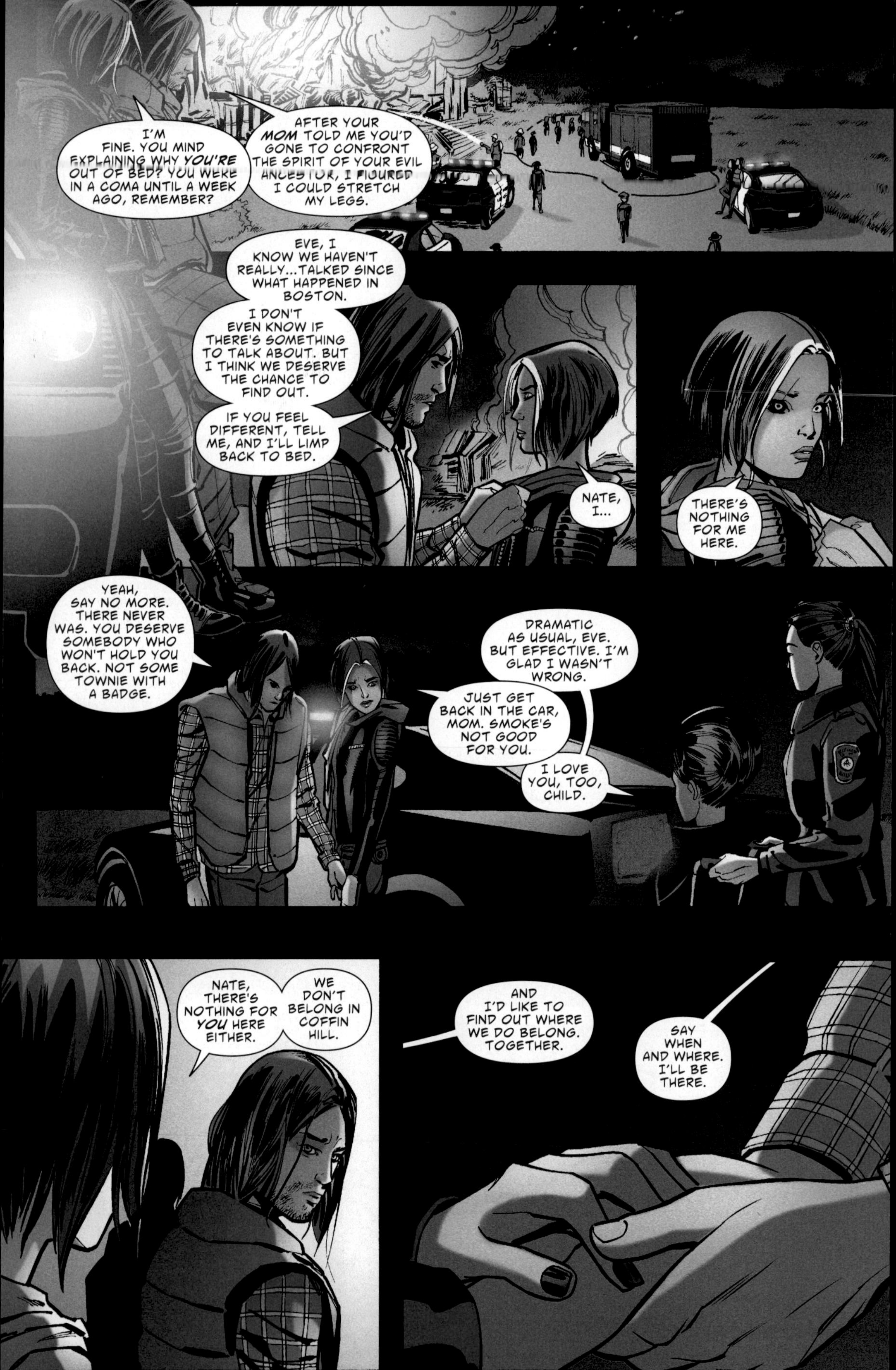
I'M FINE. YOU MIND EXPLAINING WHY YOU'RE OUT OF BED? YOU WERE IN A COMA UNTIL A WEEK AGO, REMEMBER?
AFTER YOUR MOM TOLD ME YOU'D GONE TO CONFRONT THE SPIRIT OF YOUR EVIL ANCESTOR, I FIGURED I COULD STRETCH MY LEGS.
EVE, I KNOW WE HAVEN'T REALLY...TALKED SINCE WHAT HAPPENED IN BOSTON.
I DON'T EVEN KNOW IF THERE'S SOMETHING TO TALK ABOUT. BUT I THINK WE DESERVE THE CHANCE TO FIND OUT.
IF YOU FEEL DIFFERENT, TELL ME, AND I'LL LIMP BACK TO BED.
NATE, I...
THERE'S NOTHING FOR ME HERE.
YEAH, SAY NO MORE. THERE NEVER WAS. YOU DESERVE SOMEBODY WHO WON'T HOLD YOU BACK. NOT SOME TOWNIE WITH A BADGE.
DRAMATIC AS USUAL, EVE. BUT EFFECTIVE. I'M GLAD I WASN'T WRONG.
JUST GET BACK IN THE CAR, MOM. SMOKE'S NOT GOOD FOR YOU.
I LOVE YOU, TOO, CHILD.
NATE, THERE'S NOTHING FOR YOU HERE EITHER.
WE DON'T BELONG IN COFFIN HILL.
AND I'D LIKE TO FIND OUT WHERE WE DO BELONG. TOGETHER.
SAY WHEN AND WHERE. I'LL BE THERE.

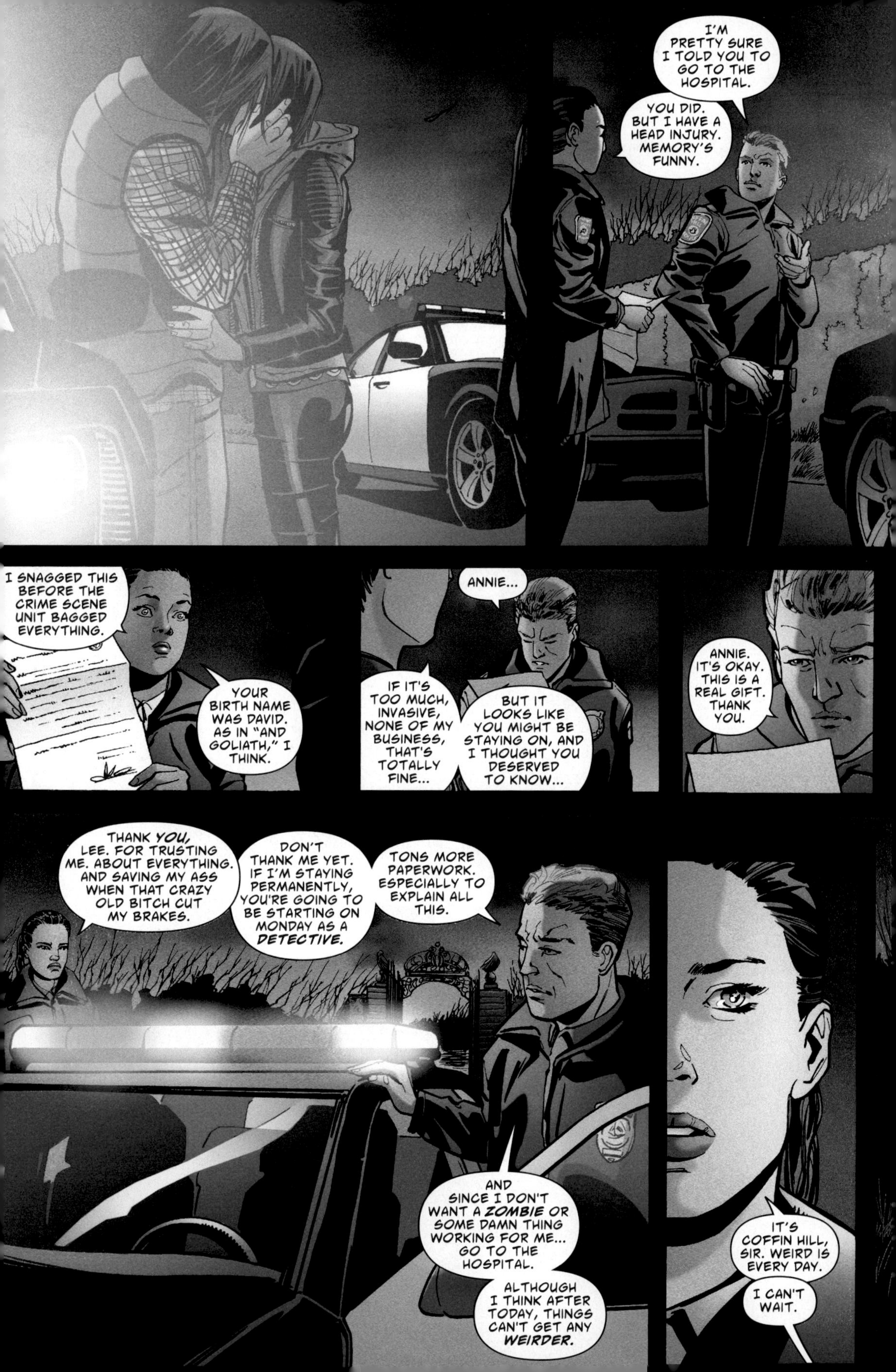
I'M PRETTY SURE I TOLD YOU TO GO TO THE HOSPITAL.
YOU DID. BUT I HAVE A HEAD INJURY. MEMORY'S FUNNY.
I SNAGGED THIS BEFORE THE CRIME SCENE UNIT BAGGED EVERYTHING.
YOUR BIRTH NAME WAS DAVID. AS IN "AND GOLIATH," I THINK.
ANNIE...
IF IT'S TOO MUCH, INVASIVE, NONE OF MY BUSINESS, THAT'S TOTALLY FINE...
BUT IT LOOKS LIKE YOU MIGHT BE STAYING ON, AND I THOUGHT YOU DESERVED TO KNOW...
ANNIE. IT'S OKAY. THIS IS A REAL GIFT. THANK YOU.
THANK YOU, LEE. FOR TRUSTING ME. ABOUT EVERYTHING. AND SAVING MY ASS WHEN THAT CRAZY OLD BITCH CUT MY BRAKES.
DON'T THANK ME YET. IF I'M STAYING PERMANENTLY, YOU'RE GOING TO BE STARTING ON MONDAY AS A DETECTIVE.
TONS MORE PAPERWORK. ESPECIALLY TO EXPLAIN ALL THIS.
AND SINCE I DON'T WANT A ZOMBIE OR SOME DAMN THING WORKING FOR ME... GO TO THE HOSPITAL.
ALTHOUGH I THINK AFTER TODAY, THINGS CAN'T GET ANY WEIRDER.
IT'S COFFIN HILL, SIR. WEIRD IS EVERY DAY.
I CAN'T WAIT.

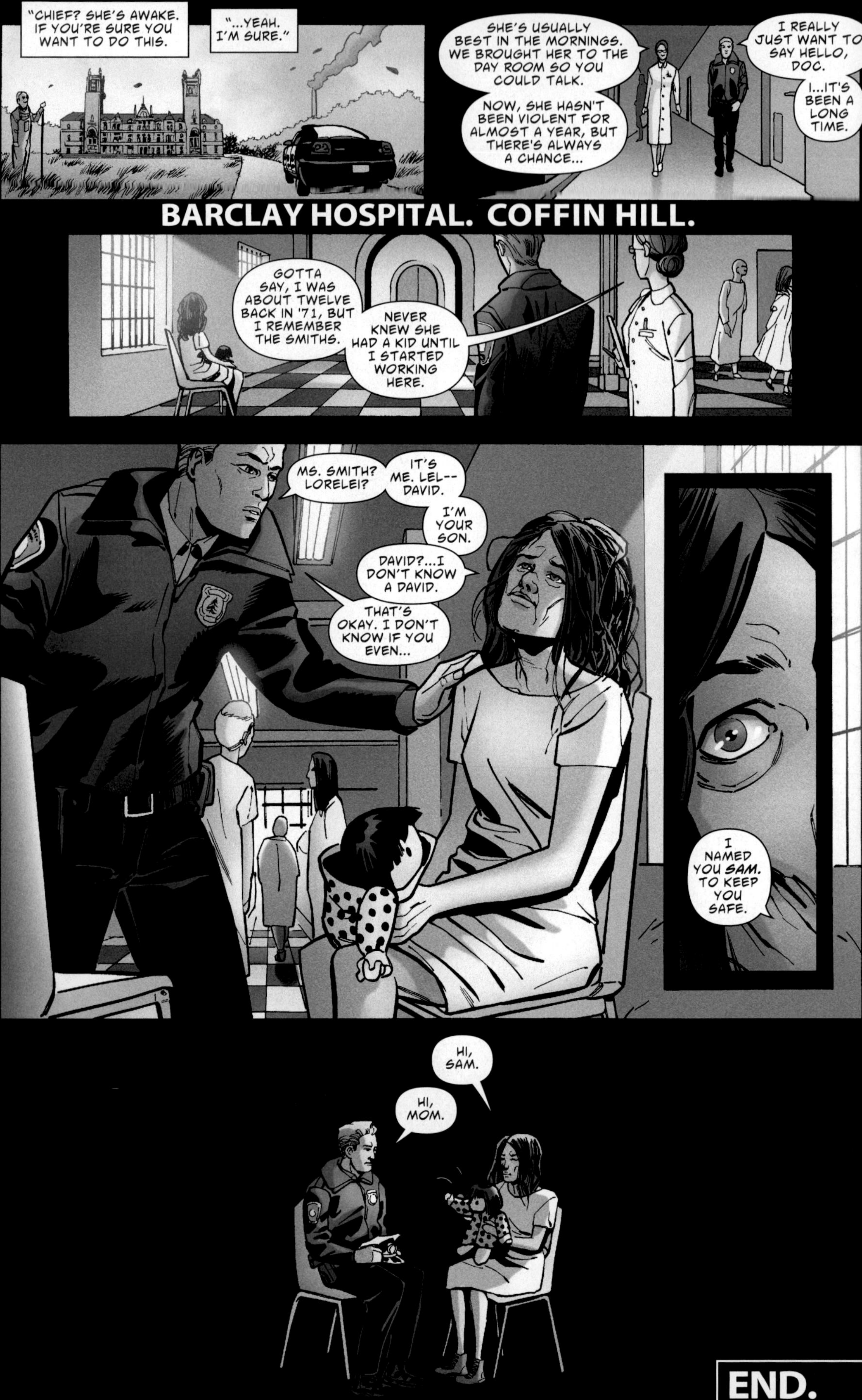
"CHIEF? SHE'S AWAKE. IF YOU'RE SURE YOU WANT TO DO THIS.
"...YEAH. I'M SURE."
SHE'S USUALLY BEST IN THE MORNINGS. WE BROUGHT HER TO THE DAY ROOM SO YOU COULD TALK.
NOW, SHE HASN'T BEEN VIOLENT FOR ALMOST A YEAR, BUT THERE'S ALWAYS A CHANCE...
I REALLY JUST WANT TO SAY HELLO, DOC.
I...IT'S BEEN A LONG TIME.
BARCLAY HOSPITAL. COFFIN HILL.
GOTTA SAY, I WAS ABOUT TWELVE BACK IN '71, BUT I REMEMBER THE SMITHS.
NEVER KNEW SHE HAD A KID UNTIL I STARTED WORKING HERE.
MS. SMITH? LORELEI?
IT'S ME. LEL-- DAVID.
I'M YOUR SON.
DAVID?...I DON'T KNOW A DAVID.
THAT'S OKAY. I DON'T KNOW IF YOU EVEN...
I NAMED YOU SAM. TO KEEP YOU SAFE.
HI, SAM.
HI, MOM.
END.

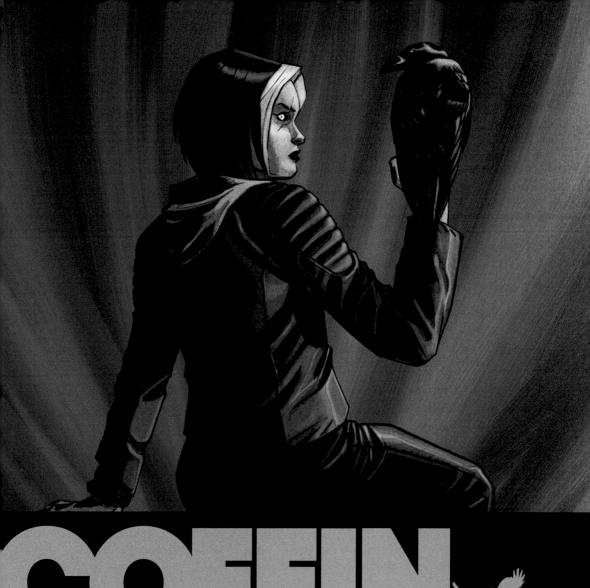

COFFIN HILL

Unused cover art
by Dave Johnson

AFTERWORD

"Buy the ticket, take the ride."

Hunter S. Thompson said that, and while at the age of thirteen I didn't know any other kids who'd read *Fear and Loathing in Las Vegas*, I did know plenty who read comics. Me, I was a sporadic comics reader — having an intellectual mom who didn't police my reading habits had its upsides, but one downside was that superheroes and spandex weren't high on the list of things I "should" have been reading. It wasn't until college, when someone lent me a copy of THE SANDMAN, that I realized comics were where I belonged. Professionally, creatively, as a reader — I was meant to be right here.

That kind of revelation at nineteen can be good, but it can also be terrifying — the weight of the certainty was something I carried for years, as I tried and failed to become a screenwriter, a comics writer, a game designer and finally succeeded as a novelist. I accepted this lateral path, because everything happens for a reason, I figured — and hey, at least I was writing for a living, which I was never ungrateful for. Still, I felt that same tug any time I opened a comic, and it just got stronger as time went on. This was the ride, I reasoned, but maybe I was in the wrong car.

Then, out of the blue, I got a call from Shelly Bond at Vertigo. (The previous pitches I'd submitted hadn't quite made it, and at that point I figured I'd probably given it my best shot and lost out.) They were looking for new comics, my eventual editor said, specifically, comics with a supernatural bent — but no vampires, werewolves or zombies. I knew, the same way I'd known when I opened my copy of THE SANDMAN: PRELUDES AND NOCTURNES on the bus almost a decade earlier, that this was my last chance and that I had to knock it out of the park. So I pitched COFFIN HILL over the phone: a labyrinthine, magic-fueled tale of a monster in the woods and the teenage girl who summoned it — only all grown up, and coming home in disgrace to pick up the pieces.

Even though it was, at heart, a family drama with a tinge of witchcraft, COFFIN HILL was the most intensely autobiographical story I'd ever put out into the world. I had nothing to lose — I knew this was my shot to break into comics and my chance to share some of the rough, bumpy parts of the ride with readers. I'd struggled with deep, crushing depression through most of my twenties, and it just seemed to be getting worse, so into the book it went, at least metaphorically — a heroine with witchy powers that could literally eat her alive, not to mention a liberal dose of survivor's guilt. I grew up in a town very much like Coffin Hill — most of the kids around me were from hugely wealthy families, while we struggled to pay the rent, and I'd held down odd jobs since I was fourteen. Into the comic went all the privilege and bad behavior I'd witnessed, as well as Nate Finn, a "townie" kid with none of the advantages of his peers and the simmering resentment to go along with it. Unlike Nate, I moved away and let go of my anger over the inequities between my so-called childhood friends and me, but just like Eve, I eventually came back home… older, wiser, but still more in the shadow of my past than I realized.

I was terrified when the first issue of COFFIN HILL emerged (for that's the right word) into the world, brought beautifully to life by Inaki Miranda, the inhumanly talented artist Shelly found to draw the book. Seeing the visuals hammered home that I was absolutely naked on the pages within; not only was a lot of my life in the story and open for comment, but my prowess as a writer was already being tested as I tried to hold dozens of story threads close to my chest while spooling out others in that delicate balance of reveal and shadow unique to horror stories.

As I took Eve deeper and darker into her world and her psychological disintegration (and recovery), a strange, *Dorian Gray*-style sequence of events started to happen in my real life. For the first time in years, I wanted to feel better. I wanted to be able to do more than write, sleep and sit on my sofa. I found a therapist I could work with. I got on new medication. I'm not suggesting that the act of creating COFFIN HILL cured me — because outside of comics, mental illness doesn't work like that — but stepping into comics as a creator was the push I needed to finally get some help.

Writing the book got harder — and that was a good thing. I'd grown so much as a comics writer in just over a year that I was having the creative equivalent of the creaky knees and elbows I got when I shot up six inches as a kid. The readers of COFFIN HILL made me want to be better, to stay awake at night figuring out sticky plot points and to keep going farther along the road that I had chosen even though I might run out of gas — and for the first time, I didn't care if I ended up stranded, because at least I tried.

Buy the ticket, take the ride.

As COFFIN HILL went wider and wider, attracting amazing fans on a level that I'd only dreamed about when I was very drunk back in my novelist days, there were ups and downs outside of writing that would have crushed me before I finally made it to comics. But now, in the right car, with the right people riding shotgun, I was able to hang on over the bumps — not always gracefully, but who the hell cares about grace as long as you're still around?

When Shelly told me that, unfortunately, COFFIN HILL was ending, it wasn't the hammer blow I'd been dreading. I was disappointed, and downhearted that I wouldn't be able to commune with fans once a month about the latest issue of the book. But when I turned in COFFIN HILL #20, I felt like I had reached, if not the end of the road, at least a rest area with clean bathrooms and a great diner where I could hang out for a while. So many writers never get to end a story their way, and the privilege of deciding how to stop was one that I'm still holding close to my heart — because while beginnings and endings are what most people remember, it's the trip that really counts.

I got to share the ride with all of you for three stories, twenty issues and two wonderful years, and best of all, I know that somewhere down the road I'll meet you all again.

Safe travels.

— Caitlin Kittredge
July 2015

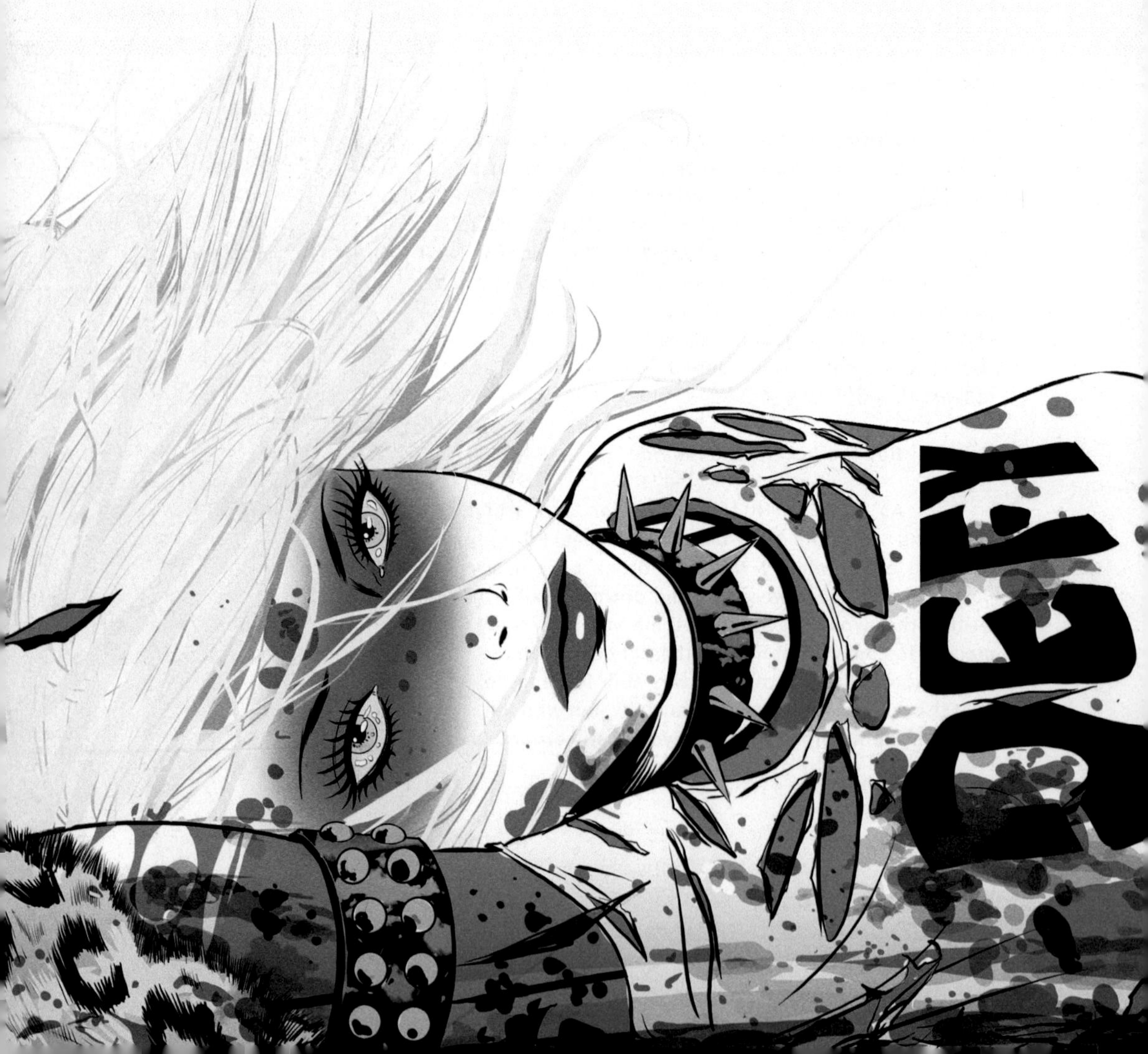